THE CLASSIC BEERS
OF BELGIUM

World Travel Market 1999

sabena **()**

With Compliments

THE CLASSIC BEERS OF BELGIUM

CHRISTIAN DEGLAS
in collaboration with
Professor GUY DERDELINCKX

The information in this book is true and complete to the best
of our knowledge. All recommendations are made without
guarantee on the part of the author or publisher. The author
and publisher disclaim any liability in connection with the use
of this information.

Published by: G.W. KENT, INC.
                  3667 Morgan Road
                  Ann Arbor, Michigan 48108 U.S.A.

Printed in Belgium

ISBN 1-887167-01-3

CONTENTS

FOREWORD

Cycling tours are sporting events that require a full and intensive training program.

The tours of France and Italy, as well as the Valetta, are races that I know very well, for the very good reason that I won them several times during my career. The intensity of such moments which were very demanding is undeniable, with the need to dig into one's physical reserves and being pushed to the limits physically each time. And yet, what lives on in the memory, is only the joy, for the tiredness is quickly forgotten.

The Tour of Belgium was less demanding, but in a different style, and doing the rounds of all the breweries in the country has to be looked upon as an amazing challenge.

Our country is truly a paradise on earth when it comes to beers, with a tremendous variety in taste and style.

I would need a different form of stamina to come out on top in that kind of race. Fortunately, however, there are those who are better equipped than me to confront the difficulties of such a testing course.

It is definitely an achievement to finish such a course.

There is no doubt that anyone who succeeds in tasting all the beers deserves a " yellow jersey ", traditionally worn by the leader of the Tour de France.

Eddy MERCKX

ACKNOWLEDGMENTS

To the Confederation of Belgian Breweries (the C.B.B.) and all the breweries throughout the country for their cooperation, documentary assistance and kind welcome.

To Jan De Brabanter, Secretary-General of the C.B.B. for his excellent advice.

To all the brewers for their kind welcome.

To Guy Derdelinckx, professor at the Catholic University of Leuven where he holds the chair of brewing, for his technical assistance in the glossary as well as the chapter " Beer And Its Production Through History ".

To Pierre Verlent, Régis De Jong, Studio Berger, and Bart Diependaele for their photos.

To Eddy Merckx, a champion without peer and renowned ambassador for Belgium throughout the world, for his kind cooperation in the foreword.

To Martine Boutin (colored drawings), Louis-Michel Carpentier *Poje*, Raoul Cauvin *scriptwriter*, François Craenhals *Chevalier Ardent, Les 4 As, Pom & Teddy*, Curtis, Jacques Debruyne, Dupa *Cubitus*, Michel Greg *Achille Talon*, Marc Hardy *Pierre Tombal*, Kox *Agent 212*, Malik *Cupidon*, Jean-Claude Servais, Turk, Michel Weyland *Aria*, and François Walthéry, *Le Vieux Bleu*, for their kind contributions to the cartoons.

To the publishers Casterman, Dupuis and Lombard.

To the St-Just, not-for-profit organization, Place du Jeu de Balle, Brussesl 1000, for the interest shown in putting a face on beer.

To my wife Béatrice, my children Harold, Emily and Tim for putting up with my many absences when I was away visiting breweries.

To Saint Arnold and long may he watch over brewers and their work.

INTRODUCTION

Not more than a few short years ago, when I was scribbling these lines, it would never have occurred to me to write a book, even less so on a subject where I had only a cursory knowledge at the start.

I have always been a great beer lover for its many qualities, and what triggered off this book were my futile attempts one New Year's eve to find some kind of guide to the different beers available in our country, the different types of glasses into which they should be poured, and above all the special nature of their ingredients as well as a description of their tastes.

I did, of course, come across some wonderful works devoted to my favorite beverage, which also dealt with the breweries which brewed them, but a complete work of the full range of Belgian beers, as I imagined it, apparently did not exist.

From that moment on, there was only one solution; to write my own beer guide. That is how my destiny as a writer came to be linked to that of the drink protected by Saint Arnold.

There is no denying that the task was complex and involved, as you can imagine, tasting a multitude of beers, irrespective of whether or not one likes such a type of beer.

New horizons were opened to me, for during the many months of "work" I made many discoveries, and by adopting a methodological approach as a beer taster I was able to gain a new insight into certain beers, the quality of which I did not doubt, but which nevertheless never managed to seduce my palate.

If the round of all the breweries in Belgium entailed covering hundreds of kilometers, I will spare you the details of the number of hectoliters of beer which I swallowed, not to quench a raging thirst, but above all to get the best possible feeling for describing the beverage. The first contact and initial impressions were made in the company of the brewer himself.

Certain beers came as a pleasant surprise, because they were the kind of beers I would not normally have expected to appreciate. Others served to confirm all the good I thought of them, and above all strengthened my confidence in a national drink that has all too often been neglected.

BEER LOVERS

Writing a book on beer is not simply a form of literary self-satisfaction, only to find it one day languishing as part of the fittings in some dusty library. It is above all a way of expressing one's enthusiasm for a beverage which goes back to the beginning of time, and which has always contributed to man's well-being. When it comes to beers, Belgium is very much a paradise on earth. Unfortunately, its inhabitants have not always treated their beers with the respect they merit. If beer has often been the source of popular jubilation, it has never been elevated to cult status, at least not until today. And to top it all, as yet there is no true beer culture in this country. Thousands of us are beer connoisseurs, and yet we do not understand what we are drinking. Contrary to the great French wines, which have pride of place in culinary or other academies, beer is always treated in its own country as the poor relative from a gastronomic view-point, and is considered as being out of place by those who keep a good table. Yet, it should be at the top of the list of drinks served to accompany meals, since not only does it lift the food during a meal, but it also facilitates digestion. It is also a pleasant and sociable companion. It brings out the good humor in guests and this is infectious.

The image of a beer lover is someone who is sociable, mature and cheerful at the same time. The " Birrophile " to use a term which does not yet exist but which conveys the subtle difference, lives life to the fullest and intends to live to a ripe old age. It is well known that Belgians are digging their own graves with their forks, but a glass of beer can postpone the appointment. Obviously, all excesses, in whatever domain, have disastrous consequences on the whole. That is why this book is far from being an incitement to drinking binges, but is intended rather to encourage people to taste what is the healthiest of drinks.

Throughout my numerous visits, all the people I met, despite in some cases going through a difficult period financially, were always available, enthusiastic and unfailing in their praises for a beer to which they have dedicated their whole life.

In the name of all those who will one day taste the fruit of your art and your imagination, thank you!

No matter how well-organized one may be when setting off to visit all the breweries, there are always a few surprises. However, my journey, which took almost four years, was based on a combination of factors. Initially, the motivating factor was the idea of discovering a new brewery. The second, practically on a par with the first, took me to regions hitherto unknown for their beer production. And finally, as part of the natural cycle of events, I found my inspiration for the journey most of the time being guided by seasonal considerations.

The outcome of this book is to some extent a log, with the finished article being a collection of bouquets that linger on as a fond memory of the many beers that I tasted. A hundred or so of them will stay imprinted on my memory, principally thanks to their characteristic flavor and the quality of the brewing.

Naturally, the world of brewers in Belgium is continually changing, and can be compared with the incessant activity of the yeast in the bottom of a bottle of beer in full fermentation.

My only regret, however, lies in not being able to describe all the top-fermented or bottom-fermented beers, not to mention those fermented spontaneously. Which will not prevent me from tasting them all before my days are out. By that, I mean all the different Pils, Seasonal beers and Gueuzes, which are too many to count, but which after all represent the lion's share of daily beer consumption in Belgium. Even if the latter are very similar in taste to other beers in the same category, they all nevertheless have an individual taste which makes them stand out from other beers. That is what is known as the consummate skill of the master brewer.

THE KEYS TO ENJOYING
AND TASTING BEER

Just as wine tasting has its rules, so does beer tasting. Above all, it is important to distinguish between drinking and tasting, which represent two very different notions. In the first case, one has also to draw the line between a passing thirst and the almost permanent thirst of an alcoholic.

As regards the second notion, one takes one's time, and explores fully the different characteristics of each drink. As a general rule, the initial reaction when tasting a beer comes down to " one likes it or one doesn't ". After that, the two opinions need further elaboration. A beer needs to be understood and appreciated in different lights. It is possible not to like a beer at the outset, a bitter beer for example, without needing to understand why. For that reason, I think that it is worthwhile describing the different ways of evaluating beers by taking a look at how professionals approach a beer tasting, but based on procedures which can be followed just as easily by the most mundane beer lover.

THE HEAD

The head varies according to the type of beer involved. The temperature of the beverage is critical. Equally the type of glass has to be taken into account. Glasses should always be hand washed for top-fermented beers, and in general should be dry.

When all the conditions are right, then it is time to move on to the initial tasting. The head is undoubtedly a proof of quality. Some beers have no head, as is the case of most faros, or are served with only a thin head. This is normal for bottom-fermented Pils style beers, whereas in the case of top-fermented beers the head is thick and creamy.

CLARITY

Beers can also be evaluated by their appearance, and that is why clarity is just as important, even for unfiltered beers. We shall describe it as being brilliant, clear, cloudy or dense.

AROMA

This is the key moment in beer tasting, since at this point the beer is already in the mouth. Aromas are the most difficult to define since a multitude of different factors is involved in describing a beer's aroma. A galaxy of adjectives can be applied to describe its acidity (pronounced, very pronounced, etc.), its bitterness depending upon the density of the hops and the malt utilized, or its sweetness depending upon the sugars, honeys, caramel, syrups which make up the ingredients.

Other ingredients will add to the underlying aroma, such as the yeast, the density of the alcohol volume or the spices used (coriander, aniseed, basil, mint, orange peel, etc.)

Of all the beer producing countries, Belgium is the one with the most aromas, largely owing to the imagination of our brewers.

THE SENSATION IN THE MOUTH

After the aroma, the palate plays its part by perceiving whether the beer has body. This also will vary according to the beer's recipe, which determines whether it will be very light, light, relatively strong or dense, its weight, and its effervescence (flat, normal, abundant or champagne-like).

THE AFTERTASTE

This is the stage that appears to be the most important in determining a beer's future. In a way, it is the memory that you will retain once the beer has been swallowed. This aftertaste also depends upon the ingredients. The feeling will persist longer in the mouth or in the nostrils depending upon the beer's strength. It can be soft, sweet or very bitter. But, by the time you are ready to swallow the beer your taste buds and olfactory senses will have already accumulated a series of elements which will most certainly enable you to judge its quality.

HOW TO POUR BEER

The art of correctly serving beer is part of a sacred ritual. As a general rule, for bottom-fermented beers, such as the Pils variety, it is the barman or barmaid who will take care of pouring the beer and pour it into a glass that

16

has been rinsed with cold water beforehand. The same procedure will be followed if the beer is bottled.

As regards top-fermented beers, they should be poured just as smoothly, and you should make certain that they are poured into the appropriate glass.

The glass should be slightly tilted, just as you start to pour. Then slowly bring the glass upright at which time the bottle should be practically horizontal.

If a sediment remains in the bottom, you have two choices, either you stop pouring and your beer will be slightly cloudy, or you decide to drink these dregs, which will result in your glass being full of yeast particles. This is, of course, less appetizing, but you should nevertheless be aware that, no matter the degree of fermentation, there is no danger of side effects from the dregs in a bottle; on the contrary, they are an impressive source of vitamin B.

THE GLASSES

It is an unwritten rule that a beer should be served in its own particular glass.

That may seem curious, but a Trappist beer, for example, just does not have the same taste when it is poured in a glass used for Pils.

That is why, if Belgium is a paradise for beers, the same is true for glasses.

The reasons are manifold. On most occasions, brewers select a glass according to whether or not the aroma is strong, because it should not be forgotten that beer has a nose, and this will determine the optimum shape for the glass.

A beer with only a slight aroma should be served in a glass where the top is narrower. On the other hand, a strongly perfumed brew should preferably be served in a wide-rimmed drinking vessel.

Chevalier Ardent « de Graal ! »
© CRAENHALS, 1995

BEER AND ITS PRODUCTION THROUGH HISTORY

This introduction is intended to take stock of the descriptions and virtues that have been attributed to beer since the human race started producing it. It consists of several historical notes and a paragraph devoted to the discovery of yeast, which is an essential micro-organism in the aroma, and another on the work of Pasteur, a scientist who had a passion for microbiology but remained motivated by a genuine desire to find a practical outlet for his work and improve the quality of industrial processes. This introduction has drawn on historical data quoted by:

— A. Allard, Head of Research at the *Fonds National de la Recherche Scientifique* and professor at the Faculty of Notre-Daim de la Paix in Namur and at the Catholic University of Leuven, at Leuven-la-Neuve;

— A. Devreux, professor emeritus of the Meurice-Chimie Institute in Brussels and the Catholic University of Leuven, at Leuven-la-Neuve;

— the book entitled " Beer: a culture " published in 1984 by the " Maison des Historiens "of the Catholic University of Leuven, at Leuven-la-Neuve; also not forgetting to thank the " Nouvelles éditions Marabout, Brussels " who have very kindly authorised us to reproduce in full excerpts from the remarkable biography of Louis Pasteur, written by Professor J. Nicolle.

In distant pre-historic times, before man even knew how to cultivate the land, he managed in all likelihood to produce slightly alcoholic beverages, using honey and wild plants containing fermentable sugars.

With the advent of agriculture, he was able to use fruits, edible root crops, and above all cereals for fermentation: that corresponds to the beginning of the " wine " era, made with fruits which were cultivated, and the " beer " era using grain.

If the evolution of beer in pre-historic times is blurred, the first written traces of its production were discovered in Sumer and Mesopotamia, and clay tablets which date from the year 4000 BC describe the manufacture of a beer called *Sikaru* made from sprouting barley bread. It is therefore likely that the manufacture of bread and that of beer followed parallel paths, the dough of the first being cooked while in the case of beer it was left to ferment.

In the year 2000 BC, rules and regulations were already attached to this manufacturing process, in particular the famous law of Hammourabi. In Chaldea as well as in the Egypt of the Pharaohs, beer was known as barley wine.

While on the subject of the Egyptians, Herodotus (2nd half of the V century BC) [*Stories,* Book II, Chapter 77] indicates: " The wine they normally use is a kind of wine made with barley, since there are no vines in their country ".

In Egypt, the pharaoh and important dignitaries had their personal breweries. The most widely consumed beer was called *Zythum.* A recipe from ancient times, extracted from writings which for a long time were attributed to Zosime de Panopolis (IV century AD), but which opinion today places rather in the Géoponic epoch (a Byzantine compilation on the subject of agriculture, written at the beginning of the X century), describes the manufacture of *zythum:* " Take a beautiful, pure, white stem of barley. Moisten it throughout the day, then stretch it by spreading it out or also leave it in a windless place until the next morning. Then soak it again for five hours. Put it through a riddle and sprinkle it with water after having left it to dry until it falls apart, since the rootlets (small strands) are bitter. Grind the rest into small loaves adding yeast as with bread. Heat the loaves while they are still damp, not too strongly, and when they rise, crumble them into sweetened water and strain them through a sieve or a finely woven fabric. Others heat the loaves, before casting them in a vat with water and heating them slightly, without allowing them to boil nor become lukewarm, then take them out and strain them, before pouring them into another vessel, re-heating and straining once again." The process is a mix of baking and brewing.

Still on the subject of the Egyptian *Zythum,* in *Talmud,* [Misna, Pesachim III, Chapter 1]: " Rabbi Joseph points out that it is made up of one third barley, a third of saffron [*Carthamus tinctorius* L.] and a third salt. Rabbi Papa replaced the barley with wheat... it is left to soak, it is grilled, milled and drunk. Its effects lead to constipation for those with diarrhea. It is dangerous for sick and weak people."

Thus Babylonians and Egyptians were already familiar with not only fermentation, but also malting, which is the basic procedure for making beer.

Aeschylus, a Greek poet of the second half of the V century BC, put the following words into the mouth of his hero in the *Suppliantes* [(verses 950 to 953)]: " The Herald: Be wary that you are stirring up an uncertain war. May victory and conquest be for the males!

The King: Males, you will find them also in this country, and they do not drink wine made from barley! "

Xenophon also wrote at the same period in the *Anabase*, [4th book, chapter 5], when referring to the Armenian houses: " We also found wheat, barley, vegetables and barley wine in the craters. The edges were awash with barley grains, mixed with straw without nodes, some very long and others very short. Every time we were thirsty, we had to place these straws to our mouths and suck them. This drink was very strong, if no water was added. As soon as we were accustomed to it, it was extremely pleasant. "

Diodore of Sicily, a writer from the 1st century BC, wrote: " When a region cannot produce any vines, one finds a drink prepared with barley, which is not far behind wine in terms of its strength and the pleasure it gives. " (1st Book, Chapter 20).

Pliny, a Roman author from the 1st century AD, points out when discussing leavens in his work entitled *Natural History*, [Book 18, Chapter 104]: " The millet is primarily used to prepare leavens; filled with wort, it keeps for a year. A similar leaven is made with the most delicate bran and the best wheat [*Tricitum turgidum* L.], which is filled with grape must which has been left to ferment for three days, before being put out in the sun to dry. This is made into tablets which are watered down to make bread and then warmed up with finest " *zéa* " [*Triticum dicoccum* Schrk.]; the whole is mixed with flour. [...] The types of leavens of which we have just spoken are be prepared at the time of grape harvests. But one can make some at any time with barley and water: the balls which are two pounds in weight are roasted on a very hot hearth or in an earthenware plate, on the ashes or the embers, until they become reddish; then they are placed in sealed vessels until they turn sour; in that way one obtains a leaven which simply needs to be watered down.

In the *Géoponiques*, [Book 2, Chapter 23], the following words are to be found: " The day before we are due to bake bread, bunches of grapes are thrown into water and pressed the next day; the froth which overflows is collected as leaven and used to make pleasant and light bread. If we want to make leaven for the whole year, as the grape must is fermenting in the jars, we take the froth and fill it with millet flour; with this we make balls which are left out in the sun to dry before being stored in a dry place. "

If the first tangible proofs of beer's existence are to be found first in Samur, then in Babylon in Egypt, the rest of the world was included. Everywhere cereals were being cultivated, beer was brewed.

Traces of cereal-based beer have been found in Denmark, dating from the Nordic bronze age (1500 years BC).

In 300 BC, Celts and Germans were drinking barley wine, with grape wine being the domain of classical Greece and Southern Italy. In Asia, China led the way with innovations, both from an agricultural point of view as well as in the utilization of metals. That country was brewing 2000 years before Christ, a beer which was completely fermented and well clarified using millet. This beer which was called *tsiou* contained, according to writings from that time, the two opposing elements dear to Chinese philosophy, the liquid element which descends and nourishes the body and the element which rises and gladdens the soul.

In the II century BC, the Chinese empire produced beers made from millet, rice and wheat, whereas the rice beer known as *saké* was the only beer produced in Japan at the same time.

In America prior to Christopher Columbus, corn was the sacred cereal, the basis of all human food.

Corn beer was not only a local beer but was also used as a ritual offering to the sun god and the dead. In South America, and primarily in the Amazon basin, beer was made with manioc, while sorghum was the main raw material used to produce beers in Central and Southern Africa.

To ferment all these beers they used wild yeasts which were inherent in the leaven from a previous " mash tub " which was added deliberately, and they also added fruits; but fermentation also came about accidentally through the container, through the surrounding air and above all through bees or other insects attracted by the sweetened juice.

The transformation of starch into sugar caused more problems. If the majority of primitive tribes understood that the germination of cereals produced sweetened products, others used less appetizing but nevertheless effective procedures.

That is how " the sun virgins " responsible for the Inca food in the palace at Lake Titicaca in Peru, were entrusted with the task of chewing the corn before it was fermented. When the enzyme from the saliva of these pure virgins was no longer considered satisfactory, they were sacrificed to the sun god to whom the priests also offered beer at the same time. This process of saccharification through saliva was also used on cassava by the Indians in the Amazon basin, where this " production " method was also entrusted to young girls.

Prior to our era, beer was primarily brewed by women. Brewing and fermentation, while appearing to be a very uncertain and almost magical process, were considered to be sacrosanct in that period.

Beer played a role in all important ceremonies, whether civil or religious.

BEER'S FIRST APPEARANCE
IN WESTERN EUROPE

The first reference to beer in Western Europe is to be found in Pliny [*Natural history,* Book 22, Chapter 164]; this Roman author from the first century uses the term *cervesia* amongst others, when describing the many varieties: *ex iisdem fiunt et potus: zythum in Aegypto, caelia et cerea in Hispania, cervesia et plura genera in Gallia aliisque provinciis, quorum omnium spuma, cutem feminarum in facie nutrit...*that is to say: " using these as a base [i.e. cereals], they make zythum in Egypt, celia and cerea in Spain, ceruisia and several others in Gaul and other provinces. The foam from all these drinks is used by women for facial care... " and the author adds: " as for the drinks themselves, it is better to move on to the wine! "

ATHENEE de NAUCRATIS, [*Banquet des Sophistes IV,* Chapter 36], author from the end of the II century, writes on the subject of the Celts from the heart of Gaul: " The rich drink wine from Italy or Marseilles which is imported and drunk pure; they sometimes add a drop of water. The poor prepare *Zythum* from wheat to which they add honey, or more often than not, drink it as it stands; it is called *corma. "*

ISIDORE De SEVILLE writes in the *Etymologies,* [Book 20, Chapters 16-17]: " the generic name given to all intoxicating drinks , except wine, is *sicera...*The *ceruisia* draws its name from Cérès, that is to say cereals. It is in effect a drink that is manufactured in different ways using corn grains. The " celia " gets its name from the fact that it is heated. It is a drink extracted from common corn juice [*Triticum vulgare* Vill.] by using special skills. The fierce hear is achieved [germination] by soaking the wheat, then drying it. It is reduced to flour and then milled. The fermentation gives rise to a harsh taste and an intoxicating heat.That which is gathered from the overflowing vessels is called " faex " [sediment]. "

STRABOB (early 1st century described in his *Geography* different peoples and their traditions regarding beer; on the subject of the Ethiopians, he points out that: " They live off millet, and barley, two cereals from which they extract a drink. " [*Geography,* Book 17, Chapter 2]

— As regards the Egyptians: "The zythum is specially prepared; it is a very common drink of which there are a great many different varieties." [*Geography,* Book 17, Chapter 2]

— As regards the Portugese: " In general they drink zythum, rarely touching wine (the wine they have is reserved for festive occasions.) " [*Geography,* Book 3, Chapter 3,6]

— Finally, quoting Pythéas de Marseille on the subject of the inhabit ants of Thule - probably the Faroe Islands, Iceland or the Norwegian coast: " They are totally devoid of food-producing plants and they have very few domestic animals, so much so that they live off millet and other pasturage, fruit and roots; those who have corn and honey extract their staple drink from them. [*Geography,* Book 4, Chapter 5,5]

At the time of Caesar, *Nerviens* and *Suèves* forbade the import of wine: traffickers used it as a bargaining tool to exchange for slaves.

TACITUS, [*Germania,* XXIII, 1], points out on their subject: *" Potui umor ex hordeo aut frumento in quandam similitudinem vini corruptus ;proximi ripae et vinum mercantur. "* (" As a drink they have a liquid made from barley and corn, which when fermented is not unlike wine; those living close to the shore also buy wine. ")

While drawing attention to the liking which Gauls had for drink, Tacitus reports that they produced a " fermented liqueur " extracted from barley and corn; the same expression " umor " (" liqueur ") was applied to beer throughout the Middle Ages.

As for Pliny, he recounts how people got drunk on drinks made from grains which had been dampened. Different processes were followed in Gaul and Spain. The names were different but the effects were the same.

Deckers points out that excavations carried out in the area around Namur in Belgium, have revealed Roman villas dating from the third and fourth centuries which were equipped with annexes where beer was manufactured. In addition, Gallo-Roman goblets in terra-cotta with clear inscriptions referring to beer have been found.

In the same way, at the Arlon museum in Belgium a bass-relief dating from the third century is on show and shows the " *cervisiarii* " at work. All this leads us to believe that beer was manufactured and drunk in Gallo-Roman times. But one has to then wait almost another five centuries to find further traces of beer production. In the capitular " *De villis* " [M.G.H., *Capitularia regium francorum,* t.I, n° 32, *Capitulare de villis,* Chapter 45, pg. 87; chapter 61, pg. 88; Chapter 62, pg. 89.], which in all likelihood was written shortly before 800, mention is made of beer production: Charlemagne ordered that the workers and craftsmen necessary to ensure that the farms functioned correctly should include those who knew how to brew barley beer. But there is no mention of breweries. It is also interesting to note that, before the year 800, this term is never used when listing all the different elements which made up the domain. However, from the year 800 onwards, the term brewery occurs, regularly albeit under different names depending upon the era and the region. Thus in the IX century, one comes across the word *camba* and the more popular expression " *braxina* "; this word was derived from *buecis* which means malt, or sprouting barley. This was an essential ingredient in manufacturing beer. These expressions, being part of popular expression, were replaced during the XIII century by *cambe* or *bressine* in the Roman regions, and by *bruwers huse* or *panhus* in Germanic regions. One comes across other expressions, but which are in less frequent use, namely: *braciarum, braciatorium, braxatorium* and *brassina.* In fact, in the early Middle Ages beer was always mentioned in connection with monasteries. It is mentioned in connection with the life of Saint Colomban, an Irish monk who died in the year 615 and founded the Abbaye de Luxeuil, but above all with reference to Bobbio. The presence of breweries in monasteries as soon as they were created is confirmed in numerous documents (charters, settlements, narratives).

The role played by the abbeys in improving and helping to transfer knowledge is primordial. The extent of knowledge that reigned there, the transmission of know-how through writing, the social structure and finally the means at their disposal turned the abbeys into centers of " intelligence and experience " and their archives are a valuable source of information concerning habits and customs of the era. Several elements explain and/or confirm this pre-eminence: the role played by monasteries in the economic life and the knowledge of the advantages of the three-year rotation of crops. The best known are in Germany (Niederalteich, Metten, Prüfening, Kempte,etc.) and in Switzerland (Saint-Gall). The detailed plan of this last abbey, drawn up in the IX century, shows three breweries set up inside the convent. It included a brewery for pilgrims (*bracitorium*), an inn with a brewery (*domus conficiendae celiae*), and a brewery for the monks (*hic fratribus conficiatur cervisia - hic coletur celia*), lofts and a malt warehouse (*granarium ruri mundatum fromentum serveteur et quod ad cervisam praeparatur*). The three breweries were built along similar lines four hearths, a cooling tank and a mash tun for fermentation. The malt warehouse was equipped with an area for germination in the shape of a cross that enabled four layers of barley, grain or oats to be germinated simultaneously. Next to this was situated the high tower: this was where the sprouting barley was subjected to heat treatment by being spread out on wicker trays fixed around a hearth.

In a nearby room, there were pestles to crush the malt. Each brewery produced a different kind of beer. The best, called *prima melia* or *celia*, produced from barley, was reserved for important guests. The second, *cervisia*, less dense and produced from oats, was drunk on a daily basis by the monks. The third, the most ordinary, was served to pilgrims. In addition, there was a beer made from honey, *cervisia mellia,* very similar to mead. It was so popular with the monks that the Council of Worms (868) was obliged to limit its consumption to festivals [B. Hell, *Man and Beer,* Rosheim, 1983, 21-23]. It has to be emphasized, however, that during the Middle Ages, poor crops and poor yields had an influence on beer production, in that such production was no doubt limited, if not forbidden, during periods of great famine. It was a period which saw a great many technological improvements, but produced little by way of innovation.

The Cistercian monks were producing beer as early as the XII century, and it was consumed in particular in the abbeys in Northern Germany, Holland, and especially in England and Ireland. There is nothing surprising in all that, if one is aware that William the Conqueror, victorious at the Battle of Hastings (1066), was the illegitimate son of Robert, the Duke of Normandy and a brewer's daughter. Several statutes from the Order's general rules often came as a reminder to the abbots of these two countries that drinking wine and beer in the barns where the lay brothers worked was prohibited. But beer was also drunk in the monasteries in France, even in Champagne, the country of vines *par excellence,* when there were wine shortages. An anonymous author of the thirteenth century has left a description of the Abbaye de Clervaux in which he mentions a brewery. At the Abbaye de Villers-en-Brabant, the ruins of which represent one of the most beautiful group of monastic buildings in Belgium, one can still see the remains of the brewery built between 1270 and 1278 alongside the river Thyle which provided the necessary water. The building is 42 meters long and 12 meters wide, divided into 2 naves covered with groined vaults, supported in the center by a row of 5 circular columns holding up the crown-shaped arches of the hearth's hood. Although initially, the Cistercian monks brewed beer only for consumption by the monks, they subsequently began to sell part of their production to neighboring villages. Afterwards, they turned it into a genuine money-making industry, which grew and grew.

The discovery and utilization of hops were decisive steps which gave to beer the flavor and bitter taste which we associate with it today. It seems highly likely that this discovery was made in one of the monasteries itself. It was around 1070 that the abbess HILDEGARDE de BRINGEN, in her book on natural science, indicated, apparently for the first time, that the bitterness of the hops could provide an antidote to certain harmful effects of fermentation when added to drinks and that it also enabled them to be preserved for longer periods. These characteristics were soon put to good use in breweries and gradually hops took the place of aromatic herbs, which had until then been prevalent since, according to a legend which dies hard mistakenly claims, westerners had developed a taste for spices during the crusades.

In reality, brewers had always used numerous aromatic plants in order to add taste to their beers. Even in the time of the Egyptians, one of the spices frequently used with ginger was honey. This honey beer was to be found in Europe during the Middle Ages. There were also a great many spicy beers. However, in certain episcopal towns, the bishops had rights over the aromatic plants used for beer (dues from gruit). The first *jus grutae* dates from the year 974 and disappeared during the XVI century when the utilization of hops became standard. At the beginning of the XV century, Jean sans Peur, the Duke of Burgundy, played a decisive role in this respect by creating the Order of the Hops.

After the invention of printing techniques in around 1450, written tracts on producing beer began to circulate. We are aware of a treatise in French dated 1530 and another in Latin from 1549.

That is why, from 1453 onwards, the end of the Middle Ages and the start of the modern era, events of note regarding brewing relate above all to the organization of the profession:
- the important role, as we have indicated, of the monks-cum-brewers who produced beer for their own consumption and also for their hospices;
- gradual transformation of family-style breweries into artisanal breweries, often in association with an inn;
- associations formed by brewers to fix rules and regulations for the industry and ensure the respect of such rules.

Production and quality were more and more controlled; inspectors-tasters made their appearance entrusted with the role of controlling quality, but their methods were archaic (e.g. verifying the presence of the sugar extract by reference to the " sticky " powers of the beer); from a scientific point of view, a great deal of knowledge was either not applied through ignorance, or was simply lost.

A brewer's life was not easy in that period, not only on account of the controls which were nit-picking and inaccurate, but also because the manufacturing process itself was very demanding physically and required a lot of intuition.

THE ANCIEN REGIME AND THE REVOLUTION

What stands out in the period from the XVI to the XIX century is the multiplication of breweries, which were more spacious and better designed, and the slow but steady improvement in techniques.

Under the Ancien Regime, breweries began to attract the attention of the authorities. In 1693 the King of France had created and officially appointed sworn brewers in Flanders, Hainault and Artois. These jurors, whose titles were hereditary, were granted a monopoly for brewing beer, while innkeepers were prohibited from carrying on this activity. But, in certain districts, these authorities were not appointed. Accordingly, the King gave innkeepers the possibility of acquiring such rights, and accordingly of producing their own beer. To ensure that the regulations were respected, the authorities deemed it necessary to create posts referred to as " d'égards " or " gourmets " entrusted by magistrates with the task of tasting, in the event of a dispute, and verifying the quality of the beers.

Amongst the Cistercian monasteries, the abbot of Rancé introduced in the XIII century, in his monastery of Trappe, in the Orne, a reform that became well-known on account of its extreme austerity. Other monasteries very quickly adhered to his school of thought and the new followers of this strict code of observance quite naturally took the word " Trappe " in their name and became known as the " Trappists ". The suppression of the cooperative system, the looting of abbeys during the French Revolution and the lifting of constraints attached to brewing gave a new impetus to what was to become an industry.

The century will be remembered for the important technological progress in brewing techniques: it is very worthwhile consulting the monumental *Encyclopedia* of Diderot and d'Alembert [DIDEROT - D'ALEMBERT, *The Encyclopedia,* Paris, 1772, Vol. II, Chapter: Brewing, page 403] to read a summary of the knowledge of that period regarding the production of malt and beer, while at the same time admiring the most interesting illustrations of workshops in those days.

THE XIX CENTURY AND THE BEGINNINGS OF THE MODERN BREWERY

As in all domains, it was the second half of the XVIII century and the XIX century in particular, which represented a turning point in the history of brewing. After a long period in which technical progress was slow, empirical and confused, there was a period of sudden change. Not just one change, but a whole series of radical changes occurred, sometimes seemingly unconnected, but which together resulted in far reaching changes in the processes used to produce beer.

If one is aware that thermometers were only introduced into breweries in 1760 by Baverstock, and the saccharimeter in 1805 by Richardson, it makes one wonder about the methods used at the time to saccharify malt, to take just one part of the process.

An amusing example is given in the following description of the method employed at Queen's College, Oxford, which was founded in 1340: " Boiling water is poured into the mash tun which is made of oak and left to cool until, the steam having cleared, the brewer can see his face clearly reflected in the water's surface. " It is clear from subsequent phases that the water, at that stage, was at approximately 75° C/167° F. Then the malt flour was poured in, thereby using the method of brewing by infusion. Because there were no precise ways of measuring density, taxes were often calculated on the capacity of the mash tun, thus encouraging brewers to use very thick coatings.

The veritable industrialization of brewing really only began with the invention of steam engines. The development of railway networks was not only advantageous from a sales point of view but also a boon to the transfer of natural ice, which was used in large quantities by brewers.

The steam engine itself replaced the furnaces in 1784 at the Whitbread brewery. Everything was therefore in place at that time to produce and commercialize beer in large volumes, while practically nothing was known as to the nature of the changes which turned barley into beer.

Yeast had long since been considered as an insoluble deposit, the volume of which increased during the fermentation process and which was able, by an as then unexplained process, to transmit this property to other sweetened solutions.

In 1680, Antoon van Leeuwenhoeck observed through his microscope that yeast was made up of small particles which were joined together and could only imagine that it was a question of living organisms. The gas released during the fermentation process was also a mystery. In 1755 J. Black considered that it was the same compound as that formed through the combustion of charcoal and through respiration. Carbonic anhydride was only identified in 1789 by Lavoisier, who established the purely chemical nature of fermentation, during which part of the sugar is oxidized into CO^2 and the rest reduced to alcohol.

It was during this period that scientists began to understand that fragments of plant or animal tissue, as well as extracts from such tissue, could stimulate certain chemical reactions.

Research was actively carried out to trace the active constituent, at that time called the " fermenting agent ", in particular in the malt barley and in beer yeast which at the time were both considered to be potentially very active sources.

Payen and Persoz in 1833 were thus the first to isolate a " fermenting agent " by precipitating to alcohol an aqueous malt extract.

The white powder thereby obtained was capable of liquefying starch, which it had recently been discovered (by Saussure in 1814) was made up of glucose. This fermenting agent, the purification of which is seen as the beginning of bio-chemistry, will be called diastase. Utilizing the same technique of precipitation into alcohol, Bertholet succeeded in 1860 in isolating the sucrase of the beer yeast extract. From this the important role played by brewing in the development of enzymology is clear.

However, in our view, it is particularly interesting, and accordingly indispensable, to give some background information at this stage concerning the discovery of yeast. In fact, it was Van Leeuwenhoek (1632 - 1723) who, when observing beer, noted the presence of small spherical or ovoid globules; then in the eighteenth century (1799) the French Institute made the following question the subject of a competition: " What are the characteristics which, in plants and animal matter, differentiate those which act as fermentation agents and those which undergo fermentation? " In reply, Thenard published in the year XI a work devoted to the nature of fermentation: " This yeast, he said, is by nature " animal ", that is to say it is nitrogenous and when it is distilled it produces a good deal of ammoniac. " During the fermentation process, the yeast loses its nitrogen and partially disappears. Finally, at the end of the process a white residue remains, with " ligneous " properties and which no longer produces any reaction when applied to a fresh quantity of sweetened water. The question still remains to be answered what becomes of the nitrogen from the fermenting agent since, contrary to the opinion of the German chemist, Döbereiner (1780 - 1849) he did not accept that yeast was transformed into ammoniac. Shortly after the publication of this thesis, Gay-Lussac announced that a grape must, which was carefully preserved without modification during a year in accordance with Appert's process (1750-1841), the inventor of a process used to manufacture canned foods, could be used as a fermenting agent when placed in an appropriate environment. The scientist concluded that oxygen was necessary to start the fermentation process, but not to continue it.

Between 1835 and 1837, Cagniard de la Tour then Schwann concluded that yeast was a vegetative organism: they had in effect recognized that " yeast " was made up of a mass of globules likely to reproduce through budding and not through a simply organic or chemical matter. In particular they drew attention to the following: " It is very likely through some effect due to their vegetative nature that the yeast globules give off the carbonic acid of sweetened liqueur and convert it into spirituous liqueurs. " Liebig (1803-1873) a famous German chemist and the spiritual father of agrochemistry definitely did not share this theory, which he held up to ridicule, declaring: " The facts which we have just exposed demonstrate the existence of a new cause.... which is simply the movement which a body in decomposition communicates to other matter in which the elements are preserved and where there is a very slight affinity...Brewers' yeast and in general all animal and plant matter in a state of putrefaction transfer their own state of decomposition; the movement which by disturbing the balance of the elements in its own composition is also transmitted to the elements which compose bodies with which it is in contact. " Mitscherlich indicates that " the globules of the fermentation agent behave towards sugar and water, which contains the elements of carbonic acid and alcohol, exactly like platinum sponge with regard to hydrogen peroxide ". The latter also confirmed the work carried out by Cagniard and pointed out that the budding process came about through the development on the surface of the cell of an excrescence which appears on the surface of the globule, with a new globule forming and then separating from the first. This is the scientific background against which Pasteur commenced his scientific experimentation on fermentation and as early as 25th February 1821 [*Works,* Vol. II, pg. 136] in a written presentation to the Academy of Sciences he pointed out for the first time the existence of " animalcules which live in liquids " with the capacity to exist without free oxygen gas and also to act as fermentation agents. (He was referring to the ferment used in butyric fermentation.)

In a communication addressed to the same institute dated 17th June 1861 [PASTEUR, *Works,* Vol. II, pg. 142] he made the following comment: " (...) Alongside all the living beings known to science at the present time and which, without exception (at least that is what we believe), cannot live and nourish themselves without breathing pure oxygen, it would appear that there also exists classes of beings which respire in a way that is sufficiently active to enable them to live outside the influence of the air by taking in oxygen in certain combinations, which explains why their decomposition is slow and progressive. This second category of organized beings is apparently made up of different ferments which in every respect are similar to beings in the first category, existing in the same way, taking in their own way carbon, nitrogen and phosphates and like them needing oxygen, but different in that they could, should they lack free oxygen gas, breathe with oxygen gas drawn from relatively unstable combinations. " On the 25th May 1863, Pasteur, [*Works,* Vol. II, pg. 172] demonstrated the presence of small quantities of acetic acid during the fermentation of alcohol (just as Lavoisier had noticed). He indicated that this substance was the result of an action of the air provoked by a mycoderma or by special ferments other than alcoholic yeast. During the same period, he also drew attention to the fact that putrefaction was determined by organized ferments such as " vibrios ". The paroxysm of the dispute between Liebig and Pasteur arrived in 1870 when the German chemist published in scientific circles an important thesis which not only refuted but mocked Pasteur's research [J. von Liebig, Concerning fermentation and the source of muscular energy: presented to the Royal Academy of Science of Munich on 9th May 1858 and 5th November 1869, French translation appearing in a paper Chemistry and Physics, 4°s XXIII, 1871, pg. 5-49].

In particular, Liebig contested that Pasteur could have produced brewers' yeast and alcoholic ferment in an inorganic sweetened environment into which he had introduced an extremely small quantity of yeast at the outset. Pasteur replied in the following terms: " For Mr. Liebig, it is known, fermentation is a phenomena correlative to death, if I may thus express myself...All substances, whatever they are, and in particular those which are described as albuminoid substances, casein, etc., or organic liquids which hold them, milk, blood, urine, etc. have the property of being able to transmit movement, that exposure to the air determines, to the molecules of a fermentable matter. The latter is then transformed into new products, without transmitting to them any of its own characteristics. In my opinion (L. Pasteur) on the contrary fermentation in the strict sense of the word is correlative with life, and I believe that I have demonstrated with peremptory proof that a fermentable substance never undergoes a fermentation process without there being a continuous exchange between living cells which grow or multiply by assimilating part of the fermentable substance itself. " And to reply once and for all to Liebig's sarcasm, Pasteur revealed that " I composed fermentable environments in which there were only three substances: the matter to be fermented, appropriately chosen mineral salts and thirdly germs of the fermenting agent...Then in precise detail, in a solution of very pure lactate of crystallized lime, I added ammoniated phosphates, magnesium and potassium, small quantities of ammoniated sulfate, and finally the germ of this bacteria or bacteria fully formed. After a few days, the lactate had completely disappeared, and an infinite number of new vibrios had been born. As long as the lactate of lime exists, the vibrios multiply in the liqueur. Once all the lactate is fully decomposed, the vibrio drop like bodies to the bottom of the vessel. The other fermentation agents and all the yeasts of the same family produce the same results, especially brewers' yeast, with which I began my research in this field. " And finally, in 1875, the scientist concluded: " I would add, today, as in 1861: fermentation is life without free oxygen. Yes there are two forms of beings: on the one hand, those that I shall call aerobics, which need to take oxygen from the air to live; the others which I shall call anaerobes, which can do without it. The latter are fermenting agents... Fermentation theory is well founded, of that I am certain. It will be established mathematically, the day when science will have made sufficient progress to be able to quantify on a proportional basis the quantity of heat that the activity of the yeast, in the absence of air, removes during the decomposition of the sugar, with the quantity of heat supplied by the combustion process due to free oxygen gas when the activity of the ferment is carried out in conditions where this gas is supplied in differing quantities. " The above summarizes the scientific episodes linked to the discovery of yeast, which is the essential organism responsible for the different aromas to be found in most beers, with the exception of certain special brews where the main characteristics are derived from caramel or roasted malts, or sometimes from the hops.

Pasteur's work was even more far-reaching in the benefits it brought to brewing and he pointed out, in addition to the way acidification altered the taste, that he suspected that oxidization had an influence on changes in the aroma. On this subject, Nicolle points out: " At that time (1870), Pasteur carried out key experiments in particular by using a wine glass. Taking a glass bowl of 300 cm³, with a long neck, into which he introduced beer wort. He stretched the neck using a lamp to bend it downwards. It was then brought to the boil. He then left it to cool down after having introduced into the opening in the neck a small piece of asbestos which had previously been heated. " (N.B.: In this way no dust could enter the glass and touch the liquid). If the wort is limpid at the outset, said Pasteur, it will stay so for twelve years. On the other hand, if the liquid in the glass is exposed to the air, it will very quickly become cloudy, and the same is true of urine, household cooking stock, grape must and any liquid which is either putrescible or fermentable. As part of his investigations he carried out similar experiments using wort which had this time been previously boiled in a wine glass; then yeast was added by way of a tube that had previously been heated over a flame. After a certain time, which varied from 24 to 48 hours, the yeast developed normally and one could then manufacture a beer no longer subject to oxidization, which could be preserved in the glass without any problem. However, Pasteur noticed that the product in this case " could go flat " on account of air getting in, or else owing to, he believed, differences in temperature and pressure.

We will also mention the experience which the brilliant scientist acquired during his trips to London (1871), his work in Chamalières (near Clermont-Ferrand) and finally the high esteem in which he was held by J-C Jacobsen and his son Carl who used the knowledge gained from the scientist to improve their manufacturing processes; in a book devoted to their brewery, the following words appear: " The method of pure yeast was discovered in 1883 by the head of the Carlsberg laboratory, Professor Emil Chr. Hansen. It is based on Pasteur's research work. " The Jacobsen family, convinced of the importance and the interest of scientific research and the arts, utilized a large part of their profits to create a research laboratory and to found an important art museum: the " Glyptothèque Ny Carlsberg ". On the 10th November 1878, Pasteur wrote the following lines to J-C and Carl Jacobsen who had suggested placing a marble bust of him in their laboratory: " By the creation of your laboratory and by the means with which you have placed at its disposal (the construction and a permanent endowment), you provide industrialists throughout the world with one of the most noble examples of gratitude to science, which is a fertile source of lasting progress. " Fortunately, others followed this example and without the support of the important brewing families, amongst whom we would mention: de Spoelbergh, Martens, Moortgat, Van Damme, van den Schriek, van der Stricht, van Roy, Verhelst, Wielmans, it is likely that the leading Belgian technical colleges which specialize in the science of brewing, in particular those of our Alma Mater (the Catholic University of Leuven) would never have been able to carry out their roles so efficiently. May they find an expression of our gratitude in this book. From a practical point of view, we therefore owe to Louis Pasteur the assertion that " alcoholic fermentation is a transformation to be associated with the life and the organization of the yeast cells and not its death or putrefaction ". He also contributed a great deal more to brewing. Summoned to the breweries in the North of France to solve a production problem, he noted that the problem arose from the yeast being contaminated by foreign micro-organisms. Hence the need to sterilize the material, to protect the production process from the air, for pasteurization.

He also observed that micro-organisms multiply less efficiently than yeast at low temperatures. That is how bottom-fermentation, which had already been used in Munich in 1420, developed. The yeasts used in bottom-fermentation were isolated in 1883 by Hansen who finalized the first installation devoted entirely to the cultivation of yeast.

With everybody more or less sticking to their own line, the distinction between " fermentation agents extracted from tissues " and " fermentation agents as micro-organisms " remained vague until 1897, two years after the death of Pasteur, when Büchner made a very important discovery. He demonstrated, in effect, that a yeast extract containing no cells could transform sugar into alcohol and CO_2. The micro-organism fermentation agent functions only thanks to " tissue fermentation agents ". The latter were to be known henceforward as enzymes, that is to say " in the yeast ".

Also noteworthy was the progress of thermodynamics (industrial cold production), which together with the development of industrial machinery, enabled the production of typical Central European beers (beers in the " Pils " style) in western regions. The latter, probably on account of consumer tastes, but also and above all due to the fact that they could be preserved for longer owing to the greater care taken in their production, gradually replaced local beers, of which the quality often proved to be variable.

It was therefore necessary to wait until the end of the XIX century before brewers could in principle brew all types of beer and at last ensure the microbiological stability of their products. There was still some way to go before they completely understood colloidal and gustatory stability.

THE XX CENTURY

Malt and brewing industries were at the origin of a great many scientific discoveries in the XIX and XX centuries, but brewing gained tremendously from the discoveries of Pasteur which enabled quality beers to be produced, which were stable and consistent, to the consumer's satisfaction. The production of malt and beer has become, over the years, in the space of a century, a veritable science, while at the same time respecting the traditions of a natural and healthy product.

Turning to the sensory characteristics of beer, research also made great steps forward during this century and we would point out the important work carried out by Klopper, Rudin and Sharpe as regards head on beer, the research of Verzele and de Keukeleire as regards the composites which give the bitter taste to hops; the papers of Chapon, De Cleck and Hashimoto regarding aging; Meilgaard, Tressi as regards the aromatic compounds in beer and their perception threshold; Meilgaard for the creation of a tasting jury, Hudson for coloring and caramel and roasted aromas, Verachtert for spontaneously fermented beers and Derdelinckx regarding the evolution of aromas and the taste of bottle conditioned beers.

What have been the consequences of the technical improvements made during the XIX century?

Obviously, an enormous increase in beer consumption during the XX century, but also, as we shall see, an incredible drop in the number of breweries due to the wars (requisitioning of copper for military needs), consumer preference for " Pils " style beers and the important investment required from an industrial point of view (cold production). In fact, in Belgium in 1900, there were 3,223 breweries, almost one per village! In general they were breweries-cum-farms, set up near water supplies, and autonomous: they cultivated the land in summer and brewed beer in the winter. The waste from manufacturing beer, the spent grain, was used to feed the livestock.

Today, not even 5% still exist. From 1950 to 1980, 70% went out of business. But the figures cannot be taken at face value: supposedly 140 are left, but they are really nothing more than simple brewing rooms.

There cannot be more than approximately 80 truly independent breweries still in existence. As regards craft brewers, they are far more numerous, but they are happy to own cafes where they serve their own beer. The introduction of the so-called " bottom-fermented " beers is partly responsible for this slaughter since this process requires far more precision and involves techniques which require heavy investment. Big corporations have taken advantage of the situation to acquire firms in difficulty.

Another factor which has played a part in the standardization of the market is the growing trend for people to drink at home rather than in the local café: local beers have been gradually forgotten for the simple reason they are no longer available in shops. It has to be pointed out that the big breweries own a good half of the cafés, which are obliged contractually to sell their beers. Nevertheless, special beers remain very much the trump card of regional breweries and a classification based on their basic ingredients, their coloration and the technology whereby they are conditioned in bottles to produce carbonation, is provided (see table 1). Today, even more than yesterday, family breweries are an essential part of our brewing culture, and without them, the industrial concentration that we are witnessing could, for purely economic reasons, make the world of brewing in Belgium drab and colorless. Long live all the brewers... and may they continue to produce their distinctive and complementary beers for a long time to come!

Professor Guy DERDELINCKX,
Lecturer and co-head of the brewing chair
at the Catholic University of Leuven,
Brewery Section, Leuven-la-Neuve

36

TRAPPIST BEERS

It is absolutely essential not to confuse an abbey beer with Trappist beers.

It is true that certain abbey beers are not dissimilar to our Trappist beers from the point of view of taste. However, though both are top-fermented beers, the word Trappist can only be used when Trappist monks have brewed the beer inside their monastery. There are five in Belgium and one in Holland, which we could not forget since it is the only one of its type in the world.

As regards Belgium, two are to be found in Flanders, one in the province of Antwerp and the other in western Flanders; the other three are in Wallonia, primarily located on the mountain ridges of the Ardennes: Chimay (the province of Hainault), Rochefort (the province of Namur) and finally Orval (the province of Luxembourg). As regards La Trappe, this is brewed in Tilbourg, on the border of the Dutch province of Limbourg.

If the Belgian Trappist beers are only five in number, there are on the other hand twelve Trappist monasteries, six with monks and six with cloistered nuns. Within their confines, all these religious gatherings produce different products intended for consumption, ranging from bars of yeast to cheese, and including market garden produce and fruit. The Trappist monks who live in the monasteries rarely drink the beer that is produced for consumption by the public at large. In general they drink only light beers which are no more than 3% alcohol, and exclusively during meals. Only the monk in charge of brewing is authorized to taste the beers he produces, and this is a secret he shares with God.

The WESTMALLE

The jewel in the collection of the Abbaye Notre-Dame de Sacré-Cœur de Westmalle is undoubtedly the Triple. Golden blond in color, it has all the attributes of a vintage beer. Its relatively high alcohol content (9%) plus just the right amount of hops and pale malt make it quite delightful. It is preferable to drink it at room

temperature. But slightly chilled, it turns out to be a very good thirst-quencher. It has a creamy tight head, which gives it an aura of calm. Its aftertaste is very pleasant, with a soft bitterness like butter. Its flavor is strongly alcoholic which helps to underline its fruity aroma. It is extremely good for the digestive system.

As regards the Double, it is far darker in color, being almost black, and is made from malt to which dark colored candy sugar is added. It is more aggressive in the mouth, with an aniseed aftertaste. Its characteristics are the same as the Triple, but with a more respectable alcohol content (6.5%). Its aftertaste is less powerful, but more notable, which means that it can be drunk with a cheese course.

The WESTLVLETEREN

Of the five Belgian Trappist beers, this is certainly the least well known, but on the other hand it is the most sought-after. We will use other superlatives to describe this exceptional beer. Its recipe is as mysterious, and remains a well kept secret hidden behind the thick walls of the Abbaye Saint-Sixtus, which is virtually off limits to secular visitors. In fact the beer

is only available in the porch of the monastery, or alternatively at the café opposite. These uncommunicative monks of Vleteren have in fact recently modernized their brewing equipment, which has enabled them to stabilize the quality of their three beers. The least strong is their red-capped beer (6%) which has a much softer taste than the other two. It is only slightly bitter and instead its aniseed aftertaste is prominent.

The blue-capped (8%) is similar to the previously mentioned beer but is fruitier, bringing to mind beers from western Flanders. The strongest of the three is the yellow-capped (11%) which, like all beers with a strong alcohol content, has a very full-bodied alcoholic flavor which is however offset by a marked bitterness and, once again, that licorice aftertaste. The principal characteristic of the Trappist beers from Westvleteren is the use of a dark malt which gives the brew a similar taste, while the hop presence is far more discreet.

CHIMAY

The three Chimay Trappist beers are probably the most successful in Belgium from a commercial point

of view. Despite the disapproval of purists, it is the only Trappist beer to have at one stage mounted a vast advertising campaign, which led certain people to read between the lines and claim that the beer was no longer brewed within the walls of the Abbaye de Notre-Dame de Scourmont. There is however no denying that, commercially speaking, their campaign was a great success for the Trappist brewery, since their beers were not particularly well known initially.

The quality of their beer was certainly worth the effort. The different beers have different colored crown caps. The red (7%) has a full-bodied taste. Overall it has a pleasant but powerful bouquet with only a hint of bitterness. The white (8%), which is a dark rusty color, has a stronger, more astringent taste, but with a far more pronounced bitterness.

The blue (9%), which is the most popular of the three, is a dark, ruby color. Its aroma is very complex, but very powerful also. In addition, the spices that are used in brewing this beer give it an even spicier taste. Despite its heavy density, it is easy to digest, so much so that it would not be out of place on a dinner table.

The ROCHEFORT

This is nicknamed "the Trappist beer for real men", since it is undoubtedly the toughest one to drink. All three have a powerful spicy aroma and are also noteworthy for their bitterness. Once again, different colored crown caps are used to distinguish the beers, which vary essentially by their alcohol content. The red 6 (7.5%) with its rich dark amber color is wonderful to drink. With its thick brownish head, it is well rounded and has a noticeable bitterness which will improve over the years.

The white 8 (9.5%), which in appearance is more tawny colored, is in my opinion a better balanced beer. Its bitterness is blended with a spicy taste and it has a drier taste.

On the other hand, the blue 10 (12%) is made for stronger palates. It has an aggressive aroma and in the mouth is velvety with a coppery, spicy taste. It is very much a beer of character, especially when drunk at between 12 and 14°C/54-57°F a beer that you can count on in the cellars of the Abbaye de Notre-Dame de Saint-Rémy.

ORVAL

This is the most straightforward Trappist beer, being simply a mixture of the traditional ingredients of water, yeast, malt, sugar and hops. When compared with other Trappist beers, it is unique in that the monks from the Abbaye Notre-Dame d'Orval produce only one beer; but what a beer! I must confess that of all the beers, this is my favorite. For connoisseurs who like their beer to have a bitter taste, it is perfect. Hops have been generously added, and it has a fairly modest alcohol content. It is a lively beer from every point of view. Its plentiful head alone is indisputable proof, as are the bubbles and beautiful lacework effect which it leaves on the glass. The real secret of Orval lies in the yeast, which is cultivated in the abbey's brewery. This Trappist beer is bottled at a very advanced stage in the production process since it has already been doubly fermented. This abbey, hidden away from the outside world deep in the forests of the Ardennes in the south of Belgium, holds many secrets. It is blessed with still pure spring waters, into which one day Matilda, Duch-

ess of Tuscany and aunt of Godfrey of Bouillon dropped her wedding ring, which was a keepsake of her husband who had died in the crusades. A trout brought her ring back to the surface. That is the legend of the Val d'Or, renamed more poetically Orval.

Do the spring waters of Orval have the same powerful healing powers as those of Lourdes? The answer is yes, if one listens to those who cultivate the land and who, as drinkers of this Trappist beer, claim that it has certain medicinal powers and can protect against cardiovascular problems as well as nervous disorders. Mythology, the water's natural characteristics, or is it simply a question of tales of sorcery from the druids of yesteryear?

The TRAPPE

It would be unfair not to refer to the sixth Trappist brew, which is Dutch. Brewed in the monastery of Onze-Lieve-Vrouw Van Kroningshoeven in Tilburg, on the border of the Dutch province of Limbourg, there are two versions, one is brown (6.5%) and the other a golden colored pale beer (8%). The venerable Dutch brothers have been brewing this beer, which is considerably different from the Belgian Trappist beers, since 1884.

Its taste is decidedly more exotic, and its taste is warmer. The brown has a strong caramel, almost coffee flavor, which is backed up by a very pronounced bitterness. It is very dense and relatively heavy to digest. However its taste is worth the effort.

The pale beer, which is frankly easier to digest, is made with a different malt, and uses a vanilla-scented sugar which gives it that exotic vigor. It also has lots of character, but the bitterness still comes through and is less aggressive than in the case of the brown.

44

THE ABBEY BEERS

In Belgium, there is practically a beer for each abbey. As with Trappist beers, there is an underlying mystique attached to beers known as abbey beers for their qualities, not to mention, of course, the name. But in reality the latter beers have no connection with the monks who brew beers. Most of the time they simply utilize the name of an abbey which formerly brewed one beer, or else, with the approval of the local ecclesiastic authorities, a local brewery buys the right to use the name of the religious site. The danger in this system of appellation is that many people, whether initiated or not, sometimes quite understandably confuse abbey beers with the Trappists. It is true that certain abbey beers are based on recipes which have been extracted from dust covered books of barely readable scrawl found in an old monastery, albeit updated by a master brewer. The others, however, are either simple top-fermented beers as a general rule, or re-labeled beers. By the latter, I mean that the beer made from the original recipe already exists with a different stamp of origin. Even the most delicate palate can be taken in by them, despite all the tasting rules. They are often more numerous than one thinks, but what does it matter? After all, they are all excellent in terms of quality.

It is by exploring all the Belgian breweries that one comes across them. Here also, it seemed to me to be a good idea to stick to basic essentials, by attaching greater importance to their original flavors, their character, the brewing principles applied as well as the design which is always cleverly conceived, being in permanence an allusion to the mysticism reigning within the somber cloisters of the monasteries.

AFFLIGEM

This is perhaps the beer most frequently confused with Trappist beers. This error is easy to understand, and in truth it is only half an error, since up to 1950 it was brewed by the Benedictine monks from the Abbaye d'Affligem, which is not far from Brussels, on the border of Pajottenland (in the western part of the province of Flemish Brabant). On the one hand, hops began to be in short supply, and on the other hand the dwindling number of monks, led Dom Robertus to sign an agreement with an Antwerp based brewery, De Hertog, which today no longer exists. It brewed the Affligem for almost twenty years while respecting the abbey's special character, describing it as *formula Antiqua renovata,* before turning to a brewery closer to the abbey, the Desmedt brewery at Opwijk.

The Affligem exists in three versions.

BLONDE

It is full of surprises from the first taste. Whereas one expects an unequivocal bitterness, instead the beer is rather soft without really any distinctive bitterness. Neither does it have a dry taste, but on the palate its basic softness once again flourishes. The Blonde (7%) also offers a pleasant taste of white alcohol to which pepper has been skillfully added.

There is a natural bitterness at the finish to confirm the earlier hints.

DOUBLE

This dark amber colored beer, which is also relatively soft, is based on a more roasted malt which introduces a deceptive aromatic bitterness, accompanied by an exotic hint of coriander. Its taste confirms the initial impression on the palate, with a touch of licorice in addition to release a spicy freshness which does not last. The bitterness of this Double (7%) is just as unobtrusive behind the aromatic malts, and only plays a brief secondary role in the final phase.

TRIPLE

The initial nose is more neutral, and corresponds to a natural bouquet of natural aromas from the different barley used in its recipe. However, this Triple with its intimate caramel alcoholic flavor (8.5%) endears itself on account of the fact that its bitterness is not aggressive. Its dark yellow appearance lends itself to tranquility, and leaves a peppery taste in the mouth, which banishes all bitterness.

GRIMBERGEN

This is often generously described as a "Trappist " beer. It is true that this beer and its origins owe much to the magical recipes of the monks from the Abbaye de Grimbergen, which was founded in 1128, by Saint Norbert, for the Premonstratensian monastic order.

The fathers who brewed the beers endeavored to provide comfort for the many pilgrims who came from distant horizons such as Rome or the Holy Land, by

offering them a brown beer, which even for that era had a fairly high alcohol content.

Because of the shortage of fathers to brew the beer, the brewing rights to this monastic beer are today owned and operated by the Alken Maes brewery under the Grimbergen label, which does its utmost to respect the secular recipe which was previously handed down from generation to generation. Four types of brew are offered to beer lovers, varying from the traditional Brown to the pale brownish-yellow Blonde, all of which are top-fermented beers and then conditioned for up to four weeks to stabilize the beer. Grimbergen beers undergo further fermentation after being bottled.

The DOUBLE

The Grimbergen Double, with its reasonable level of alcohol (6.5%), is undoubtedly the beer that most resembles that which was offered to pilgrims a century ago. In appearance it is a pleasant reddish-brown color, and it develops a powerful aroma of roasted malts, which in fact represent the essential ingredients, together with a mix of pale and caramel malts, but which is more subdued from the point of view of its odor. Its taste confirms this impression, but reveals a very specific caramel malt aftertaste, while at the same time there is a pleasant degree of bitterness. Also worthy of note is a very slight hint of sugar in the aftertaste, which for a beer of this density is absolutely normal.

The TRIPLE

To begin with, its volume of alcohol is much higher (9%). Its color is also lighter, being a slightly amber shade of blonde. The pale malts used to produce this beer, and left to germinate for a long time in the cold, explain this aspect. The ingredients also include candy sugar and a liberal dose of hops, while nevertheless being well rounded. Its aroma is less powerful than that of the Double, but on the other hand its aftertaste, where the bitterness dominates, is longer lasting.

GRIMBERGEN OPTIMO BRUNO

Contrary to what its name would suggest, it is not at all dark brown, but rather copper colored. Here the volume of alcohol is very high (10%). Its ingredients also include a variety of different malts, pale and roasted. Its taste however is strongly alcoholic and soft. There is a perfect balance between the bitter and aromatic hops.

It is a beer with character, and to appreciate it at its best it should be drunk at room temperature. Its bitterness is lighter than the two previously mentioned beers, but its flavor is distinctly drier with fruity and licorice tangs.

The BLONDE

This is the most recent creation from Grimbergen. It is brewed primarily using pale malts, which gives it a delightful bright golden appearance, which could lead to it being confused with Triple style beers (7% vol. alcohol). Its other ingredients, aromatic hops and candy sugar, give it enough bitterness and roundness to underline its fairly round but dry character. It appears to be extremely easy to digest, and can be consumed at a considerably lower temperature than the other three.

The CUVEE DE L'ERMITAGE

" Honesti laboris fructus divinus ", in other words " the divine fruit of hard work " is the motto which appears on the beer label which embellishes the bottles which contain the Cuvée de l'Ermitage. This beer evokes the solitude of a monk living as a hermit of his own volition, and who thus relied upon himself to meet his own needs. One cannot really talk of the hermit's recipe, but the brewers in the province of Hainault (the Union brewery in Jumet) based their brew on secular notes.

It is very complex in its make-up, and uses three different types of malt and four varieties of hops. It is therefore unique in character, with a distinctive flavor and an excellent bitterness. Its dark amber appearance accentuates its mysterious aspect, as does its thick head that seems to last forever in its own huge glass, which is the ideal vessel in which to appreciate in full its rich, complex aroma. Indeed one could even go so far as to say that such a glass is essential in order to appreciate fully this beer.

The Cuvée de l'Ermitage has won gold medals in world beer competitions on several occasions.

The SAINT-BERNARDUS

For a very long time beer lovers were confused by the appellation given to the beers emanating from the Saint-Bernardus brewery in Watou and the Trappist Westvleteren beer from the Abbaye Saint-Sixtus. It is true that there were grounds for confusion, since for many years (from 1946) the monks of Westvleteren had authorized the owners of the Saint-Bernardus brewery to utilize the name of the abbey for the local brewery's beers. That is how three Saint-Sixtus beers, the Pater, la Prior and the Abt came to be readily available to the public at large, who consequently assumed that they were genuine Trappist beers, all the more so since the veritable Trappist beer was almost impossible to find outside the abbey.

Once the Trappist monks had modernized the brewing equipment at Westvleteren, they decided to recover their property. From that time on, it was

50

necessary for the beers produced at the Watou brewery to be re-named. Henceforth, they were to be known definitively as Saint-Bernardus. Today, they are four in number, since the most recent creation, the Triple, in effect launched the name for the series.

Their different qualities have not changed. It is also worth noting that in appearance they are very similar with their dark amber color.

PATER 6

Its name has become a reference. Very often, it is described or ordered by its " first name ". Although its volume of alcohol is 7.1%, it is light in taste with a very slight fruity aftertaste, which is just enough to remind drinkers that it is a beer brewed in West Flanders. It should also be pointed out that the Saint-Bernardus brewery uses local hops.

PRIOR 8

Cast in the same mold as the Pater, the Prior 8, which has a higher volume of alcohol (8.3%), is a more noble and distinctive beer. Its aromatic flavor brings to mind the Trappist beer of Saint-Sixtus. What makes it stand out are primarily its qualities as an aperitif.

ABT 12

This represents the top of the range in the Saint-Bernardus portfolio of beers and it has undoubtedly the highest alcohol content too (10.4%). It is also the beer that is closest in taste and distinctive characteristics to its Trappist beers. It has a good deal of character and is well rounded, with at the forefront an impression of smoothness which rapidly creates a rapport between its taste and your palate. Its strong volume of alcohol does not diminish its flavor, which truly remains amongst the best in this category.

TRIPLE

Neither pale colored, nor too strong in alcoholic content (7%), this Triple Saint-Bernardus is decidedly less aggressive in its taste than other beers in the same category. Nevertheless its aroma is very present, and its mellow flavor is subtly reinforced by a discreet bitterness, which strikes a balance between malt and hops, with a fruity taste. To a certain extent it corresponds to the wish expressed by the brewers of Saint-Bernardus to produce a beer likely to please women.

The TONGERLO

All the signs are that this beer was being enjoyed as long ago as 1133, in Tongerlo, which lies on the present border between the provinces of Antwerp and Limbourg. In the small commune (more part of Limbourg than the Campine region), the prelate Waltman

of the Abbaye Saint-Michel d'Anvers and the bishop Burchard de Cambrai founded a religious community under the aegis of Saint Norbert, the Norbertins. Over the years, this Premonstratensian abbey, similar to that of Grimbergen, became an important center of worship and rural exploitation. Regrettably, all the secular work of the monks, as well as their patrimony, was destined to be swept away by the French Revolution. But in 1840, several monks returned and rebuilt the abbey, which lay in ruins. Everything was rebuilt, except for the brewery adjoining the abbey. However, for these gallant monks, it was impossible to imagine monastic life without beer. Consequently, the monks sought a brewer. They found salvation at Haecht, with a beer faithful to the gastronomic traditions of the Norbertins. Two versions of the Tongerlo were produced, the Double and the Triple.

What sets both types of beer apart from all other beverages of the same style is the use of a special strain of yeast.

DOUBLE

With its alcoholic density of 6%, this beer, which has a dark reddish-brown color, is full of panache. Creamy to perfection, it is well rounded from every point of view, with only a touch of bitterness. Its charm essentially lies in a long-lasting aftertaste, which is tinged with aniseed and fruity at the same time. At room temperature, it can also be sometimes soft and sugary, sometimes sharp. It is certainly an effective thirst-quencher, and is renowned for its generous head in a chalice shaped glass.

TRIPLE

This Triple, which is naturally the strongest from the point of view of its volume of alcohol (8%), is both appetizing at the outset, and provides a total contrast with the basic characteristics of the Double. The first impression is a taste of malt and yeast, against a background of bitterness, which is cushioned by a very dry but powerful aftertaste. Its equally rich head does not succeed in hiding its alluring and charmingly intoxicating aroma. It is equally successful as a thirst-quencher, but is less effective as a digestive.

DOUBLE BLONDE

This is the most recent creation, and naturally this is a child of the other two, and as such is bound to have certain points in common with its parents. From the point of view of appearance, it is amber, the result of mixing brown with blonde. As regards taste, in deference to its parents, there is in effect a balance between a more roasted taste, which is somewhat lacking in character, and a bitterness. And yet youth innovates, and it is distinctly livelier on the tongue, with a pleasant spicy taste accompanied by a dash of exoticism, which comes from the coriander and a zest of orange peel. It is clearly more a digestive than its parent beers, and should age well. There is however an aroma of chicory at the bottom of the empty glass, whereas this sensation was completely absent when the beer was tasted.

L'ABBAYE ENAME

Many years ago, the river Escaut, the second longest river in Belgium, which flows along the valleys of the Flemish Ardennes in the region of Audenarde, the whims of nature caused it to burst its banks and change slightly the course of its slow journey to the North Sea. As a consequence of this abrupt change in the river's natural course, part of a small riverside village called Ename was left under water. The turbulent waters of the river claimed the cemetery, a few houses belonging to fresh water fishermen, but above all the splendid Benedictine abbey of Ename.

When it disappeared under the weight of the bursting river, all the secrets of a terrestrial life full of promise were lost with it. However, since relatively recently, the ruins of the secular abbey have started to re-appear above the water level. This renaissance has encour-

aged many local craftsmen to carry out intensive fresh research in the archives of the town of Audenarde, which already has a very rich artistic patrimony, but also a very considerable brewing and farming tradition.

In 1545 in particular, the Roman family was already brewing beer, principally for its staging post, the inn "la Cloche ", in the small village of Schorisse. This was all the encouragement that the descendants of this well-known family required to update an astonishing recipe from days gone by, the Abbaye d'Entane, which also is brewed in two versions.

DOUBLE

Dark colored like most Doubles, it is a beer strong in character. Reddish-amber in appearance, the Double Ename has a smooth, creamy taste, and a bitterness that is only slightly aggressive. Its aroma is distinct and fruity. Its flavor is dense and even discretely sharp with an aftertaste redolent of licorice. It seems to be a beer that has discovered the secret of eternal youth.

TRIPLE

The Blonde Triple from the Roman brewery definitely has a much stronger volume of alcohol (9%) than its fellow beer, the dark colored Double. Its taste is drier, and strangely enough there is just a passing hint of sugar. It is bottled after being left to ferment for the relatively long period of two months. It is then conditioned in the bottle. The Triple Ename is very soft in the mouth, and is also very refreshing when it is drunk at the appropriate temperature. Moreover, largely on account of the ferruginous spring water from the Flemish Ardennes, it is also very good as a digestive.

Both Ename beers, even if their lacework is relatively modest, have magnificent white heads.

The STEENBRUGGE

Whenever anyone speaks of the Abbaye de Steenbrugge, which is to be found in the leafy suburb of Brugges, they will inevitably evoke the name of Saint

Arnold. At a period in history when epidemics were decimating the population, this splendid fellow was

responsible for beer being recognized as the only healthy, life preserving drink.

Since then he has become the patron saint of brewers. In accordance with a request of the 58th Abbot, successor to Saint Arnold, the Steenbrugge double and triple beers are brewed in strict conformity with the monastic rules.

DOUBLE

In appearance the Double is a shimmering ruby color, it is well rounded in the mouth and voluptuous on the palate. Its volume of alcohol is 6.5%. In accordance with the monastic traditions, it is brewed from pure malt and hops. It was launched in 1980, that is 10 years before the Triple. It is brewed in one of the oldest breweries in Belgium, the Gouden Boom, and like the classic beers of ancestral times, it has a magnificent taste. The master brewer responsible for the Double, Paul Vanneste, is a giant in the world of brewing in Belgium (more than 2 meters tall!). He is a walking encyclopedia of the magical recipes and secrets of the monks and their brews. He is also nicknamed "the star of the Triple ", as you will understand from the following paragraph.

TRIPLE

With a spiritual father such as Paul Vanneste, the Triple Steenbrugge could not help but be born under a lucky star when it was launched in 1990. It has a very handsome 9% volume of alcohol. It is almost transparent, being a deep blonde color with attractive lacework, and topped by a generous head. From a tasting point of view it has many attractions, including a rich bouquet as well as a powerful flavor which conjures up images of the rich historical past of Bruges. Its bitterness releases two diametrically opposed tastes, a slightly sugary taste which lingers on the tongue, just the time it takes to savor the quality of the hops, which are excellent in quality for this dense but extremely subtle tasting beer. It is excellent as an aperitif, and it is

also perfect by way of a digestive, with the promise of a good night's sleep to follow.

If laid down in a cellar it will gain even more in character, which will be even more noticeable when the beer is served at an ambient temperature.

The TRIPLE DE BRUGES

It goes without saying that we could not fail to devote a few separate lines to the Triple de Bruges, that classic beer from the city that is known as the "Venice of the North ". It is a masterpiece in its category, full of roundness and rich in taste. It has a subtle bitterness wrapped in a strong aroma of alcohol (9.5%). Its aftertaste also evokes the presence of different aromatic malts, all of which is rounded off with a good amount of hops. One is almost tempted to describe it as having a certain exotic style, but perhaps this is simply one's imagination being given free rein to explore the historic past of the city of Bruges, which used to be a sea port, and a calling port for the great sailors of the southern oceans.

The SAINT-ARNOLDUS TRIPLE

It was quite odd that, despite the long and prestigious history of beer in our country, no beer existed as a tribute to the patron saint of the industry. Since 1985, the brewery Riva has been producing a beer bearing this name, but it is only by chance that we discovered its existence, but what a discovery!

In fact, as was often the case in the early days of beer production in Belgium, beers were more amber colored before the yellowish tint of Pils style beer took over. The Saint-Arnoldus beer is the traditional color, but in addition it is double fermented. It would not be out of place in the category of "abbey " beers, not only because of the description of its name, but also on account of its quality. With a more than correct volume of alcohol (7.5%), it has a very distinctive aroma which is not dissimilar to the strong English " ales ". Its taste is based on a bitterness in the back-

58

ground, but which for a few moments gives way to a discreet hint of caramel and spices. There is a slight tingling feeling on the tip of the tongue and at the back of the throat. However, its aftertaste is both powerful and full of character. This touch of amber in its appearance and the caramel taste in the mouth are achieved by using an amber malt.

Ideally it should be consumed at a temperature of between 10 and 12° C/50-53°F to discover its full qualities. At that temperature it will demonstrate the panache which makes it worthy to bear the name of its patron Saint, Saint Arnold.

SAINT-SEBASTIEN

Here also the brewers have sought to pay tribute to a saint, this time, Sebastien, a Roman martyr who was executed by arrows. That is why he became the patron saint of archers. However the brewer gives no indication whether this beer was initially aimed at a guild of archers. Whatever the answer, it is a veritable " abbey " beer, distributed in magnificent stoneware bottles, brown in the case of the Dark variety and white for the Grand Cru.

DARK

It has a very pleasant caramel sensation, which is backed up by a fruity, sugary tang. It retains a perfect balance, with a slight bitterness, which is only detectable in the mouth, since it is the first two impressions that dominate its aftertaste.

As its name suggests, it is dark colored.

GRAND CRU

It is blonde in appearance and naturally is slightly more bitter in taste than its dark, fellow beer.

This is a result of being blended with pale malts. However, after a period of adaptation, a fruity flavor is discernible on the palate, but this remains a hint and nothing more. The secrets of this brew are just as impenetrable as its bottle.

It is very much a beer that displays a little more of its charm every day.

The TRIPLE PETRUS

With its jovially designed label, which encourages conviviality, the Triple Petrus cannot but belong to the famous family of abbey beers. Its name serves as a reminder that not all monks were melancholy. Its label bears excellent witness to this observation, with a religious figure looking like a very sweet tempered Saint Peter, and who, with a broad smile on his face, and a glass in his hand, inspires optimism.

And there are certainly reasons to be optimistic, for this superb heady Triple has all that is necessary to warm you to the bones of your body. Its volume of alcohol is high (7.5%) and it is a beer which is full of character and is uncompromising. It leaves a lingering bitterness on the tongue and in the throat. It is very rich in flavor and there is a very discreet but noteworthy fruity touch.

Other than its convivial qualities, this triple Blonde is good for quenching a thirst and is also an above average digestive drink.

The ABBAYE DE BONNE-ESPERANCE

At least with the Bonne-Esperance, there cannot be the slightest doubt concerning the aptness of its name. This beer, which evokes the site of Vellereille-lez-Brayeux near Binche in the province of Hainult, was at the outset virtually invented for the pilgrims visiting the abbey. Very quickly its reputation spread beyond the confines of the abbey and it became a beverage that was much sought after by laymen also. It is a very accomplished beer and its recipe appeals to lovers of beers that have a certain depth of character. There is a strong caramel aroma. This is confirmed by the flavor, while the aftertaste leaves a very strong bitterness, which thus lessens the initial impression. Its amber color corresponds perfectly to the roasted malt utilized. Its subtlety and the spices that are discernible make it an abbey beer which is in perfect symbiosis with the Holy Spirit.

ABBAYE de FLORETTE

Another beer which makes direct use of the ecclesiastical appellation in its name. This magnificent site overlooks the unassuming Sambre at the entrance to Dinant. This abbey cultivates, with great dignity, a legend according to which in 1204, during the feast of the Holy Cross, at the time of the service, drops of blood flowed from this relic. The same phenomenon occurred again fifty years later in 1254. Since then, it has become a place of pilgrimage, and it welcomes many pilgrims who come perhaps to see another miracle. However, thus far, the only wonders that the faithful pilgrims have observed are inspired by the pleasures of this beer, which is served to visitors to this famous abbey.

There are three versions of this beer, the Blonde, the Double and the Meilleure, which are all very different in taste.

BLONDE

With its 7% volume of alcohol, its aroma is fairly neutral and not particularly strong. Its bitterness in the mouth is full but is not harsh and does not last, but there is however a slightly spicy bite to it on the tongue. It is also slightly fruity (orange peel), but this is minor in relation to the overall taste.

The bitterness reappears in the aftertaste, but it does not last, nor does it develop any further flavor.

It is a little lacking in body but is extremely pleasant to drink, especially when it is served fresh at a temperature of between 8 and 10°C/46-50°F.

DOUBLE

It is dark brown in color with a brownish head. It also has a volume of alcohol of 7%. Its aroma is just as weak as its bitterness which, it has to be pointed out, is nevertheless made more pleasant by a slight taste of licorice against a background of sugar and coffee (roasted malt).

It also has a spicy tang on the tongue and develops very little aftertaste.

TRIPLE

Its 8% volume of alcohol gives it more of a kick than the other two, with however a nose which remains relatively sober. Its bitterness is of short duration and gives way to a taste that can be described as caramel, spicy and fruity at the same time. Its aftertaste is subdued and does not add anything. It is nevertheless a very pleasant beer to drink for an evening, on condition that it is served at a temperature between 12 and 14°C/ 53-57°F.

MEILLEURE

To justify its name, it is undoubtedly the most spectacular of the Floreffe. Its volume of alcohol is not measurably higher (8%), but its bouquet is most pleasant, with a powerful aroma of aniseed, which is amplified by a head that like the beer's color is a deep reddish brown.

If one were to close one's eyes, its aroma could be confused with the bouquet of a glass of pastis.

Its taste confirms this impression but is even more powerful with an added touch of brief exoticism, which results from a well-judged combination of aromatic malts. Its bitterness is relegated to the background but reappears at the end and is enhanced by a licorice flavor. With each mouthful, subtle new secrets emerge. It justifies its name the " meilleure " i.e. the best.

AUGUSTIJN

On the few occasions we are confronted with beers that do not bear the names of abbeys, we often find instead the names of those who lived there. This time the beer involved is called Augustijn. Apparently, even the brewers are not totally certain why it was christened thus. In reality, it probably refers to saint Augustine, a writer of the Latin Church. The link between the beer which bears his name and the tribute paid to his memory is somewhat tenuous.

However, the choice of the name Augustijn is not merely a matter of chance, since if the saint brought his letters patent of nobility to Latin, the beer is not far behind in terms of winning acclaim in its own category. It exists in two versions, the Augustijn forte (8%) and the Grand Cru (9%).

AUGUSTIJN FORTE

Slightly amber in color, there is a well balanced bitterness that is both well rounded and delicately spicy. It retains a very well judged balance, in other words, despite it being full tasting none of the ingredients is overpowering. Its taste is neutral against a malt background. The aftertaste will confirm this impression.

AUGUSTIJN GRAND CRU

This is very much based on the above Augustijn Forte. Indeed the latter name would perhaps have been more appropriate for this beer, which deliberately has a greater depth of character with an aroma which is more present, as well as a far more noticeable bitterness. Its higher level of alcohol is also more present in the aftertaste. One can also detect a slightly exotic touch through the intermediary of orange peel, but this is the only artifice used. Its generous head is pleasing on the eye and whets the appetite. It can be consumed at fairly cool temperatures (8 to 9° C/46-48°F).

MAREDSOUS

When I was a young man discovering the joys of brewing, the Maredsous was always an enigma. Perhaps it is simply the memories of wonderful times spent with my parents on childhood outings, which often ended with a supper of bread, cheese and Maredsous beer. Whatever the reason, this name will always have a special place in my memory, and I remain convinced that this beer would have found a place amongst present day Trappist beers, if at least a monk had discovered that he was a brewer to the core. There is no need therefore to elaborate on whether the description of an " abbey " beer is appropriate.

And as if to reinforce the idea of an important presence, in accordance with the secular tradition of

abbey beers, there are four varieties of the Maredsous, while for many years it was available in only one version. The most common is the 8%, which is dark amber in color, with a certain depth of character and a base of licorice. The other three Maredsous beers (6% blonde and brown and 9%) stand out immediately by their color, always on condition that they are poured into a large glass with a curving rim almost like a large flute glass, since at the abbey the beverages are served in earthenware vessels. Their tastes are, of course, also distinctive.

The Maredsous beers tend to be blonde in color, and are fairly well rounded but also dry in flavor.

The first of them (6%) is fruity but this fades in the aftertaste. On the other hand the 10% (9.5%) cannot hide its strong alcohol flavor with a body, which when all is said and done, is fairly soft. There is also a slightly fruity tang, which adds to its flavor.

The two other versions are more distinctive because of a tendency to taste like wine, but without any acidity. The correction occurs during the second fermentation. There is almost a suggestion of exoticism against a licorice background. Now, they are also filtered, which makes their color even more brilliant.

The POSTEL

Founded in 1138, this abbey, situated at the cross-roads for travelers between Antwerp and Cologne, Leuven's Hertogenbosch welcomed many visitors who wished to withdraw for a certain time to a monastery.

This retreat, which can be seen as the equivalent of a present day anti-stress therapy, was accompanied by a vintage beer, called the Postel. The dark years of the French Revolution led to the closure of this magnificent abbey, which only opened its doors again in 1847. By the same token, the fate of the Postel was sealed, since it was no longer brewed.

It took almost another hundred and twenty years for it to be reborn, this time no longer at the abbey, but well and truly in a brewery in the Brussels suburbs. This brewery rediscovered the precious monastic recipe and gave a new life to the Postel, which continues today, with an extra version as a bonus.

That is how there came to be a classic Double (brown) with a volume of alcohol of 7%, as well as a Triple, which is not very far removed from the initial version with a volume of alcohol of 8.5%.

DOUBLE

It has a velvet bronzed color, and hides a marvelously soft aroma that develops even more fully in the mouth, and leaves two sensations in the aftertaste, one of wine and the other bitter. It has an impressive subtlety and is rich in flavor. It is ideal to accompany soft cheeses, and is a good aperitif.

TRIPLE

It makes little impression with the first taste, but it very quickly asserts itself in the mouth. It bears no resemblance to its fellow beer, the darker Double. This whimsical pale beer which appears inoffensive, very quickly shows its mettle, through a lingering but never aggressive bitterness. It leaves a lingering after-taste as with the bitterness, but is spicier and makes a very good aperitif, while its digestive capacities are not to be ignored.

The KAPITTEL

Neither the name of an abbey, even less that of an influential person from the ecclesiastical world, the Kappitel qualifies as an abbey beer by the indispensable accessory represented by its name. Brewed close beside the abbey of Saint-Sixtus from where the Westvleteren, the most mysterious Trappist beer in the country originates, it describes the spirit of monks during congregations. It champions a mystical rather than a convivial role. There are four chapters, the Pater (6.5%), the Double (7%), the Prior (9%) and finally the Abt (10%).

PATER

It may seem a contradiction, but the " father " of the Kapittel beers is the least strong in terms of percentage of alcohol; however, that is not the case as regards the density of its taste, which is extremely surprising. This dark beer is relatively soft tasting with very little bitterness, but the surprise comes from its aftertaste in which a very discreet bitterness develops secretly in the glass.

The way in which the taste changes between only two phases in the tasting leaves a strange impression. At room temperature it improves even more to develop almost the same tangs one would find in a young red wine.

67

DOUBLE

It starts off on the same basis as the Pater, but more acid and with a similar softness. It becomes even more pronounced in the mouth and does not change in the aftertaste.

PRIOR

This, the third chapter in the Kapittel family of beers, cannot deny its origins and links with the first two. It is identical to the Double in its characteristics, with a more velvety and stronger alcoholic flavor.

ABT

This is the top of the range beer for the Kapittel series, again with certain similarities with the other beers. Its alcohol content gives it a more neutral taste than the other three with a far more distinctive bitterness, which remains very present in the aftertaste. Its full flavor warrants a more moderate consumption compared with the three above-mentioned chapters.

The TRIPLE MOINE

The Triple Moine has no historical background, as such, it exists to please connoisseurs of a good strong pale beer. Its aroma is malty accompanied by a very generous measure of dry bitterness. The beer fully asserts itself in the mouth and the aftertaste is very long-lasting.

It also has a slight yeasty flavor, which means that it can be described as a beer of spontaneous good taste.

The SAINT-BENOIT

A French penitent, Benoît-Joseph Labre could never become a monk. He traveled throughout Europe begging. The harshness of his existence and his good works were only recognized long after his death.

The Saint-Benoît is certainly not the reflection of his life, but rather a symbol of eternal hope.

And yet, the key characteristic of the taste of this beverage is the softness, whereas in all logic we could have expected a far harder beer.

Two versions are brewed, one brown and one pale (both are 6.5%) and they are very similar in taste, but develop differently.

The BRUNE

Almost with no bitterness, its essence is a languid softness crowned with a subtle bouquet redolent of the forest. It is brown in color and betrays very few of the secrets surrounding its ingredients. There is no surprise in the tangs in the aftertaste, as though it was satisfied with its humble but honest destiny.

The BLONDE

The same comment applies as for the Brune, and its clear color is no more communicative as to its ingredients. Its taste differs however on the edge of the tongue, with a fruitier but unobtrusive flavor, just enough to prepare the way for a more distinct and assertive bitterness at the end of the tasting.

SAINT-HERMES

Between Hermes, a Greek god on the one hand, protector of travelers and also patron of merchants, and on the other hand the saint, the connection is very remote.

In truth only Belgium granted him this title, in particular the town of Renaix in western Flanders, of which he is the patron saint. An old abbey, formerly

occupied by the Jesuits in the region, serves as a reminder today of the role of this famous individual in the town's history. It is also certainly an abbey beer since the name of Saint-Hermes is also linked to this former abbey which is still situated in this commune in Flanders.

The Saint-Hermes (8%), amber through its special malts, leaves only a little room for bitterness. It is certainly present, but very delicately. The subtlety of the taste could even be described as spicy and invigorating. Its aroma is peppery and dry. Its aftertaste reveals no new impressions. It should be drunk at relatively moderate temperatures (12 to 14° C/53-57°F).

The SAINT-IDESBALD

Saint-Idesbald, which is a very popular holiday resort on the Belgian coast, with its main attraction being its sand dunes, was in bygone times the site of the Abbaye des Dunes, which was built on the very dunes which form this vast coastal hill range.It was built in 1107, but very rapidly the natural elements conspired to totally destroy this Cistercian abbey. At the beginning of the XII century the buildings could still only be de-

scribed as precarious. In 1127, the abbot Foulques, successor of the Benedictine monk Ligier, the first investigator of the abbey, set to work to construct a decidedly more solid edifice. Nevertheless, the passing time would show that this abbey was never destined to expand as it should have, and was never to become the place of prayer that the fishermen had so badly wanted.

Today, all that remains are a few ruins, including the foundations, and a beer which bears the same name in three versions.

BLONDE

With its low volume of alcohol of 6%, this is one of the weakest abbey beers. What emerges is a beer with relatively little dimension. Its taste is really very soft against a fruity background. It reveals very little depth in character, and does not develop at all in the mouth. Only a slight bitterness makes up for the thinness of the aftertaste. On the other hand, as a digestive drink, it lends itself willingly to this role. It should ideally be drunk fairly cool.

BRUNE

Though the Blonde should have shown more character, it is the Brune that reveals the veritable character of the Saint-Idesbald. Its volume of alcohol is more than correct at 8%, and it has a great many similarities

71

with the old Flemish brown beers, that is to say sharp against a background of well balanced bitterness.

It thus respects the taste which North Sea fishermen appreciated in bygone days, especially after long days exposed to the salt waters and their old tubs, where even the food they ate was covered in salt. Far from being a thirst-quenching beer, it shows itself to be a true friend, on whom one can count. Its aftertaste sometimes has an edge to it, in which the bitterness is clearly dominant.

TRIPLE

Very similar to the Brune, the Triple tones down the acid aspect with a touch of caramel. This impact is reinforced by a flavor that is also higher in alcohol (9%). It is easier to drink, but on the other hand its effect is more immediate. It cannot boast of its digestive qualities, but when it is served at 12° C/53°F, it shows its claws, and could cast a spell over you.

The LEFFE

Situated at the threshold of the gateway to the Ardennes in Dinant (Province of Namur), the Abbaye de Leffe was built in the XIII century and could never have imagined for a second that its fame would spread to the four corners of the earth thanks to a bottle of beer. It cannot be denied that the Leffe is the abbey beer which has made the biggest break-through internationally. This success of Leffe is primarily due to the largest brewing group in Belgium, Interbrew, recognizing its worth, and consequently using the considerable means at its disposal to promote its expansion throughout Europe and the world.

For example, the Japanese regularly enjoy Leffe, as do the Canadians deep in the heart of their forests. Leffe has become such a phenomenon that there now exists a veritable chain of cafés which are confused as one with the name of the beer; for two cents its ecclesiastical origins would be forgotten.

In total there are five versions, and there can be no denying that it is a brilliant product, perfect throughout the range. The different beers are available under the following labels: Blonde, Brune, Radieuse, Triple and Vieille Cuvée.

BLONDE

To begin with, its name describes its color. It also implies that it is made with pale malts to which are added an average amount of hops, which slightly changes its bitterness but not in any exaggerated way. It develops well in the mouth and the bitterness, which it leaves in the after-taste, is only slightly more noticeable. It is one of the least strong (6.5%) amongst the five. It is certainly a friendly, welcoming beer, but it should be drunk with caution, because it quickly goes to one's head.

BRUNE

This is almost black in color, and brings to mind certain dark English beers. It is to our very good fortune that its aroma is by far superior to those beers from across the Channel. Its alcohol content is also greater than the latter (6.3%). It retains a good balance between softness and bitterness, which are the two tastes discernible in this beer. The dark malt which is used also gives it an aftertaste of strong coffee. It is alas fairly heavy to digest, that is why it is better suited to be savored during relaxing moments, and preferably at a moderate temperature.

RADIEUSE

Its strong alcohol content (8.2%) develops a powerful, dense flavor against a background of bitter caramel. It is most attractive to those who have a taste for slightly peppery beers. It has a great deal of distinction with notably a concluding spicy bitterness, which to a certain degree overpowers its caramel flavor.

It should be drunk at room temperature, and although from a digestive point of view it is somewhat

heavy, this can easily be forgiven since it remains the most accomplished and personalized in the range.

TRIPLE

The Triple (8.1%) is only slightly darker than the Blonde, and the initial impact in its taste is its density, which gives way to a fuller taste against a malt background. It becomes richer as the taste develops fully, but does not develop further in the aftertaste, although a spicy tang does linger in the mouth.

VIEILLE CUVEE

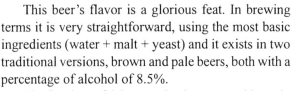

This is the classic vintage full of maturity. Its appellation also emphasizes a certain maturity in its delicate syrupy flavor. Its bitterness is more than discreet and in no way influences the aftertaste. This is a beer for genuine connoisseurs to enjoy as a way of rounding off a pleasant evening.

The MOINETTE

Contrary to what people may think, the Moinette is not an allusion to the feminine side of monks. In fact, its name dates back to a place of prayer in a small village in west Hainault, Tourpes, not far from Tournai, and called in the local dialect " moënette ", which became over the years, moinette.

This beer's flavor is a glorious feat. In brewing terms it is very straightforward, using the most basic ingredients (water + malt + yeast) and it exists in two traditional versions, brown and pale beers, both with a percentage of alcohol of 8.5%.

The first has a fairly complex bouquet, with a mix of bitterness, a slight acidity in the background, yet soft at the same time. It develops even more in the mouth, and as a result the aftertaste is wonderfully full and bitter.

On the other hand, the Blonde goes all out for a deep bitter taste with a hint of fruit in the flavor. In the mouth there is an even stronger acrid taste which never disappears throughout the drink. It leaves a very bitter and dry aftertaste. In addition it is extremely easy to digest, and is a relaxing beer, on account of its generous use of hops. It is a superb abbey beer, simple, forthright and effective.

It should not be forgotten there exists a special Christmas version, " Avec les Bons Voeux de la Brasserie " (9.5%) and which is even denser than the other two versions.

There are also organic brews available, with however the same taste. These are brewed in accordance with strict biological hygienic standards. The raw materials (hops and malts) are not treated with pesticides or other products used to protect them against insects, and are left to grow naturally outdoors. In addition to the Moinette Biologique (also 7.5 vol. alcohol), other organic beers are the Saison Dupont Biologique (5.5%) and the Biolégère (3.5%).

It must be pointed out that only beverages which are approved by " Nature et Progrès " a European association for agriculture and biological hygiene are allowed to describe themselves as organic, and only after very strict tests have been carried out.

We knew that beer was good for the health; with biological hygiene as a bonus, it is in the process of being almost indispensable for our organism.

Excellent vintage!

PATER VAN DAMME

Throughout time, a multitude of individuals has played their part in writing the history of Flanders Real or imaginary, those who have participated have always managed to preserve an element of mystery, causing a certain perplexity amongst the population.

The flat lands of Belgium have had their share of invaders, principally Spanish, who left many vestiges behind them, not only from a human point of view, but also artistically and architecturally. During the period of the Spanish occupation, apparently amongst the

inhabitants of a small village situated in the inner suburbs of Bruges there was a dauntless and courageous young man, who answered to the name of Tijl Uilenspiegel. Single-handedly he harassed the invaders to such an extent that he became a wanted man with a price on his head, dead or alive.

If one believes that this brave and likable young man existed, then one will accept just as readily the history of father Van Damme. Who was he and what was his importance during the years of Spanish occupation? Absolutely nothing is known about him, and yet according to stories of present day inhabitants he actually did exist and, apparently, gave help to the young Tijl. Whatever the truth may be, a beer exists today which bears his name, which confirms that he belongs to this village in Flanders. Irrespective of whether or not he really existed, the Pater van Damme beer can without doubt be classified amongst abbey beers.

It is a relatively young beer since it was created in 1992, inspired by the ingenuity of one of the villagers with a great love of beer and history. Apparently, his recipe comes from a manuscript in the Damme museum. The Pater Van Damme which has a volume of alcohol of 7.5%, is a beer which is filtered and pasteurized, and is reddish-brown in color. Its ingredients are Belgian hops, which are turned into dough, and a dark malt.

Its taste is relatively fruity but without acidity, which gives it a certain discreet bitter taste, but which is not at all overpowering in its conclusion, where it is well balanced by a suggestion of brown sugar, which does not however linger. It is also a thirst-quencher when it is consumed at cellar temperature. It is served in an earthenware vessel with four finger holds engraved into it as with traditional drinking vessels. The only drawback is that you must be right-handed.

It is generally served with a slice of bread (wheat bread) spread with cheese (soft cheese), and can be found in only two places, direct at the micro-brewery or in the restaurant " Tijl Uilenspiegel ", which is where two legends meet, if there really is a legend!

WITKAP

Literally the name of this beer alludes to the white cape which monks were obliged to wear during prayer. Nevertheless, the brewers have not hidden their intentions in producing this abbey beer.

The three versions, with their very discreet labels, have very special tastes and, in the case of the two with the lowest alcohol content, lack the real character one would expect from a beverage in this category.

PATER STIMULO

Its taste is sparkling and slightly fruity, especially in the nose. It does not develop any more character in

the mouth, but the fruity impact is lessened and gives way to a balanced bitterness. Its alcoholic flavor (6.2%) is barely discernible.

PATER DOUBLE

It tastes of caramel and is bitter at the same time. There is a certain suggestion of licorice but this does not last. Only the well-rounded bitterness lingers at the end. Preferably it should be drunk at moderate temperatures.

PATER TRIPLE

This has much more character than the two above-mentioned beers. The suggestion of a fruit flavored perfume is still very much present, but the bitterness is far more in harmony with its alcoholic taste (7.5%). It is also drier in its bitter aftertaste.

ABBAYE D'AULNE

Its name evokes the numerous alders that surround it. The Abbaye d'Aulne was built alongside the Sambre in the very heart of Hainault (Gozée), looking out towards the province of Namur. It is one of the oldest abbeys in the country, since it dates from 657, the year when a certain Father Landelin, while walking in the woods amongst the alders, built a small chapel there as well as several cells for monks looking for a place to meditate. Over the years it became prestigious and very important, mainly under the aegis of the Cistercian monks of Clairvaux who assumed responsibility for the destiny of the abbey.

Alas, the winds of violence of the French Revolution destroyed a large part of this splendid place of prayer. Some of the ruins still exist which stand majestically tall amongst the alders which, if they could talk, would be able to recount the tragic events which the sans culotte inflicted on the Abbaye d'Aulne.

The recipes of the different beers that were brewed there have on the other hand remained intact, and have not changed one iota throughout the centuries. There are five varieties available, but it is highly likely that in former times the monks brewed only two sorts, a light beer and a strong version.

SUR LIE

The lightest beer in the range is also one of the most traditional. It is gently spicy and sugary, and there is only a very discreet but effective bitterness, which carries through to the aftertaste. Its alcohol content is 6%.

SELECTION

With 8% volume of alcohol, it is just as sweet as the 6, with also more of a caramel flavor and accordingly has more roundness. Again the bitterness does not stand out and appears uniquely in the aftertaste.

SUPERBE

This version is decidedly sugary (candy sugar). There is no bitterness detectable, only softness with a strong alcoholic flavor (10%). This is probably the version which was brewed by the monks in the abbey. It is not to be recommended as a digestive drink, or if it is, then only at the very end of the evening. The presence of a sugar in its ingredients also makes it a beer rich in vitamins, but makes it also fearsome for the rapidity with which it induces a state of intoxication.

BLONDE DES PERES

Its basic ingredient is pale malt, and this Blonde, which is nevertheless fairly strong (7%) does not develop much bitterness. From a personality point of view it is somewhat passive, and while it undoubtedly asserts itself in the mouth, there are no real surprises in the conclusion. It should be consumed cooler than the others, and as a digestive has certain qualities.

TRIPLE

The initial impact on the taste buds comes from its alcoholic flavor (9%). This impression is accompanied by a malty taste.

When all is said and done, its general nature is based on its softness. Its bitterness is neutral and has no impact on the initial impression. This should be drunk very cool since it has no new subtleties to highlight.

SAINT-PAUL

Apostle of the good, Saint Paul was destined to appear on the label of a beer, which is welcoming and cheerful in spirit. The Saint-Paul and its earthenware bottle does not suffer at all when compared with another beer from the brewery, the Saint-Sebastien. Naturally they have certain points in common but uniquely in the basic yeast used, and of course the receptacles. But that is where any comparison stops. It exists in two versions, which are much sought after by pilgrims from Limbourg.

DOUBLE

Dark in color, it is very soft and at the same time has a sugared coffee flavor. From the point of view of bitterness it is also interesting, and this aspect develops especially in the aftertaste.

Its volume of alcohol is 6.9%.

TRIPLE

The initial impression is that the Triple (7.6%), which is brewed alongside the Double, seems to have less character than the latter. Its ingredients (pale malt and hops) appear however more limpid in the mouth. The amounts are very well balanced, and no aspect is overpowering. It is in the aftertaste that its bitter character stands out. It has two diametrically opposed roles, aperitif and digestive. It can be drunk cool or at a moderate temperature depending upon individual preferences.

SAINT-FEUILLEN

In the 7th century, Feuillien, an Irish monk, arrived on the continent to preach the bible. It was at Roeulx

in the Hainault that he took his last dramatic steps to meet his destiny, but also towards his canonization.

While he was crossing a coal forest, he was set upon by brigands, who tortured him before decapitating him. His disciples erected a chapel on the very spot where he was murdered. This same site then took on a

far more important dimension, and became an abbey, that of Saint-Feuillien. This met the same fate as its patron saint, and was razed to the ground during the French Revolution.

The monks who brewed the beer there nevertheless took great care not to lose the recipe of their beverage, which today is available in two versions, brown and blonde.

BRUNE

This is the least known to the general public, since the Blonde's success has somewhat forced it to play second fiddle. And yet it has all the qualities of a strong Brune (7.5%).

Its taste has a few hidden subtleties from every point of view, soft without almost any perceptible bitterness. At the first taste it appears slightly peppery, it leaves a suggestion of dryness despite a velvety feeling.

BLONDE

In reality this Blonde (also 7.5% vol. alcohol) is rather reddish-brown in color. It is less spicy than the Blonde, but develops slightly more bitterness against a malt background. In the mouth it develops no new aspect, despite a fruity and peppery aroma. Its aftertaste is not long-lasting on account of its dry taste.

It is very much a digestive drink, and it is easy to drink, but quickly becomes intoxicating.

L'ABBAYE DES ROCS

Originally built at the summit of Montignies-sur-Rocs to the south of Mons, all that remains today of the abbey is a section of wall concealed beneath piles of secular stones and the undergrowth.

In truth, the Abbaye des Rocs is rather a large monastic farm.

The brewery, which has the same name was, on the other hand, built using stones from the ancient edifice. Its qualification is therefore fully justified and its credibility in this matter is beyond reproach.

The Abbaye des Rocs (vol. alcohol 9%) is a pure malt beer, without any added sugar. All the aspects of its taste are directly linked to the phenomenon of double fermentation, precise amounts of malt as well as a mix of three different types of hops (Belgian, German and Czech).

Its color is a papal, dark ruby and is majestic. Its taste is rich and full of subtlety. It should be tasted like a red wine (it also has the same color) without the tannin.

It develops a very powerful aroma of sugary tangs. In the mouth it confirms the initial impression with in addition a layer of deep bitterness, but is well balanced with a certain fruity flavor. It asserts itself on the palate, and develops an impressive density of flavor. One can detect a tang of burnt wood, but there is no suggestion of roasting, even if the ingredients include a malt of this type.

The aftertaste which develops in the mouth is dense and creamy; a sensation which is very long-lasting. The bitterness and sugary aspect (although there is none amongst the ingredients) are in perfect harmony and blend together to the pure joy of anyone tasting this beer.

It is a beer with a great depth of character, mystical and extremely mature, which has to be classified amongst the great classics of our native land.

SAINT AMANDUS BLONDE KORTENBERGS ABDIJBIER

The particularity of this abbey beer is its volume of alcohol (5%) which is low for a beer of this type, and usually is above 7%. It is thus a pale beer, and could be assimilated with a Pils style beer, if it were not so strong in bitterness. Without being excessively bitter, the harshness of its bitter taste seems more distinctive in the aftertaste than in the mouth, since in the recipe there are also softer aromas which are only detectable on the palate and then only for a fleeting moment.

It is good as a thirst-quencher and can also be drunk as an aperitif.

An excellent initiative would be to drink it at 5°C/ 41°F.

KORTENBERGS ABDIJBIER

Its description as a pale beer goes no further than the label, and it is dark in color. The fragrance of its bouquet also changes, and a smoky and slightly fruity softness becomes apparent.

A suggestion of velvet caresses the tongue in the mouth and the suggestion of fruity softness is greater, almost even syrupy. Its high density is even more pronounced at the finish with an astonishing bitterness that was barely discernible in the second phase of the tasting.

84

TER DOLEN

The inspiration for this abbey beer came from a tavern that sought to offer its customers (tourists and pilgrims) a good beer rich in character and full-tasting.

Its qualification as an abbey beer lies in the stones used to construct the De Dool premises, which are dominated by a sumptuous chateau in the heart of a forest in Limbourg.

The result is an excellent pale beer with a volume of alcohol of 6%, effectively dense in its taste with a suggestion of angelic softness. Its flavor is unique. There is a tiny hint of bitterness, just enough to show its character. Contrary to other abbey beers, Ter Dolen is pasteurized and filtered twice. It is therefore very pure and lively, thanks to a remarkable lacework that produces a tickling sensation on the tongue and goose-bumps, such is its consistency which is used to maximum effect in the mouth and in the aftertaste.

It is amazingly good as a digestive, often welcomed in inns where meals are undoubtedly of high quality, but above all copious and occasionally even difficult to digest.

CORSENDONK

The history of the small brewery of the same name dates back to 1398. It adjoined the priory of Corsendonk, which subsequently became a monastery. Brewed by the monks of the period, the beer was however taken over by professional brewers who upgraded the mash tuns to produce a superb Patersbier, the direct ancestor of the Corsendonk Pater. The Corsendonk's presentation is itself quite delightful. The bottles all bear the Corsendonk seal, which dates from the 15th century. The accompanying logo is nothing

less than the manuscript of a monk from the priory of Corsendonk. The 75cl bottles are also wrapped in paper, which indirectly protects them better against the light and helps to preserve them longer.

AGNUS

Its initial impact is not very discreet. It is very fortunate that its aroma is not representative of its flavor. Its volume of alcohol is solid at 8% which makes it fairly dry in the mouth, and this effect is heightened by a good dose of bitterness, which naturally produces an identical tang at the finish. It is very easily digested, and convincing as a pale beer with a deferential disposition.

PATER

With the same volume of alcohol as the Agnus, the Pater is very much darker in appearance, and its aroma is based on a traditional softness. The first hint of bitterness appears only at the start of the tasting phase in the mouth. It takes on a new dimension on the palate in particular with this soft bitterness, but also a fruity flavor with a discreet trace of orange. As with many other abbey beers, it will be remembered for its unique bitterness, which is very thirst-quenching and comforting.

It is worthy of its ancestors.

VIEILLE BON SECOURS

In addition to its other functions, the basilica of Bon-Secours was an excellent frontier post on the Franco-Belgian border.

Built on top of a high hill overlooking on one side the plain of Péruwelz in the province of Hainault, and Saint-Amand-les-Eaux in France on the other, this site has throughout the ages attracted a multitude of pilgrims, both from Belgium and France, seeking the blessing of Notre Dame de Bon Secours, for a rapid cure for their illnesses which were generally more of an inconvenience than incurable.

Often those who came seeking a miracle did find a new optimism for life, but this was often due to the beverages served in the many establishments.

The Vieille Bon Secours is at the top of the list of these beverages that provided consolation to these eternal pilgrims.

Its color, which is exceedingly amber, is in perfect harmony with the dark clothes worn by those who visited the (church) tower. Its volume of alcohol is 8% and its bouquet offers a gentle welcome. Its ingredients, with a roasted malt and a brown candy sugar, have much in common with a cold cup of sweetened coffee offered to persevering pilgrims. Its bitterness is in the background, but nevertheless does provide a touch of harshness which corresponds to the serious contemplative side of life in this watching post on a high hill overlooking the border.

The final blessing is the reappearance of a pleasant softness with the tang of sweet, not too strong, coffee.

This classic beer which is neither pasteurized nor filtered is available in either 75cl or 33cl bottles with a catch top, ready to be taken away on other pilgrimages.

CRAFT BEERS

If most abbey beers are based on traditional recipes, such recipes are also often the basis for craft beers, which are also called special beers.

The ingredients used in craft beverages have, however, numerous different sources. All that excludes some of them from qualifying as abbey beers is the simple fact that no allusion is made to an ecclesiastical link. That did not necessarily mean that the recipes were not handed down by our ancestors. The recipes, and often the end product, are almost identical with abbey beers. In addition, family traditions often play a role. In fact, it must not be forgotten that the profession of brewer was handed down from generation to generation, from father to son, or son-in-law, as were the ancestral secrets. Certain craft beers have evolved in their basic nature, while others are an integral part of our brewing heritage, and therefore have not changed one iota.

Craft or special beers as a whole (and even fantasy beers) are top-fermented, with a relatively high volume of alcohol. However, there are a few local, not particularly well known, beers which are bottom-fermented, but not pasteurized, which means that they cannot be preserved for long once they are bottled. When the cork (or the cap) is popped, they have to be drunk in one session.

The LEGENDE D'AUBEL

There is no hiding the fact that this beer, which is reddish in color, originates from the village of the same name which is situated to the east of Liege.

Its flavor is simple and complex at the same time. It can be summed up as a soft and spicy beer, which is not aggressively bitter.

Its tone is therefore more velvety but not without character, since at the finish, there is a bitter tang, to prove itself a good companion.

Its volume of alcohol of 7% leaves its mark and gives it a certain roundness.

It goes down very easily when served at room temperature, without really asserting itself in the mouth, despite a top quality malt.

VAL-DIEU BLONDE

Without being classified amongst the strongest Blondes, the Val-Dieu Blonde possesses several strong points that help it stand out from traditional Blondes.

First of all, it is top-fermented, and its volume of alcohol is 6.5%.

Its bitterness is very well balanced and is in perfect harmony with its spices, which are apparent from the first taste, characterized by a tingling sensation on the tongue. There is a suggestion of acidity in the background, but which has no impact on its status as a bitter beer.

There is practically no aftertaste, all the action takes place on the palate.

To be drunk between 7 and 10°C/45-50°F.

VAL-DIEU BRUNE

By its color, it is the opposite of its fellow beer, but the differences go beyond this aspect. For example, its bitterness is almost non-existent, the accent being placed on a sharp taste which expands in the mouth. This is moreover very surprising for this type of beer, where one would expect more of a taste of licorice with a touch of bitterness.

It could almost be compared with an old Flemish Brown beer, if its discreet bitterness did not reappear, albeit just as timorously as in the initial impact, in the aftertaste. It can be served cool.

CUVEE D'ARISTEE

There is nothing at first glance to suggest that this beer is brewed with honey, and yet, that is the case.

But on further examination, one realizes that its name is not simply a matter of chance. In reality, within this micro-brewery in the region of Peissant near Binche, there is also a family of beekeepers. By christening their beer " Cuvée d'Aristée ", the brewers are alluding to Greek mythology, since Aristée, the son of Apollo, domesticated bees. This is therefore a wonderful tribute. But this civility extends beyond a mere name.

The Cuvée d'Aristée is a wonderful example of how to succeed with limited resources.

This beer is totally natural without any spices, composed solely of aromatic malt, and there is absolutely nothing secretive about it.

It is naturally honey colored and the immediate bouquet is very rich. The first noteworthy aspect is its discreetly fruity, but effective, aroma. It has a very good bitterness, spontaneous and robust, but which does not linger in the mouth. Its different malts also produce a touch of exoticism.

On the other hand, the taste of honey is never detectable, as it is overshadowed by a full- bodied spicy, sparkling sensation. The powerful alcoholic flavor (9.5%) gives it an even greater depth of character.

It is in the aftertaste that the different sensations are even more interesting. There is a freshness, like mint without sugar. It is only after the finish that it justifies the name of malt beer. This ultimate flavor

91

remains nevertheless very discreet and is only discernible on the tip of the tongue and lips, but not at the back of the throat. It lingers a long time.

The full-bodied effervescent aspect makes it a lively beer, and accordingly very easy to digest. On the other hand, its fairly high volume of alcohol will leave you groggy after finishing a 75cl. bottle.

You are certain to spend an excellent night in the arms of Morpheus.

The MONTAGNARDE

The inhabitants of Montignies-sur-Rocs, to the south of Mons in the province of Hainault, are called the Montagnards. It was therefore completely normal that a beer brewed within the walls of this city should be called the Montagnarde.

This beer, which is strong in taste and alcohol density (9%), has a very accomplished flavor.

Its bouquet is very sharp with a suggestion of fruit and spices. Its taste is harsh, with the influence of a sharp bitterness and a caramel flavor. There is no sugar. This pure malt beer is a complex mix, but overall the different aspects make the bitterness less one-dimensional. It is slightly peppery in the back of the throat, and there is a tingling sensation on the tongue. It is even more impressive in the mouth, with each element of its flavor coming into play individually. It is very active in the glass, which gives it a long-lasting head.

Its finish is long and emphasizes a bitterness that is just as remarkable but with less of a caramel backup.

The finish brings to mind a kind of sugarless ginger-bread.

BLANCHE DES HONNELLES

Very much a local beer when it was created in 1991, this white beer has since spread its wings beyond the banks of the river after which it is named.

The Blanche des Honnelles cannot be described as run of the mill. It is amber in color, which after all is the traditional color of bygone ages. Next, its volume of alcohol (6%) is superior to what we expect to find in white beers. And finally, its taste is surprising and is not at all comparable with other beverages of the same style that are presently available.

If its initial nose is relatively discreet, its early flavor is overtaken by a harsh bitterness against a peppery background. Three different cereals (barley, wheat and oats) are used in the production of this white beer which has no acidity whatsoever. Its taste is stimulating, with a discreet, but refreshing, finish. Lots of character and somewhat curious.

DUVEL

One day not very long ago, the brewer of Breendonck asked the village baker to taste his new pale beer in order to have his opinion on the beverage. His reaction was as spontaneous as the beer that he had just drunk. " Diable ", he exclaimed in his Flemish dialect from the province of Antwerp, that is " Duvel ". It was thus baptized Duval as a tribute to this heart felt

reaction. The Duval is the veritable front-runner and yardstick amongst strong Belgian pale beers.

It is gloriously bitter, and its aroma is powerful and heady, with a plentiful, lively and lasting head. Its initial nose is slightly apple flavored.

Its flavor is full-bodied but the omnipresent bitterness is predominant. With its lively lacework, it is also extremely easy to digest, although it does cause stomachs which are not familiar with it to become knotted as an initial reaction. Its aftertaste is just as bitter and dry, and its alcoholic flavor is present (8.5%).

Should be drunk fairly cold (5° C/41°F), without this being in any way detrimental to its flavor.

The CAMPAGNARDE

The old-style Brunes are typical beverages from Flanders. Wallonia also has a few stereotype beers of the same color, which could easily lead one to believe that people from the south of Belgium are particularly fond of amber colored beers which taste of licorice.

The Campagnarde, discreet with its odor of burnt wood, belongs to the special category of beers that have character with a strong licorice flavor. It is not however too coarse, and this trait does not make it especially robust in the mouth. It is rather its strong level of alcohol (9.5%) which takes over in the mouth. The aftertaste is sharp from the keen taste of licorice and the bitterness is relative. The bitter taste, which remains in the mouth, is the logical conclusion of its main taste.

It could be more robust with a few more concentrated scoops of hops.

On the other hand, apart from the fact that it is quickly intoxicating, it is very easy going on the digestive system.

The BLONDE DE PRAILLE

More hazy gold in color than blonde, this beer, which is very artisanal in nature, is named after the place where it is brewed.

Its spicy aroma, which is accompanied by a flavor that is sharp and peppery on the tongue, is not particularly harsh. Its bitterness is not immediately discernible on account of the spicy taste on the tongue.

However, the bitterness is well and truly present, but will always be overshadowed by the acridity of its neutral taste. It does not really develop at all in the mouth.

The Blonde de Praille (7.5%) lacks just a little personality and character, in particular in the mouth. We cannot insist too much on its artisanal nature, and that is precisely where its charm lies and above all why it is appreciated, in the image of the magnificent countryside around Praile, between Binche and Beaumont (province of Hainault), which is well known for its discretion and natural charisma. The brewer has succeeded very well in getting his message across.

It goes down very easily, and can be served cool (5 to 8°C/41-46°F).

SLOEBER

Little imp or rascal is the translation for this beer, which is brewed in the Ardennes, near Audenarde in eastern Flanders.

With an alcohol content that is appropriate at 7.5%, it is nevertheless slightly lacking in body. Its aroma is discreet, and its taste only develops slightly in the mouth. It has a well-rounded bitterness that is dry towards the finish.

In the aftertaste there is a further suggestion of bitterness which reappears in the mouth. It should be consumed relatively cool, at 8°C/46°F, in order to appreciate its primary flavors, principally at the end of the glass.

The BLANCHE DE CHARLEROI

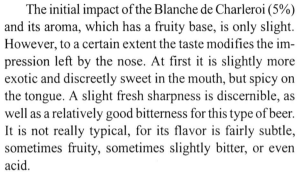

A white beer as a tribute to the "black country"; we have seen it all and drunk it all in Belgium.

The initial impact of the Blanche de Charleroi (5%) and its aroma, which has a fruity base, is only slight. However, to a certain extent the taste modifies the impression left by the nose. At first it is slightly more exotic and discreetly sweet in the mouth, but spicy on the tongue. A slight fresh sharpness is discernible, as well as a relatively good bitterness for this type of beer. It is not really typical, for its flavor is fairly subtle, sometimes fruity, sometimes slightly bitter, or even acid.

One can almost detect the wheat and barley used in its manufacture, but perhaps this is an illusion induced by its label which shows that it is an organic white beer.

Its aftertaste is somewhat disappointing, since it fades rapidly, leaving simply a taste of freshness on the tongue, whereas the nose will appreciate its exotic perfume.

DOBBELIN BRUINEN

Here is a Double which is a genuine thirst-quencher from every point of view, from its initial bitter softness to the first taste, which confirms the impression made by the nose.

Its flavor develops very quickly in the mouth and the nostrils are filled with a certain sharpness that is never aggressive since it is accompanied by a predominant, but admirably well-balanced, bitterness, just sufficient to refresh the palate.

Its aftertaste will be harsher on the breath, but the wonderful bitterness will linger.

MATER

A traditional white beer from the village of Mater (eastern Flanders), where it is brewed.

The principal characteristics of this beer, that is intended primarily as a thirst-quencher, are a discreet aroma, a fresh taste and an acidity in the aftertaste.

One must underline the great quality of the ferruginous water used in this brew, which reduces its acidity to a level seen in few other white beers.

HOEGAARDEN

This is the leading white beer in Belgium and is known throughout the world.

In appearance it is yellow and cloudy and has a wheaty aroma. This is completely normal for a white beer, as the basic ingredient is wheat.

Its taste confirms the initial impression, while the sharpness only appears during the second phase of tasting, which enables it to assert itself on the palate.

In the third phase in the mouth, that is in its aftertaste, a lingering bitterness is apparent with a sour tang.

The Hoegaarden (5%) should be served very cool (5°C/41°F).

L'ECUME DES JOURS

Named after Boris Vian's novel, l'Ecume des Jours is a highly expressive beer starting with its very distinctive bouquet with a malty tang against a fruity background.

Logically, for a beer made from spelt it has a characteristic taste, that is to say a malt flavor and a secondary bitterness which is principally apparent in the aftertaste, whereas in the initial taste there is a tingling sensation on the end of the tongue.

Its volume of alcohol of 7% has no impact on the taste, but rather plays a secondary role by quickly inducing a feeling of ephemeral well-being.

It finishes strongly with a lingering bitterness which replaces a slight acidity.

Extremely good for drinkers with a thirst and very easy to digest.

To be drunk relatively cool, at 7°C/44°F.

The MYSTERE DROSSAARD

If Drossaard, which can be written differently, is a relatively common surname in the region of Diest, in Flemish Brabant almost on its border with Limbourg, it is in reality a relative newcomer to the world of brewing. No doubt generations of Drossaard, or Drossaert etc., brewed beers in the small but bustling market town

of Diest many years ago. At one point in time this town had the highest number of breweries per square kilometer, to the extent that the town's name could only be used within the city's walls.

Drossard takes its name from a character who is typical of the region. Whenever his master was away he carried out all of his functions. At the end of the XVIII century, the last Drossaard, Dr. Juan de Paramo, built the house of the " Drossaard " which has since become the town's youth hostel. It is also the edifice that appears on the beer's label.

This beverage is strong in character, its volume of alcohol is shown as 7%, whereas in reality it is 7.8%. It is full-bodied with a strongly developed bitterness with an alcohol flavor. In addition, with its reddish-brown color, it brings to mind the great Trappist triple beers. It has lovely lacework with a smooth, creamy head. It is never aggressive in the mouth, but has a dense aftertaste in which a new bitterness develops. On the other hand, its maturity and authenticity are to be admired. It is well liked by connoisseurs of strong beer.

It should also be noted that when drunk at moderate temperatures, it has a slightly sweet flavor, just enough to cushion its bitterness a shade.

The MONEUSE

Antoine-Joseph Moneuse (1768 - 1798) died young and was guillotined publicly in Douai (in Northern France); today he has a beer named after him.

Who in fact was this Moneuse? Quite simply a highwayman, who robbed not just stagecoaches but also houses, while forcing his victims to reveal where they had hidden their valuables, by putting their feet in the hearth of the fireplace.

He was sentenced to death shortly after his arrest. His brewer is in fact a woman who is one of his descendants.

The Moneuse (8%) immediately conjures up images of bygone times with its perfume and its very hoppy bouquet. Its taste confirms this impression and is even more apparent on the palate. That is the overall impression left by this beer, which is as harsh as the person after whom it is named. Fortunately, its strong finish does not come to an abrupt end like Antoine-Joseph, and lingers long beyond the tasting.

It keeps well, but with the passing years its bitterness will diminish. It goes well with game.

The MONDE D'UNE CAMPUS

This beer is not at all a " prop " for students, without which, with its fairly high volume of alcohol, 6% for

the Blonde and 7.5% for the Ambrée, the evenings would be very short.

The two beverages are both pure malt and strongly spiced.

BLONDE

It combines two aspects. One is specific to Blondes in general with a strong bitter taste, which are intended as thirst quenchers. However, the second aspect is more prominent, while the bitterness is preceded by a very slightly spicy fruit taste, which reinforces its second function. But it does however have character, thanks notably to a peppery spice which makes it more astringent in its aftertaste. To be served cool.

AMBREE

Over and above its color, which is darker than the Blonde, this Campus (7.5%) is different in its taste, which is distinctly more syrupy with fruity overtones and a malty flavor. It is illuminated by lacework that is generous and develops fully. Its impression of softness very much tempers its bitterness, but the aftertaste will bring out a bitter and dry caramel aspect.

The CHOUFFE...(BLESS YOU!)

Achouffe, a small village high above the Vallée des Fées near Houffalize (province of Luxembourg) is beginning to gain a very good reputation in Japan, while in Belgium the beers from this brewery hidden in the Ardennes are still a well-kept secret.

LA CHOUFFE (8%) is very characteristic of a type of beer akin to Scotch Ale. Gloriously amber-colored, this beer makes a strong initial impact with its sweet aroma, with an element of caramel malt, and a very delicate spice. Its bouquet is complex and direct. It does not hide the beer's character. Its bitterness is almost non existent, for the Chouffe is far too mischievous to confine itself to a single objective. Overall, it is the (candy) sugar that plays the leading role, which does not mean to say that it is a sweet brew. The complexity of the flavors, where there is a solid dose of alcohol to combat the sweet effect, is truly incredible. Of course there are lashings of hops, and indeed top quality hops too, from the Czech Republic, the former Yugoslavia and naturally England, to justify comparisons with Scotch Ale. It contains a special yeast that is highly resist-

ant to alcohol, which results in a healthy fermentation in normal conditions. After several years this results in the very special aroma that is the pride and joy of the whole valley, through which the river Cedrogne runs, and from where the brewers draw their near miraculous water supply.

SAISON DE SILLY

Originally created to slake the thirst of farm workers, primarily during the harvest season, seasonal beers have become a part of the legend of traditional beers.

Generally, they are not too strong, and their role, other than serving as a thirst quencher, is mainly convivial, although they have more character than beers brewed specifically for that function.

The Saison de Silly (5%) is a classic beer in this category. It has a slight acidity against a background of bitterness and largely fulfills its different roles. Its acidity, which is kept under control, is very much appreciated in hot weather, on the other hand its bitterness will help to quench a thirst due most of the time to the hard work put in throughout the harvest period. Its taste develops even more in the mouth, and it will finish with a bitter flourish.

It is naturally drunk cool, and traditionally it accompanies the dish of rice pudding served to celebrate the last bale of hay of the summer harvest.

SAISON DUPONT BIOLOGIQUE

The Saison Dupont Biologique is very much an artisanal beer in its conception, and has the double social role of all seasonal beers, that is to be thirst-quenching and convivial.

There is also a certain acidity against a bitter background, but more acrid and spicier. It asserts itself more in the mouth and its bitterness will be felt only in the aftertaste.

102

The Saison Dupont Biologique (5.5%) can also be drunk cool, but its drier taste gives it also a depth of character without too much of a tang of alcohol.

SAISON DE PIPAIX

This is an exception as regards seasonal beers. The Saison des Pipaix (6.5%) is based on spicier ingredients, almost hot, despite a strong bitter presence, but on the other hand there is no trace of acidity. There is rather a spicy softness complemented by aniseed. The latter element makes it highly refreshing, which is an essential quality for a summer-time beer.

In the mouth it becomes even fuller tasting, but there is a good element of bitterness in the aftertaste with an occasional hint that confirms the presence of aniseed.

JUDAS, (A DIVINE BLONDE)

" What a mischievous beer, what divine pleasure " is a saying which captures to perfection the character of the Judas.

Like a young girl full of self-confidence, the Judas first attracts by its strong but delicate perfume. Its charms are immediately apparent, starting with its golden color topped by a white head which you cannot resist placing to your lips in order to taste its special pleasures, before being led blindly to your rendezvous with fate, which never disappoints.

This wonderful, strong pale beer (8.5%) was launched in 1986. Since then, it has continued to mature but nevertheless its reputation remains discreet compared with traditional beers. It has however all the attributes necessary to win over connoisseurs of bitter beers.

Its bitterness is moreover very distinctive without the taste being too long-lasting, just in the mouth. Its layer of flavors conceals certain peppery spices, and some extremely tasty pale malts. There is no artifice about this beer. This beautiful pale beer willingly reveals its attractions and should be tasted slowly to enjoy its full range of flavors, and the sensation of perfect harmony which it evokes is ideal whatever your mood.

Its smooth creamy head adds even more to its beauty in a glass that one raises to one's lips to caress, almost like a lingering kiss with your loved one.

A very great classic.

DOUBLE D'ENGHEIN

Enghein, which is a small locality in the province of Hainault, is located on the linguistic border which divides Belgium, and was for many years the hub of a great many activities linked to its key geographical location. Not too many years ago, this small locality had a tram depot, which linked the city of the Dukes of Arenburg to Brussels, or to the coal mines in the center, or at Borinage. In other words many workmen's feet have trodden the cobble stones of this small station and, above all, have drunk an incalculable quantity of hectoliters of beer, which as early as 1858 was brewed by a family of local brewers. The locality's spearhead was initially the Doublette, a seasonal beer, relatively low in alcohol. But with the passing years, certain economic crises badly hit the workers who were left more and more to their unhappy fate.

Unlike salary levels, the consumption of the beer d'Enghein increased, as did the alcohol strength of its beer, with the Double (8%).

DOUBLE AMBREE

For many years, this was the only beer available to an impressive number of drinkers to slake their thirst.

Its aroma is highly perfumed, but its taste unveils a bitterness against a background of caramel which rounds off this beer of character. There is also a hint of sharpness at the start, but this is very quickly covered by its initial layering of flavors. It becomes even more full bodied if it is retained in the mouth for an instant. The finish is dominated by the bitterness, with a very long-lasting and harsh bitter aftertaste.

DOUBLE BLONDE

This meets local needs for a more traditional pale beer, that is to say with more bitterness and drier in flavor. Its malts are different from the Ambrée, with which it does however have certain points in common, in particular a light acidity when it touches the tongue. Its taste in the mouth has greater depth and is less aggressive than the Ambrée, with which it shares the same aftertaste, but is less long-lasting.

TITJE

One of the most recent white beers to appear in the country (1990). It is one of the most acid, but not disproportionately so however, as it is not at all aggressive. It makes up for its lack of bitterness by this characteristic. It also leaves a slight trace of spiciness on the edge of the tongue that is rapidly overpowered by a certain spontaneous freshness, and a taste of cereals (wheat).

It is also most certainly one of the most effective thirst quenchers.

STEENDONK

The idea of two highly regarded independent brewers (Moortgat and Palm), it is based on the classic white beers with a slightly acid taste and a restrained bitterness. The result is perfectly in line with expectations, it is convivial and helps to slake a thirst.

BLANCHE DE NAMUR

This is a very original white beer, or rather it represents a return to source, in terms of color and taste.

First of all, its appearance, with its amber color, is a reminder that white beers were formerly brewed with cereals other than wheat (spelt, for example). Next comes its taste, which is different from all other brews of this type.

In fact is has no acidity whatsoever, on the contrary, the basis of its flavor is a slight bitterness. It has however a very comforting texture, and is powerfully soft. It develops even more on the palate, and for the finish undergoes a transformation to be pleasantly bitter.

Very original and captivating.

OUDEN TRIPEL

With its very evocative label, this is a convivial beer but along the lines of traditional Flemish brown beers, so beloved in the west of Belgium, in the region where linen craft workers drank this beer as an accompaniment.

It is characterized by a sour and very fruity flavor, without any alcoholic overtones (5.5%). In the mouth however it does produce a very slight touch of sweetness, which is overpowered by the acidity. At the back of the throat, this same sugary hint re-appears.

No bitterness, but a good thirst quencher for the summer months.

MC CHOUFFE

Obviously it is related to the Chouffe. Its ingredients however are different. Here we see elements such as candy sugar and honey, as well as lashings of hops and dark malts. The whole provides a powerful aroma redolent of the Ardennes, with a strong taste and a very alcoholic flavor. All the ingredients play a full role in the taste, since they are all discernible individually, from the layering of hops to a dose of sugar and aromatic malts topped by alcohol (8.5%). However, in the aftertaste the bitterness is dominant. It plays several roles, depending upon the season, the place and the circumstances in which it is consumed. The con-

centration of sugar allied to the alcohol is an explosive cocktail for the body. It should therefore be consumed with moderation.

ZOTTEGEMSE GRAND CRU

In the charming little village in eastern Flanders, almost everything revolves around the famous Count of Egmont who was beheaded in 1568, along with the Count of Hornes during a revolt of the Dutch against Philippe II. He is also the hero of Goethe's tragedy set to the music of Ludwig van Beethoven. That will give you an idea of just how proud this small village is

of its famous ancestor, who is still buried there, and its eloquent historical past.

It is therefore perfectly normal that we should find effigies of the count everywhere locally and, not surprisingly for Belgium, on a beer label.

Zottegemse Grand Cru (8.4%) has inherited a noble assignment, that of providing the future with a taste of history through a classic beer.

Despite its allusion to a harsh past, this beer has very soft tangs that give way to a well-balanced combination of softness and bitterness. The latter will come fully into play in the final phase, but its harshness will however be tempered once again by a flowery soft-ness and a bouquet of hot spices which enhance the balance of the beer's primary flavors.

It is best drunk in plush surroundings at a temperature between 12 and 14°C/53-57°F.

OERBIER

In its secondary appellation, the Oerbier is described as " nat en straf ", that is to say, "wet and strong".

It is certainly strong, with an alcoholic strength of 7.5% in volume, but this is amplified by its bitter-sweet softness and a strong density in the taste, which provide a velvety texture.

Its name translates an old, almost primitive recipe, which has been revised by its brewer.

It is a beer to be tasted with much skill, always allowing the tongue to caress its velvety texture. It is perfectly soft in every sense of the word, not only in its flavor but also in contact with the lips. Its head remains creamy and smooth, which is a sign of its obvious good health.

Its aftertaste is in the same vein and is long-lasting, and lingers long after the tasting.

Very hearty.

BOSKEUN

This is very much a local seasonal beer, which is drunk by the banks of the river Yser in western Flanders, solely at Easter, principally to celebrate certain pilgrimages from the tiny neighboring villages.

The Boskuen is an allusion to the wild rabbit, quick, vigilant and crafty.

These are the three characteristics to be found in this pure malt beer, as mischievous as you could wish. Its initial impact is soft but the essence is its freshness, which evokes memories of springtime with its fragrant greenery and the bitter odor of the rebirth of nature.

The shiver that it produces is a reminder that Easter is not synonymous with warmth. At the slightest sound, the fur on the back of the watchful rabbit stands on end. With this beer, it is its bitterness that is hair-raising, since there is a complex and seemingly never-ending bitterness at the back of the throat, like the interminable maze of a rabbit's warren.

SNOEK

If one day you cross the flat open country of western Flanders, you will be surprised by the number of families called Snoek. Written differently throughout the centuries, there remains an original and probably authentic version, which is that shown on the label used for the beer of the same name. The Snoek is distributed locally and is a simple beer that corresponds to the uneventful lives of those who live in the flat country. With this brew, one can enjoy its straightforward bitterness, which reflects its basic hop ingredient. There is a touch of softness to smooth out the taste, but this is not at all necessary. The Snoek (6.9%) develops quite naturally on the palate, to finish on a bitter note.

ROCHUS

The distinctive characteristic of this beer is that it is only available in casks, from 5 liters to 50 liters.

Its bitterness is very restrained, and it has a neutral taste with a certain sugary flavor just like its aftertaste, which is very soft.

The Rochus, which was created to celebrate the brewery's centennial, was put on sale at the specific request of the inhabitants of the small village of Herzelé, near Ninove in eastern Flanders.

There are no surprises with this beer, which is very convivial (5.2%).

It should always be served very cool.

BLANCHE DE BRUGES

A pure malt beer, produced along classical lines and therefore inevitably a classic beer. Its conception avoids complexity: malt, wheat, oats and hops. However, it is slightly less acid than other white beers. Its alcoholic strength is normal (5%).

Its role is simply to act as a thirst quencher.

VILLERS SAINT-GHISLAIN

Brewed in the region around Mons, the Villers Saint-Ghislain very quickly found a place in the hearts of the local population.

It is very dense and its nose has a superb bouquet. It has a slight caramel taste on top of a good amount of hops. It improves in the mouth and leaves a marvelous bitterness at the finish. It will keep easily for three years.

It should be served at a temperature between 8 and 12°C/46-53°F.

BIERE DU CHÂTEAU DE RAMEGIES-CHIN

With its red-brick facade, the Château de Ramegies-Chin is a fine example of an impressive piece of recent architecture, dating back to the beginning of this century. Its imposing aristocratic presence in the region of Tournai (Hainault) explains the creation of an amazing, and above all very strong, beer. With volume of alcohol of 12%, the beer of the Château de Ramegies-Chin is one of the strongest beers in Belgium.

It is very much akin to a red wine, with sugary tangs. If you take into account its very distinctive bitterness, it is well-balanced despite its very strong taste. Its level of alcohol blends in perfectly and does not at all undermine the taste of the different malts used. It develops even more on the palate, and once the beer has been swallowed it leaves a feeling of emptiness in the mouth.

Its effects are therefore immediate, the only memory left behind is linked to its bitterness.

It very quickly and dangerously goes to your head, and is not particularly easy to digest.

It is therefore to be drunk with moderation and with care. It is not a beer that is readily approachable, but it leaves its mark.

Its bottle label is more reminiscent of a wine bottle than a beer bottle, but its approach is exactly the same.

A vintage year.

FACON EXTRA STOUT

In very much traditional British style, this average size brewery produces a Belgian style stout. The end result is very similar to the English product. It is black in color, which hides a soft dry taste, without bitterness. The roasted malts play their role to perfection. Low in alcohol (5.4%), it does not hold many hidden surprises.

It is uniquely intended for the inhabitants of the village of Courtrai in western Flanders. Several of the British tourists visiting the First World War cemeteries in the area feel quite at home with the Facon Extra Stout.

The SCALDIENNE

This beer is a perfect illustration of a superb region, through which the river Escaut flows, which is growing increasingly popular.

Its name comes from the Latin " scaldis " for the river Escaut. The Scaldienne (amber colored) is a fresh beer, however, the initial nose is slight. On the other hand, the first mouthful is a pleasant surprise. Its bitterness delicately weaves its magic like the river Escaut meandering through the flat lands of Flanders. Once the palate has become accustomed to this

bitterness, there is a slight spiciness that becomes somewhat acrid against a caramel background. It is best drunk served cool (5 to 8 C/41-46°F) to appreciate the deep but subtle bitterness.

Very pleasant to drink sitting on one of the many wonderful terraces alongside the river.

The GAUMOISE

The Gaume is a region of contrasts, very hot during the summer, while being cold during the winter, but for those who discover it the region's landscape is wonderful to behold. Logically it should offer visitors an outstanding beer. In fact, it does have its own beer, but which is banal. The beer in question is the Gaumoise, which is available in two versions, a pale beer and a brown beer, with a modest 5% alcohol level.

These two beers do not create a strong impression. The Blonde is reasonably amber, but its taste is very straightforward. On the other hand, the Brune has more body because of its roasted malt.

Unfortunately, it does not leave much of an impression.

SPECIALE PALM

This is one of the real classics of Belgian brewing. This marvelous amber colored beer which should be served cool is, as it is eloquently described in its advertisements, a flagship Brabant beer. Its bitter, dry caramel taste is special.

With its convivial nature, it is above all ideal for drinking on festive occasions, but a Spéciale Palm can also be appreciated for its maturity.

It has more character and more spice to it when bottled, but most of the time it is served cool (5%C/ 41°F) as draft beer.

AERTS 1900

The Aerts 1900 was created to celebrate the hundred years of existence of a Brabant brewery, with the name as the beer chosen to reflect the occasion. Its success was totally unexpected. Today it has become one of the great classics.

It is proud of its volume of alcohol of 7%. It is russet amber colored in the Belle Epoque tradition. Its nose overflows with nostalgia bringing to mind the image of a woman splendidly reminiscent of the period with her bodice and plunging neckline.

Its caramel flavor brings back memories of bygone days when people, unaware of what the future held, were discovering the dawn of a New World, with its scientific discoveries.

How pleasant it must have been during the sweet days of the Belle Epoque! However, its caramel flavor provides a hint of reserve before giving way to a dry bitterness that dominates the finish, like a warning of the changes lying ahead.

Very subtle and full of surprises when drunk at room temperature.

ALEXANDER RODENBACH

The Rodenbachs, a great family of Flemish brewers, are proud of their family traditions (more than a hundred and fifty years of brewing).

The place of honor in this family of master brewers goes to their ancestor, Alexander.

The Rodenbach beers are a yardstick for beers brewed in the traditional style of the old brown beers, but with Alexander Rodenbach (6%), the different perfumes are increased tenfold in harmony with a syrupy bouquet against a background flavor which is more sour than soft. However, the balance is spontaneously re-established on the palate. Here there is also a slightly sweeter element that at times brings to mind a port wine. The production cycle is very strict for this beer, which is top-fermented in oak tuns where it is kept for at least 20 months.

There are no surprises in the aftertaste, simply a persistent sharpness with a thirst-quenching touch.

RODENBACH GRAND CRU

In a long line of traditional brown beers produced by the Rodenbach family, they undoubtedly felt the necessity to produce a vintage beer that stands apart from the others. This heavy responsibility has been entrusted to the Rodenbach Grand Cru (6.5%) which, as its name indicates, is made to last.

It is distinctly more sour than the other beers produced by the family, but the taste improves over time. Like a good wine it is easy to lay down, but it must be preserved at a constant temperature and away from light.

STREEKBIER BOSBIER

Typical wild strawberry flavored beer. It is reddish in color, it has a rich head and a natural strawberry aroma.

There is a slight hint of bitterness amidst the sugary flavors, just enough to prepare you for the very soft, fragrant aftertaste.

Very densely sugared, and fairly low in alcohol content (5%). It must be served cool and during the right season (summer).

114

BOKKEREYER

This beer, which won a gold medal in 1991, was originally intended for local consumption, and is very popular in the Antwerp-Limbourg province.

Its name evokes a goat rider.

Against an amber filtered background, the Bokkereyer (5.8%) has a generous head through which a discreet perfume of softness reaches the nose. It is soft and sweet, with a similar taste on the palate, where it does not last long.

At the finish its softness disappears almost too rapidly, leaving the temptation to taste it again, but only through greediness.

Served cool, or at room temperature, its charisma shines through.

HOMMELBIER

From simple ingredients, brewers can produce a very good beer, full of character. That holds true for this Hommelbier from Poperinghe, which is situated in the furthermost western corner of northern Belgium.

Initially it is soft, with a generously flavored bouquet. However, its taste is profoundly bitter and dry. The taste becomes more full bodied in the mouth and leaves behind a final logical and long-lasting acute bitterness.

CAVES

This is a historical beer for the town of Lierre in Antwerp province.

This densely colored beer is fairly low in alcohol at 5.1%. This soft tasting beer nevertheless has character. Its nose gives an early idea of its underlying softness, which is confirmed in the taste. It has also a velvety texture on the tongue and is not heavy to taste. Nothing new develops in the aftertaste.

DUCHESSE DE BOURGOGNE

Despite its name, there can be no comparison with any wine from that region, or indeed any wine whatsoever.

Brewed along the most traditional lines, it belongs to the family of great Flemish brown beers, and has that same bitter-sweet taste. Yet, it is more dense than other beers in the same category. Despite a fairly acid taste, it leaves however a sweet taste at the back of the throat.

VAPEUR EN FOLIE

This is produced by the only brewery in the world that still uses steam-power to brew its beers. The Vapeur en Folie is to a certain extent a unique specimen amongst the exceptional beers produced by this brewery.

This pale beer has a rich and varied aroma, with a hint of wild abandon, as in its name. From the start it is very distinctive, with a sharp spicy softness. Nevertheless its taste is very convivial, with a touch of bitterness which persists to the finish until it is interrupted by a dryness. The Vapeur en Folie (8%) can be served either cool or at room temperature, but in either event it pays to be wary of its secondary effects.

LEGERE

One would imagine that this beer is similar to its stable-mates, with less spice. In fact, the Vapeur Légère (4.5%) is a beer brewed along the lines of white beers, incorporating fermented wheat and using ginger, which guarantees a strong sharp taste that is cushioned in the mouth by a trace of bitterness. It develops only a little flavor on the palate, before flourishing in the throat, and leaves a strong lingering bitterness in the aftertaste.

ROUSSE

Of all the Vapeurs, this is the one. It is the most distinctive of all the brewery's beers, with all the spice you could possibly want, slightly acid, a suggestion of exoticism, just enough alcohol (8%) and a very intelligent mix of hops, and the result is complex but full flavored.

It is an amusing beer to drink, not just simply because it reaches all the parts of your body, but also because it has great sensitivity and warmth. It encourages a spontaneous yet intimate conviviality. Its exotic aspect inspires optimism.

Its bitterness brings us somewhat back to earth, and the roasted flavor in its aftertaste inspires caution and is thought-provoking. As a beer it is complete and every taste reveals a little more of what lies hidden behind...its russet color, quite naturally!

COCHONNE

After the Folie and the brown beers, it is the turn of the Cochonne. Leaving aside all allusions to aphrodisiacs, the Vapeur Cochonne is a superbly spiced beer, with caramel tangs highlighted by a bitterness that appears during the second phase. It leaves a sharp aftertaste but does not affect the overall impression.

It is to be noted that the first label was banned in Canada by the censors, for reasons of public decency.

MARCKLOFF

In around 1560, Philippe Marckloff, butler to Antoine de Metz, who was governor of the Seigneurie de Durbuy, subsequently Officer and Clerk of the High Court, owned a brewery in Durbuy.

He built the " Au Chesne " house on a site overlooking the Ourthe.

That is how the Ferme au Chene, the old homestead of the Marckloff family, came to be built. Today, the brewery is again active, as a genuine homage to its famous owner.

The brewers are not members of the Marckloff family, but they are people who love and respect gastronomic traditions as well as rural products.

The Marckloff beer (6.5%) is russet colored, just like the autumn leaves in the forests of the Ardennes. Its initial bouquet is in perfect harmony with the fragrance of the dense woods that cover the high hills overlooking the valley. But its flavor inspires no such imagery, being more neutral and less astringent than its nose suggested. This reduced sensitivity is offset by a lingering spicy bitterness.

Can only be drunk at the farm, and is often served with home-produced cheese.

LES SAISONS D'EREZEE

It was a superb idea to flavor the basic brew with the fragrance of the seasonal flowers. The basis is the same for all the beers, but the volume of alcohol varies according to the seasons, to reflect their harshness or gentleness.

VERSION AUTOMNE (FALL)

Gloomy looking with its reddish color, its volume of alcohol makes it more lively (7%). A dry fruity flavor and a well-balanced bitterness provide roundness for the basic ingredients. Sometimes, a sensation of burnt wood is perceptible.

VERSION HIVER (WINTER)

The harshness of the coldest season probably explains its high level of alcohol (8%). In his inspiration the brewer has introduced smoked and spicy aromas. This strong fragrant bouquet softens its flavor which is concealed beneath an over abundant head, which will disappear once the warmth returns, and its spicy, acrid notes will flourish to the fullest. The bitterness only appears at the finish and it will leave you with a warm glow.

VERSION PRINTEMPS (SPRING)

This stands apart from the other seasonal beers by its quartet of fragrances, smoked, spicy, bitter and caramel. Their aroma reflects the freshness associated with rebirth and blends cold and warm notes. Its contrasting aromas contrast sharply with a straightforward taste, which is naturally soft. The alcohol content of this spring version is 6.2%. It finds a new lease on life as it bows out on a bitter taste, which is the basis of the four seasons.

VERSION ETE (SUMMER)

Its composition based on flowers from the undergrowth in full bloom produces a restrained fresh bouquet. A heady softness (7%) slowly approaches the nostrils which are receptive to this drink which is thirst-quenching in its own way, but that is not necessarily the beer's unique attribute.

Its spicy note dominates the softness, while at the same time tickling the palate, which encourages you to roll the beer around its tulip shaped glass. It becomes more full-bodied on the tongue and leaves a smooth bitter taste on the palate.

The VIEILLE SALME

It is uniquely its amber colored appearance that makes this beer look somewhat old-fashioned. The Vieille Salme (8.5%) is in fact rather young and refreshing, which gives it a fruity aroma.

It is light in palate with no acridity. It becomes more full-flavored on the palate with its well-balanced bitterness, which will only taper off in the back of the throat. If left to age, its taste will improve, as its name suggests.

ALDEGONDE BRUNE

This would be a wonderful first name for a dazzling young girl. She would be auburn if she were eighteen, with a dark dress and an exotic flavored perfume.

Delicately raising a zest of dried orange to her lips, on which there will still remain a trace of wet caramel... however, she will look at us through stern eyes as if questioning our bold intentions, but with neither bitterness nor regrets.

When tasting the Aldegonde brown beer (7.2%) one can not help reflecting that it is part of the better things in life.

ALDEGONDE SPECIALE

With an additional touch of alcohol (7.5%) it becomes truly bewitching, all the more so with its dark color. Its airs and its aroma make it " British ", both by its nose and in the mouth. Occasionally when drunk at moderate temperatures the aftertaste has a hint of chicory.

MARLAGNE BLANCHE

The adjective in its name describes it as a white beer. Its appearance cannot deny this. And yet its flavor is far richer than other beers in this style. The Marlagne Blanche is less acid and the use of coriander in its ingredients adds a touch of balm, giving its nose an instant aroma, whereas white beers are somewhat subdued as regards their nose.

MARLAGNE BLONDE

In appearance, it looks like an ordinary pils style beer. It has much in common with the latter and is a kind of top-fermented pils, which makes the first description inappropriate. It is also more aromatic with pure malt as its basis. The Marlagne has a very subtle bitterness, which places it in a category above traditional pale beers. It is not pasteurized, but is sterilized in the bottle to enable it to be preserved without any problem for six months.

KUURNSE WITTE

The white beer from the town of Kuurne near Courtrai (western Flanders) has taken over from another beer of the same type that was called Witte Ezel (the white donkey). As its name indicates, it is part of the family of white beers. And yet, apart from its cloudy yellow color, it has many qualities that make it an exceptional beer.

Naturally, all the traditional elements associated with white beers are present, in particular its base of cereals, including wheat.

However, with the aroma, there is a powerful sharp perfume, like a concentrated acidity. In fact, however, the first taste demonstrates the opposite. This sour aspect is more than masked by a very good bitterness, and is also lessened by a level of alcohol that is on the high side for a white beer (7%). This cocktail is extremely refreshing on the palate, even when the beer is served at a relatively low temperature. Its strong thirst-quenching qualities are welcomed, and it is a soothing beer that it is a great pleasure to taste.

On the other hand it has almost no aftertaste, which in no way detracts from its rating as a classic beer.

HELLEKAPELLE

The Helleketelbos woods, which grace the low lands, lie in the Watou region, not far from the Saint-Sixtus Trappist abbey.

In contrast with the strong beers for which this region is reputed, the Helleketelbos (the chapel in the Helleketel woods) has a modest volume of alcohol of 5%. This considerably reduces its bouquet, but its taste improves with the bitterness based on hops from Poperinghe. It is neither filtered nor pasteurized. It is looked upon as simply a thirst quencher, but its after-dinner qualities are not to be ignored.

HELLEKETELBIER

Part of the same family of beers that is named after the woods in the middle of the countryside, which witnessed several fierce battles during World War I. The Helleketelbier (7%) reflects the traditions of this part of Flanders with first of all its color, which is a deep amber, and a softer taste and a bitterness which is distinctly more rounded. The flavor is pleasantly fruity but other than that it is uninteresting. It does justice to the region's hops only in the final taste.

DE ZATTE BIE

Literally translated, De Zatte Bie means the drunken bee. In other words, one should expect to find these two elements in the beer's ingredients. As regards the drunken aspect, it is true that with a volume of alcohol of 9.5% this can induce strange hallucinations fairly quickly. On the other hand, as regards the bee, there is no honey in this brew that has an admirably well-balanced taste. In place of the honey, candy sugar is used. Its black color, which makes it resemble a stout, absorbs the sugar to provide the smokier taste of roasted malt. However, the mix of six different malts, from a pale malt to darker ones, gives the Zatte Bie a richness of taste which is very much appreciated by serious beer drinkers. The whole is soft and dense, and for those who are alert to bitterness, it finishes with a touch of bitterness. It is definitely an endearing beer.

122

'T ZELFDE

" Bartender, the same again! ", is the translation of the original version of the title of this beer, which is amber, convivial, and based on the traditional brown beers from Brabant province. For a craft beer, it must be pointed out that the 'T Zelfde is a bottom-fermented beer with a volume of alcohol of 6.1%.

It goes down very easily, but it will lead you unwittingly to a land of sudden drunkenness. So be wary!

VLETERN ALT

The monks at Vleteren are the source of much envy in this region in western Flanders, close to the French border. Many brewers feel obliged to brew beers with a strong percentage of alcohol. The Vleteren Alt has however a respectable 8%, which represents a good average, without necessarily being low. The word " alt " (German for top) in its name, alludes to the fact that it is a top-fermented sediment beer.

In appearance it is dark colored and its head is like an overcoat, which nevertheless gives way to reveal a strong tanned side to a drink which has velvety tangs. The bitterness is slightly drowned by the softness of the aromatic malts that influence the beer's taste. There are no spices in its body. It matures peacefully in casks, and there is no obligation to produce large quantities. The end result is a very accomplished beer, both from an esthetic point of view as well as in terms of flavor. A pleasant bitterness will develop in the aftertaste, without however being able to free itself from an irritating softness.

VLETEREN SUPER 8

For all those who have enjoyed the Vleteren alt, there is every reason to suppose that more than one of them will be surprised by the Super 8.

First, in appearance it has nothing in common with the former. Only its volume of alcohol is similar (8%). Its aroma is rather malty, and the underlying tangs are distinctly more bitter with a suggestion of acidity and coriander. The initial taste sensation fades to leave a brew which overall is soft, with a very normal level of bitterness in the aftertaste.

SCHWENDI

Once again, this is a beer that is named after a local character with a rich historical past. Schwendi was the first governor of the town of Philippeville in 1855. It was not the brewer who had the idea of giving this name to a local brew, but rather it came from a brotherhood of gourmets who call themselves the " Confrères de l'Ambassade du Lapin à la Bière ".

This brotherhood, dedicated to different ways of cooking rabbit in beer, needed a beer corresponding in taste and which would blend with the gastronomic ingredients used in this dish. The brotherhood decided upon a bitter-sweet flavored beer, but with a not too long-lasting flavor.

The Schwendi which, in addition, is amber colored, can thus been seen as a culinary ingredient, but it also has its qualities when served as an accompaniment to meals. After a period of incubation in the mouth, the first impression ends with a bitter note. When used in the cooking of rabbits, it is essentially the beer's acidity which impregnates the meat.

The recipe for the beer includes three different malts, 1/3 barley, 1/3 winter barley and 1/3 special barley. It can be compared with a strong seasonal beer. It is filtered and pasteurized before being bottled in 75cl bottles.

The BIERE DE BELOEIL

It would be the last straw if one of the most beautiful chateaux in Belgium did not have its own beer named in its honor, when other edifices have been granted this honor.

Beloeil, in the heart of western Flanders, is in the middle of a triangle formed by Tournai, Ath and Mons, which are equidistant from the Château des Princes de Ligne.

The Bière de Beloeil was destined to be a noble beer which would be acceptable to blue-blooded palates, and at the same time would go down well with the common people during the festival season.

This amber beer, which is something of a cross between an amber colored pale beer and a more roasted brown beer, is somewhat a mixture of all those elements. Despite its aristocratic bearings, the end result is a blend of classic tastes. Its flavor is never aggressive, and it plays the role of a diplomat seeking to attract visitors to the site. It is not averse to flaunting its volume of alcohol of 8.5% to achieve its ends.

CERVESIA

It would appear that during an excavation carried out in the historical site of Aubechies in the region of Leuzen-Hainault, a relatively well-preserved manuscript was discovered containing the original recipe for a beer once brewed there.

The basic techniques not being the same in two distinct periods far-removed in time, it was necessary to adapt certain elements of this unknown beer which was to be renamed Cervesia (8.5%), using the Latin roots of the word beer.

In addition to the hops, its density is based on cereals, with barley and wheat being the principal ingredients. The amount of hops was just as important, as it had to blend well with herbs, which required great precision in the brewing process. The nose is spicy, and there is also a complex aroma where the bitterness blends with a discreet acidity from the wheat and a softness from the pale barley.

The bitterness dominates in the mouth and in the finish, after having demonstrated its density on the palate in between. Drunk at moderate temperatures it is a magnificent beer. One can therefore understand why the ancient manuscript was so preciously preserved.

DUPONT VIEILLE PROVISION

An enhanced seasonal beer that has even more character and distinctive qualities. Its bitterness is undoubtedly the essence of this beer, which has a volume of alcohol of 6.5%. Its convivial role having become blurred by the alcohol content and bitterness, it is a beer that cries out to assert its personality.

It is rich in discreetly acid, yet soft, aromas, but these are mixed with a bouquet of bitterness that is omnipresent. On tasting, the aromas disappear and leave behind in the mouth and in the aftertaste waves and waves of bitterness. Not an easy beer to drink, it parallels the lives of men working on the land.

JAWADDE

When popular expression plays a part in creating a beer, the result is bound to be amazing. When a brewer's imagination is given free rein, it will produce some strange concoctions.

" Jawadde " in the popular language of certain Flemish dialects means " first-rate! " and that means repeating it three times since this beer exists in three versions.

GEMBERBIER

This beer with a base of coriander is fairly fruity in its initial impact but reveals a bitter caramel presence. This is even more discernible in the mouth and overpowers the fruity element, with the bitterness becoming predominant at the finish.

Its volume of alcohol is 7%.

KRIEK

This is one of the few beers of this type to be mentioned in this book, but it is different from the others in that no Lambic is used in its fermentation. Only cherries from Schaerbeek play a role in the flavor, but in particular its dark red color conceals a volume of alcohol of 8% and the aftertaste has bitter tones.

An amazing Kriek, which probably does not find favor with purists.

TRIPEL

There is nothing original about a triple pale beer, but when its aroma is more fruity than bitter, the nose reacts immediately. In addition, the fruity aspect is dry, almost comparable with raisins, essentially on account of a peppery tone that makes the aroma less long-lasting. This is not to the beer's detriment, since the contrast with the restrained flavor of its contents leads inevitably to a more developed taste in the mouth where the bitterness is more keenly felt.

GAVERHOPKE

In alluding to the small parcels of land that certain farmers devote to the cultivation of hops, the Gaverhopke beers are a symbol of the world of farmer-brewers. The example comes from a micro-brewery which is situated alongside the Lys near Courtrai, and exists in three versions.

BLONDE

Closely resembling a strong Pils (8%), the Blonde has a malty taste against a background of dry bitterness. Despite being relatively soft, it nevertheless produces a conspicuous tingling sensation on the tongue.

BRUNE 12

With its deep softness and strong alcoholic flavor (12%), it has a syrupy fruity taste. This impression is confirmed in the mouth but its flavor is too powerful to develop further in the aftertaste.

BRUNE 8

Its base is very similar to that of the Brune 12 but the tangs are not as keen, and are therefore more pleasant on the tongue. It leaves more freedom of expression to its ingredients, which are fresher, but still fruity and spicy and thereby prevent any significant aftertaste developing.

CUVEE DU MARAIS

One day a cafe owner in Tournai who had problems obtaining supplies from his brewers decided to brew his own beer. Naturally, there are other examples in Belgium, but in this particular instance, however, the beer was to be extremely high in alcohol (13%) and intended only for consumption by the cafe's regular customers. It exists in three versions.

BLONDE BRUT

Overall it is soft despite a clear bitterness, but it will grab you by the throat and will not let go. For sensation seekers it is a wonderful beer, but it is not a beer that lends itself to a lengthy tasting session.

BRUNE BRUT

The caramel is more present and the beer is creamier, but it is preferable to drink this beer as an aperitif since, despite its strong volume of alcohol, it weighs heavily on the stomach, and it is difficult to drink more than one glass.

SPECIALE BRUT

This is more refined than the other two, and it leaves a sweeter impression, even to the extent of there being a discernible hint of honey on the palate, although there is absolutely no honey in the recipe. The verdict is the same as for the other two, that is to say the alcohol content is too high to enable the other ingredients to assert themselves fully and to allow the person tasting the beer time to appreciate it fully.

OERAL

The label on this summer beer shows a volume of alcohol of 6%, whereas in reality it is only 5%. It is a very pleasant beer for its bouquet and flavor, which are not too bitter, but at the same time are very distinctive. It is an excellent thirst quencher in summer, and it does not go to your head too quickly.

DULLE TEVE

This beer, named Dulle Teve (roguish witch), has lots of character. The harshness of its bitter bouquet provides a hint to its tone. On the other hand, its volume of alcohol is not discernible after the first mouthful. Deeply and intensely blonde, as only beautiful young girls from the north can be, its label seems to be a misnomer, unless there is a real hint of menace lurking beneath its charming exterior!

There is a lingering bitterness in its aftertaste, which will stay with you for a long time, and will even follow you in your dreams.

That must be the spell it casts!

ENGELTJES BIER

The angels with Cupid at their head can be both soft and spicy. Engeltjes Bier (10%), the beer of the angels, is more or less that combination, without the aphrodisiac effect. At the beginning, it has a spicy, special fragrance, which contrasts with its sweet flavor...

but be wary of its bitterness in readiness for a highly surprising aftertaste.

HOEGAARDEN SPECIALE

The announcement one day of the arrival of a new beer to add to the existing Hoegaarden family of beers, and on top of that a white beer, came as a surprise.

Even in the shadow of its prestigious stable companion, the Hoegaarden Spéciale stands out first of all by its color, which is more amber and thus more akin to white beers of bygone times.

In addition, its aroma is distinctly less spicy and not at all acid.

And finally, its velvety texture and creamy taste conclusively rule out any comparison with the traditional Hoegaarden beer. Its volume of alcohol (5.6%) also plays a predominant role in its conception, serving mainly to bring out the flavor of the beer's ingredients.

The absence of acidity, an unmistakable bitterness, and a darker roasted malt make this beer special and very different from all others. Its flavor is more restrained, but more complex at the same time. The coriander and curaçao give it a new and subtle taste. The curaçao is most pronounced in the aftertaste, leaving behind a slight hint of sweetness, but no more than that.

It has a lasting, creamy head with barely discernible bubbles.

It can certainly be said to be thirst-quenching, but by its relaxing and comforting character it is also a beer which makes an excellent complement to meals or can be consumed at home amongst friends. The traditional Hoegaarden does not cast a shadow over this newer version.

JULIUS

"Of all the Gallic nations, the Belgians are the most knowledgeable about beer", is perhaps what Julius Caesar might have said if he had tasted the beer named after him.

The Hoegaarden brewers never had the intention of exporting this beer to Italy, where it would doubtless have attracted attention. In Belgium it suffers slightly from the popularity of the other top-selling brews produced by the brewery. Connoisseurs of beer should not however ignore this beer, for it is full of character, and it is remarkably well conceived.

Initially it is somewhat neutral, and underneath its white toga there exists a bitter drink, which is brewed with aromatic malts that give added taste to its Latin, if not to say exotic, character.

It is sharp like a spear on the end of the tongue, and immediately reveals its special bitter flavor which is derived from traditional spices: coriander, orange peel and naturally a dash of curaçao to round out gently its character. Its flavor develops on the palate and continues in the mouth, but without being too long-lasting. The initial lacework is impressive when the beer is first poured into the glass, and once each element has been allowed to settle peacefully in the glass, then the circus may begin in honor of its emperor, who in this instance is.....you.

A work of art in the beer world which should not be missed!

131

RUBENS

In 1989, an association from Antwerp, called " Antwerpen Rubenstaad ", being dedicated followers of the great artist's work, had the idea of promoting the painter's town of origin through a special brew which would bear his name. Essentially aimed at foreign tourists in the Belgian metropolis, the beer had to please a maximum number of people, including often those who were not used to the beers of character consumed in this country. The brewers therefore opted for a beer low in alcohol, and with a restrained bitterness.

GOLD

Its aroma is very soft, very slightly fruity, and does not develop much in the mouth, whereas its vivid gold coloring hints at shades of caramel and bitterness. The latter is eventually worth describing at the finish, but remains overall bland, and this will not become a classic beer.

ROUGE

As its name suggests, the Reuben Rouge, with a lower alcohol content (4%), and even softer flavor, is amber, almost a discreet shade of red in color. What gives it this shade is the presence of apricots in the recipe, and these are also responsible for a flavor that is more exotic but without great bitterness, based on a welcoming fruity bouquet. A slight but very refined suggestion of bitterness reappears however at the back of the mouth, which will enable the tourist tasting this beer to grasp the distinctive features of Belgian beers.

ZULTE

A brown beer par excellence, this traditional Flemish brown beer was prepared in a brewery in a large village of the same name near Waregem. This was the beer that was consumed on festive occasions, and accordingly its volume of alcohol was relatively low (4.7%).

Its aroma is sour, and this is confirmed by the initial taste, in which there is also a sweet touch of softness. It very quickly stabilizes in the mouth but the taste does not develop any further. The fact that it is served very cool also prevents the beer from expressing itself fully. It also leaves a slightly spicy, but not aggressive, taste on the end of the tongue.

It goes down very well during the summer months, but is less to the fore in colder periods.

The FRUIT DEFENDU

The Fruit Défendu, a white beer descended from the famous Hoegaarden family of beers, has inherited only the sharp taste, which remains very discreet and cannot therefore be compared with a Hoegaarden white beer. First of all it is brown, and therefore does not use the same malts, hence it has more of a coffee flavor and a good dose of bitterness highlights its solid taste.

The Fruit Défendu (9%) appeals to those who like their beers strong in character. Its finish is extremely subtle thanks to the many spices, including coriander and dried orange peel, which give it an exotic touch, which is intelligent in its conception, and tremendously rich in taste. The world of farmer-brewers in Belgium can be proud of this beer.

MAGONETTE

Magonette, was a XVIII century highwayman who robbed those traveling the roads in the heart of the Ardennes. He could not have imagined that one day he

would be bottled to be served at dinner, or that he would be taken to the bosom of families in the form of a beer.

This beer is still very young, since it was created in 1994, in a tiny brewery in Comblain-la-Tour (Liège province). This brewery, although already in business, officially opened its doors in 1996, and intends to increase its range of beers, drawing inspiration from the modest historical past of the valley of the Ourthe.

The Magonette (8.2%) quickly establishes its personality with a keen sharp aroma, which is almost sour. There is a touch of acidity which is apparent from the outset. Most fortunately, this is not the only flavor, since it is accompanied by a bitterness, which is typical of the Ardennes, without being too pronounced. Although it is lightly filtered, its color is amber and in appearance it is clear and bright when exposed to the light. It also has a peppery tone which offsets the initial touch of acidity, and at the finish its bitterness is drier. Its creamy smooth aspect contains different sugars, including a liquid honey from the Ardennes, which round out the edges. The ingredients also include hawthorn flowers. It is served with an opulent white head.

MINTY

Amongst the traditional beer colors, there are many different shades, pale, brown, amber, red, black, but never green.

The Minty (4.3%) makes good this gap. It deserves its description as a mint beer. Surprising as it may seem, it must be said that it is not at all unpleasant; however it is not a beer to which one can grow accustomed.

It's mainly a fantasy beer, to be tasted in summer simply as a thirst quencher. In this it is most successful.

Its aroma naturally has a strong mint fragrance, but with also a peppery touch. On the other hand, this special characteristic is less noticeable in its taste, as there is nevertheless a touch of dry bitterness, which subdues the vigorous aroma.

Other than its natural peppermint spiciness, it is fairly sharp on the tongue.

It is generally served cool (5 to 7°C/41-44°F), but by its very nature it is cool in itself.

It is worth trying, but only out of curiosity.

The BIERE DU LION

The natural purity of the water used in the brewing process is one of the main elements in determining a beer's quality.

In the heart of the Fagnes in eastern Belgium, a small craft brewery that is even more artisanal than the others, endeavors to exploit as best as possible all the natural elements at his disposal. Situated in the shade of an impressive stone lion that overlooks the Barrage de la Gileppe, what could be more

natural than for the brewers to dedicate their beer to the King of the Forest of Fagnes.

The Biere du Lion has an impressive aroma, which corresponds to its natural setting. In appearance it is golden, with rich lacework, crowned by a very soft head. Its initial nose is very delicately bitter, and this carries over into the taste, which is bitter and rich, with different tones redolent of the fragrances of the forest. A slight smoked touch is discernible in the throat alongside the bitterness. It is immensely refreshing, with as a secondary effect digestive powers second to none.

It can be described as a talented beer which is both subtle and delicate, but which is destined to appeal to those whose palates like strong beers (8% vol. alcohol).

135

The LA ROUSSE DES FAGNES

This is a tribute to the region of Fagnes in Belgium, which is so pretty and captivating in the summer, but so unpredictable in the fall and during the winter months. The Rousse des Fagnes (9%) is the color of the fall months. It is very direct with no distinctive nose, as its aroma is so omnipresent that it leaves no room for surprises in the tastes to come. These are powerful and enhanced by the typical tastes characteristic of the Ardennes. These are not easily overpowered, for each taste brings a fresh flourish to the palate. Its bitterness dominates but allows a roasted malt flavor to develop.

Its bitter aftertaste is robust and lingers on the tongue.

Its pure water and gassy preparation, which are responsible for the lacework, greatly enhance its digestive qualities.

Despite the long harsh winters, the Rousse des Fagnes, has all the qualities to be drunk as a heart-warming beer in front of a wood fire using dry fir.

It could become a classic beer for this region where friends take great pleasure in gathering for a quiet friendly drink during the cold months.

MEESTERS BIER

This beer's name is tailormade. Meesters Bier (7.5%) means the master's beer, but in this case it also quite simply has the same name as the master-brewer who produces it.

Its welcoming bouquet, which is not too powerful, immediately evokes the coriander that is used. But that is not its only perfume, and one can detect a lingering bitterness and a strong malty effect.

This is the richest phase in the tasting of this beer, for its placid bitterness takes on a new dimension on the palate. It even adds a touch of spice to the tongue and develops with the heat on the palate. It is a pity however that only the bitterness remains in the aftertaste, for its initial nose was so welcoming

that one would have preferred to retain that particular memory.

KATJE SPECIAL

Traditionally, the second Sunday of the month of May in Ypres (western Flanders) is devoted to cats. Up until 1817, kittens were thrown from the belfry. Despite the fact that a cat always lands on its paws, from that height very few survived the ritual. The tradition was revived in 1938, but with fluffy toy kittens. In 1958 a traditional procession was added.

This festival was also a good opportunity to drink and make merry, in the name of cats. That is how the Katje Special came about.

This slightly amber beer, with its very respectable 6% volume of alcohol, is readily comparable to an English ale, by its amber color and several aspects of its taste. It is sweet on the palate, but with a sharp bitter taste in the mouth where it develops even more character. It is neither caramel flavored nor peppery. Its aroma is very neutral and does not reflect the beer's ingredients.

Its finish corresponds to its development in the mouth. Despite its principal role as a convivial festive beer, the Katje special has a lot of character and should be drunk with care since its intoxicating effects could take hold more quickly than expected.

OLD MUSKETEER

Based on the " Trois Mousquetaires " of Alexandre Dumas, this variation called the Old Musketeer (7.5%) was intended for export to France, in particular to the regions of French Flanders, which so resemble Belgium. However, it convinced few people and returned to its native land, that is Boezinge near Ypres (western Flanders).

Since then it has found its place in the cottages alongside the river Yser where it has become one of the many beverages over which the local inhabitants share their secrets.

Its main characteristic is its pleasantly fresh bouquet, which brings to mind beers from the north with the tang of a soft breeze. Its flavor brings out even more this softness with a hint of sugar, which enhances the roundness of a bitterness that is only present in the aftertaste.

It is the taste buds of the tongue rather than the palate which play the leading role in appreciating this beer. This " old musketeer " is liked for its coziness, and as a nightcap will ensure that you have a good night's sleep.

JOSEPH

This beer made from spelt, is essentially a white beer, but possesses a taste which is specific to the spelt used in its production.

Its aroma is exceptional and welcoming with an orange and honey fragrance.

Its flavor does not contradict the nose. In fact during the first phase of tasting it is the orange taste that stands out. A slight touch of acidity is also discernible on the tongue but this gives way to reveal a distinct semi-dry syrupy aspect.

In appearance it is a deep yellow color and deliberately cloudy. Its double fermentation also conveys the fruity aspect that is exclusive to spelt.

The Joseph (5%) is a very refreshing drink without being intoxicating, and thus can be drunk more frequently, explaining its description as the beer of the apostle, which accompanies the many walkers enjoying the lakeside pleasures of the Eau d'Heure.

SARA

The siren of the fields has a name, Sara. Its aroma attracts lovers of straightforward authentic beers who unreservedly applaud this beer.

Its very powerful initial aroma is the consequence of its marriage with buckwheat, which is also known as black wheat. Its taste is therefore very exclusive and very rich, but lacking in bitterness both in palate and in the aftaste. It leaves a very pleasant feeling of freshness on the tongue, which at the same time brings to mind a slight hint of licorice.

Its charm is so undeniable that I will certainly not be the last person to fall victim to its obvious attractions, which are so irresistible.

BIERES DES TRINITAIRES

For the inhabitants of the small village of Lens, near Ath (Hainault), the Trinitaire holds no secrets. It refers in fact to a congregation of monks who had chosen to settle in the town square, known as the Place de la Trinité in this town in the province of Hainault, in what is now in fact the town hall.

The brewing process of this craft beer, with its honorable volume of alcohol of 8%, remains highly secret even today.

In appearance it is amber colored with a very spicy and pungent aroma. Its flavor confirms this initial impression and adds a generous dash of red cane sugar, plus a touch of licorice at the finish. The bitterness plays only a minor role, but does serve to balance any spiciness arising from the peppery taste.

DOREE DE L'HAMIO

Its label reflects the local dialect. In this part of Belgium, in Lens (western Hainault), the local word for hamlet is pronounced " hamio ", which gives an idea just how popular this beer, with its 8% volume of alcohol, is with the local inhabitants in this area of Lens, who see in it a reflection of the harshness of country life.

Moreover, the dominant element from start to finish in this beer is its bitterness. It is long but not astringent. Its artisanal concept prevents it from claiming a place amongst the strong pale beers in the country.

It is remarkably active, with an extremely generous lacework and abundant head which will not die away. A very accomplished beer, which makes a good after-dinner drink.

MENEER

" Monsieur ", your beer is served. Its name originates from this mark of respect shown to someone in authority, or with a natural charisma, or natural authority.

The Meneer is a very pale beer with generous helpings of hops, and a very dry taste. The acridity of its initial flavor is offset by a fruitiness, which essentially develops in the mouth. At the finish it is the bitterness that dominates once again.

Despite its youth, and the fact that it was created in what were formerly milk tanks, its maturity is surprising. It has truly become a fine " Monsieur ".

Worth discovering.

The BRIGAND
(THE HIGHWAY ROBBER'S BEER)

The Brigand did not take the name of a known highway robber from the previous century, instead it implies that even highway robbers sought to quench their dishonestly earned thirst in the inns along the roads frequented by travelers. Somewhat in the manner of the secret body that it represents, the Brigand, with its strong alcohol content (9%), immediately grabs you by the throat and will not let go. On the other hand, its nose shows its true face and reveals a malty aroma barely covered by a slight hint of fruitiness. It hides behind a thick head, and is very lively. Its taste is very subtle without any real bitterness, but is very vivacious with an invigorating spiciness on the tongue. It also has a strong alcoholic flavor that becomes even stronger in the mouth.

It does not linger on the palate taking with it all its many subtle flavors, but it does leave an excellent impression behind, which certainly cannot have been the case with the highway robbers of the XVIII century.

Its secondary effects are immediate. It will surprise you by its density of taste and the rapidity with which it will go to your head. In other words, it can be enjoyed with much pleasure, but be careful that you are not being led into an ambush.

BIERE DARBYSTE

Taking the superlative form of the name Darby, the Darbyste takes us back into a world of religious upheavals, where the war of words between Catholics and Protestants was still continuing.

In fact the pastor Darby, a descendant of the famous Nelson, was head of a branch of Protestants in England. His particular ambition was to save the " Borains ", the inhabitants of the region around Mons, from alcoholism. And to think that today there is a beer named after him, and despite everything, a beer that is much appreciated for its conviviality.

Brewed according to the traditional recipes of grandmothers from those days, the Darbyiste is a refreshing drink, not too strong in alcohol in deference to the origins of its name, and its basic ingredients are barley, sugar and figs. These elements are very much to the fore in its taste and provide a rich blend of soft flavors. The Darbyste (5.8%) takes on more character in the mouth, with a sharp touch of bitterness, which continues through to the aftertaste. This is always served cool.

VONDEL (A SYMBOLIC BEER)

The famous Flemish author, although he was of Dutch origin, has considerably changed Flemish traditions. He has become the symbol of an entire Flemish culture that is richly endowed. The impressive literary inheritance that he left to the flat country that is Belgium, and what is described as the language of Vondel, is much coveted by the purists.

In addition to his literary works, there is the other Vondel, with his respect for ancient Flemish traditions.

This beer alone, in appearance a classic amber brown beer, epitomizes the flavors of the XVII century.

143

Its bitter-sweet tones dominate both the bouquet and its taste throughout the mouth. Thanks to a very sensible fermentation process, it has great maturity. It is soothing and its lively head, which seems never to die away, is astonishing.

Just like the traditional brown beers, it nevertheless leaves a trace of bitterness at the finish, which is more akin to a grand finale than a mere aftertaste.

Superb and astonishing.

WAAS KLOK BIER

Brewed in quantities which are kept secret, its origins are confirmed by the label which shows the village of Belsele (near Saint-Nicolas) in western Flanders where it is produced, there can be no doubt that it is a triple beer with lots of character.

The Waas Klok Bier (8.5%) is strongly spiced and possesses a matchless aroma that is worth dwelling upon. In the nose, one is immediately aware of the coriander, which merges into a more rounded taste, with a spicy sweetness that is offset by a layer of malt.

Its traditional bitterness serves to affirm its personality, and as if to leave its mark, it has a lingering bitter aftertaste and then the coriander appears once again.

DIKKENEK
(AN UNPRETENTIOUS BEER)

A wonderfully delicious beer, the name of which, Dikkenek, is used in all Flemish dialects to allude to someone with a thick neck, and therefore with no right to be pretentious.

It finds its origins in the province of Limbourg, at Hasselt. It is a retort to the beers that have been made in Limbourg since the beginning of the XVII century, using three grains. It is the patron saint of brewers who symbolically appears on its label.

Without being a particularly strong beer (5.1%), the dark colored Dikkenek beer accompanies the population of this provincial town in all its organized celebrations.

While its bouquet is almost insignificant, it manifests itself on the tongue, albeit briefly with a sugary flavor. The addition of juniper leaves makes its taste a tiny bit drier. They enable all the ingredients to express themselves, thereby producing a discreet pungency and a slight thirst-quenching bitterness, which adds to the initial impression.

The Dikkenek is extremely welcoming, and is straightforward without any pretensions. But after all, isn't that how we recognize true greatness?

DELIRIUM TREMENS

In effect, after having drunk too many glasses of certain strongly alcoholic drinks, it is possible to have certain hallucinations. Some see bizarre shapes, or dead, or inanimate objects, which suddenly come to life. The most poetic amongst us will see pink elephants dancing the rumba. This is nothing to do with reality, it is simply a case of delirium tremens. Such a crisis due to alcohol poisoning is also part of the early warning signs of alcohol abuse. At this stage, therapy is strongly recommended. In choosing to give this name to their beer, the brewers responsible for the Delirium Tremens have chosen to place the emphasis on drinking with care

and attention. In fact, for anyone who is tempted to overdo things, this brew, with its 9% volume of alcohol, is a fearsome drinking partner.

Most fortunately, most people are attracted by its composition.

It is presented in an ornate opaque bottle, and once poured its bouquet is discreet but authentic. Its malt and spice provide the initial attraction, and these combine perfectly naturally with a certain bitterness to provide a beguiling allusion of softness. Its peppery tone gives it a certain dryness, which means that none of the different flavors lingers on the palate. At the finish there is a touch of bitterness, but this lasts no longer in the aftertaste than it did in the mouth.

PISSENLIT

Without being included in that category, the Pissenlit is truly a seasonal beer. That can be explained by the use of what is a summer plant as one of its ingredients.

This beer has been cleverly conceived by its brewer, who is a passionate practicioner of the new artisanal brewing techniques, and as a thirst quencher the Pissenlit is indispensable. It has an enormous seasonal bouquet, with its summer fragrance redolent of nearly ripe fruit. It is a delight not to be ignored.

Its bitterness, which for once is not derived uniquely from the hops that are naturally used in its production, but is heightened by the dandelion flowers which are very bitter in taste. However, the bitterness here is closer to that found in a glass of very cold milk with a harsh, almost bitter, taste. However, on the tongue, there is a slight spicy taste, as if to banish comparisons with the smooth texture and taste of milk.

At the finish this same impression persists, leaving only a bitter dry taste, but how thirst-quenching it is, especially when served very cool (5°C/41°F).

It is a veritable nectar produced by craftsmen!

146

TRIPLE TOISON D'OR

The town of Mechelen, in Antwerp province, was not spoilt for choice as regards triple beers. The Triple Toisson d'Or therefore corresponds not only to a need, but also reflected a desire on the part of the inhabitants of the ancient capital of Belgium.

It also brings to memory its rich and illustrious historical past linked to Charles Quint.

In terms of appearance, it lives up to its name and is a faded gold, almost copper, color. This highly appropriate color is due to the addition of different pale malts. Its initial taste is peppery and caramel flavored, but with an underlying honorable, and very correct layer of, bitterness.

Its innate class makes it a fitting and honorable representative of triple beers in Mechelen, which at the present time number only one, but what a beer!

Its aftertaste leaves a impression which respects local tradition in matters of taste, being half-caramel and half-bitter.

VIEILLE DES ESTINNES

Based on a recipe from bygone times from a small village in Hainault with the same name, situated near the coal mines in the center, the Vieille des Estinnes, with its 7.5% volume of alcohol, is terribly distinctive. In character its taste is harsh, but its nose is more finely balanced with rather a certain acidity against a background of lime peel.

That impression is not long-lasting, as its true identity lies in a harsh, deep bitterness like the coal mines. Its character toughens with each taste and assumes the force of a powerful boulder capable of waking the souls of the victims of local mining disasters.

The aftertaste consolidates this impression in the mouth and is the logical conclusion. It really is extremely astringent, just as life was in the heyday of the mines.

ARABIER (AN ELOQUENT BEER)

For a beer from northern Belgium, its character really is very bitter.

The Arabier (8%), named after a chatterbox of a bird with a multicolored plumage, is guaranteed to loosen tongues, if not only to enjoy the initial impression of unflagging bitterness. There are no spices to intensify the acridity of the taste, which is constant but not wearisome. Whether the beer is served at room temperature, or cool, makes not the slightest difference to this lasting bitterness.

It is to be consumed with the same pleasure as its aroma procures, and this beer which is relaxing, and an ideal night-cap, will satisfy your stomach as well as your taste buds.

The HESBAYE

La Hesbaye, situated in the fertile agricultural region in the south eastern part of Lilmbourg province in Belgium, is essentially a grain belt before the ruggedness of Fagnes on the Belgian border with Germany.

It is thanks to this prosperity that an incalculable number of delicious regional products have seen the light of day.

The beer of the same name, the Hesbaye is living proof. It exists in three versions, which are all very distinctive and different from one another.

148

BLONDE

With its honest 6.5% volume of alcohol, the Blonde is not bitter in taste, but rather has a licorice aroma as a by-product of its fruity bouquet. It is tremendously thirst-quenching, but the brewing process used to produce it needs to be stabilized.

AMBREE

Unlike the Blonde, the bitterness in the Ambrée (7%) is restrained by a sugary but non- caramel flavor. Its softness gives way to a fruitier tone, which is there at the finish.

BRUNE

This is the leading beer in the Hesbaye family of beers and it is incontestably the most distinctive, not only on account of its 9% volume of alcohol, but also by the greater density in its aromas as well as the flourish of hops present in the bouquet at the finish. It is perhaps more appropriate to taste this dark colored beer at a moderate temperature, but this will make it heavier to digest.

EEN MOLLEKE

Sidney Bechet used to play " Little flower "; the inhabitants of Vleteren, that little village which is so wonderfully rich in brewing tradition, sing " little mole " when savoring Een Molleke.

Let us be agreed about the interpretation of the song, for everything is only supposition. In fact, the Een Molleke (8%), which is brewed in great secret, is only to be found at the far end of the cellars of the men living off this land which lies in the extreme north west corner of Belgium.

It waits peacefully to pass your lips, but before this you will have closed your eyes and breathed its smoked soft aroma. Its taste will produce the same feeling of well-being, becoming more bitter at the finish with the smoked tone reappearing at the back of the throat. The " little mole " was just passing through.

KASTEELBIER TRIPLE D'OR

The Château d' Ingelmunster (western Flanders) must indeed have very good cellars, since despite the proximity of the Lys, as well as a surrounding moat, its basements seem to be the ideal place to ensure a sound fermentation of the beers that are laid down there.

The most recent creation to emerge from the vats in the cellars of this Flemish fortress is also the strongest, with a volume of alcohol of 11%. This is immediately felt in the taste, while the aroma is disheartened by it. The latter is even somewhat discreet. Most fortunately its initial taste is immediately convincing. It really is a classic beer with lots of character. Wonderfully bitter against a strong alcohol-flavored background

flanked by an exotic layer of curaçao. You will have to wait until the middle of the glass before a good fruity aroma, which is sweet and welcoming, finally appears, with an alcoholic pungency in the nose. Its bitterness increases during the tasting, and overpowers the exotic aspect, which reappears in the aftertaste.

The Kasteelbier Triple D'Or is remarkably dense from every point of view, and despite its strong alcohol content, all the ingredients in its recipe are perfectly well-balanced, each ingredient having the opportunity to display its charms. It can also compete with the best digestive drinks, and can be laid down in the cellar for a long time, although not necessarily in cellars akin to those of the Château d'Ingelmunster.

The BIERE DU CORSAIRE (A RED BEER)

Given the lack of Vikings in Belgium, it was left to the red pirates to invade the Italian Peninsula from the north. That is, in any event the main role given by the brewers to the Bière du Corsaire, with its color, which to say the least, is close to blood red.

Aimed at the export market, it is pasteurized when bottled, and undergoes no further treatment. Its basic volume of alcohol is sufficiently high (7.4%), and it has a beautiful aroma with the fragrance of sugar cane. In its taste however there is a very manifest suggestion of burnt caramel, which is a result of the roasted malt used in its fabrication. It belongs to the category of beers known as " birra rosa " i.e. red beers, which are so coveted by the Latins of continental Europe.

It is particularly easy to digest, and can be drunk with obvious pleasure, even served cool. In all events, its finish is memorable for its sweetness against a background hint of smoked bitterness.

The BIERE DU CORSAIRE CUVEE SPECIALE

It is better if the sea is not too stormy, otherwise there is a risk that the sediment quietly fermenting at

151

the bottom of its bottle may disappear. This triple beer which is the last in the cycle, is very powerful (10%) with a constant but soft aroma, fragrant with coriander. On the other hand, it is only slightly bitter, and lets the different sugary tones, candy and sugar cane, guide the ship.

On the starboard side, that is downstream of the tasting, it takes the sweet route to the back of your throat. Its character is primarily enhanced by its deliciously sugary flavor, which contrasts with a world where the principal actors should be salt and iodine.

GILDENBIER

Its origins date back to 1389 with the archers of the town of Diest, a small but thriving trading town in the furthermost eastern corner of the province of Flemish Brabant. It was the companion of the men who, armed with their bows, were posted behind the ramparts to defend the town of Diest.

With their disappearance the beer survived only a few years, all the more so since the small breweries in the town disappeared one after another. It was reborn in the XX century and became once and for all part of the everyday life in the town, and took the role of a convivial beer, while preserving its appetizing taste.

In fact, this beer, with its modest alcohol level (6.3%), is candy brown, just like the sugar used to make it, and has a taste which in effect is very soft and sugary but without at any moment being excessively so. Underneath its small brownish head, a trace of coffee is present at the back of the throat and this leaves a pleasant thirst-quenching feeling, before finishing with a timorous hint of bitterness which is responsible for satisfying your thirst. It is drunk in a small beer mug, which brings to mind its initial vessel which was in earthenware, and was sometimes personalized by its owner, the archer who always kept this drinking vessel by his side, even when asleep. It will leave you with a very pleasant taste and happy memories, and

will rapidly convert drinkers into faithful devotees, thus hitting its target right in the middle.

CHARLES QUINT

It is said that Charles Quint preferred beer to wine, and that he had brewers concoct very special brews for his personal consumption, as well as for his guests from distant southern horizons. Whatever the truth may be, there is no head without a beer, and in all probability there is surely an element of truth in such public gossip, for many beverages in Belgium allude to this famous character, who reigned over an immense empire where the sun never set.

Naturally, the Charles Quint, which is strong with its 7% volume of alcohol, does not hide its historic symbolism. All that remained was to find a plausible recipe corresponding to the tastes which this great king could have had.

Apparently, his tastes were for things sweet. In any event this tone is very prominent in this brew, with an aroma which is not too persistent, but an initial flavor which immediately announces its colors. Its taste is effectively soft without any immediate bitterness but not at all sugary. On the palate there is a trace of lico-

rice, but not at all overpowering. Quite the contrary, it adds something extra to all the sweetness. It mingles with the bitterness, but only at the back of the throat, and persists without acridity in the aftertaste, together with a discreet sugary tang. With its brown almost reddish color, with a bit of imagination it brings to memory the opulent cosseted world of Charles Quint and his entourage.

NE KEMPENAER

Although it may look inoffensive, just like a peaceful peasant from Limbourg, the Ne Kempenaer beer has a strong volume of alcohol of 9%. Brewed for the region of Baarle Hertog, which is a parcel of Belgian land in Holland, this brew stands out by virtue of being a cross between a Double and a Triple.

It is however the Double side that dominates, with notably a slightly caramel effect which gives it a swarthy color. Its bitterness remains restrained throughout, even at the finish, when it scarcely flirts with the palate.

992 MILLENEIR 1992

This is the quintessential type of beer which was intended to be brewed only selectively, but which had such an impact on those who drank it, that today, even if its label seems out of date, it has become part of the brewing traditions of the inhabitants of Baarle-Nassau, a small strip of Belgian land lost in Holland. It was, for the organizers of the festivities organized by the inhabitants of this Belgian colony exiled in Holland to celebrate their thousandth anniversary, a remarkable piece of research to uncover a thousand year old recipe. In reality, this beer, renamed 992 MILLENEIR 1992 for the occasion, was in those days known as Barleweyn. It was a very strong beer, that the English exported illicitly into Great Britain.

The thousandth year anniversary celebrations were the occasion to brew anew this beer, which has a volume of alcohol of 8.5%. Its recipe is plentiful in ingredients, which include Pilsener malt, German hops, water from the Cedrogne (a river which flows through this region), yeast, spices, ginseng and horseradish roots, the latter being a plant which is cultivated for its thick peppery flavored root.

Its taste is however relatively simple, and even fruity in its aroma. There is however a spicy touch on the tongue but this is short-lasting. Its bitterness is present throughout, but remains in harmony with the beer's softness. It is a beer that enables everyone to identify the tastes that most suit them. That is true diplomacy, especially in a land of exile.

BRAVE BROEDER

Despite its name of Brave Broeder, this beer should not be confused with an abbey beer. It has neither the historic roots, nor the olfactory character.

It has more in common with a seasonal beer, but with more bitterness, with a caramel aftertaste to the finish.

It is not particularly easy to digest, but it is pleasant to drink, especially when viewed as a simple thirst quencher.

LAZARUS

Lazarus was resurrected by Jesus. Now it is brought back to life by a cunning brewer, who did not fail to point out on his label that in the Bible, it was explicitly stated that the blind would see again, and that the ears of the deaf would function as before.

If one is to believe the Lazarus (7%) beer label, those who drink two glasses of this brew will have the impression that their life will be eternal.

To invoke such an argument, it surely required some heavyweight ingredients. Yet, apart from the hazelnut extracts used in this beer, only the traditional flavors, bitterness and a fruity flavor, are present.

It is true that it communicates easily with the tongue, but it leaves very few memories in the mouth, and leaves one feeling unsatisfied, so much so that one has a second beer to test one's memories of the first. Perhaps that is what is meant by resurrection?

SCOTCH SILLY

Scotch ales are not really a Belgian speciality, and yet certain brewers do not hesitate to introduce them it into a land that is spoilt for choice for diverse bitter beers.

The Scotch Silly, with its brown candy sweetness, is different in one immediate respect from English drinks of this style, and that is its relatively strong volume of alcohol of 8%.

It also has a different taste with a smoked tang in the aftertaste. It also has a good bitterness, which is felt at the back of the throat.

This scotch is however very intoxicating, and can be served at a fairly cool temperature (8°C/46°F) which is not traditional.

The BIEKEN
(FROM THE NEST TO THE BOTTLE)

The label on this beer would not look out of place on any jar of honey. In reality, you would not be far off the mark, as the Bieken (little bee) is equally a honey beer. Of all the drinks made with honey, it is probably the one that is closest to honey by its concentration. It

157

is at the same time dense in honey, and in hops and alcohol (8.5%). Moreover, it is not filtered, and it is top-fermented, which makes it very cloudy in appearance, certainly not particularly attractive in its large " hostelry " glass, which rapidly attracts dogged insect invaders. But, in accordance with the traditional rule applying to drinks brewed with honey, whereby the honey and the hops are completely merged during the fermentation process, the honey remains more or less in name only. The initial impression when tasting this beer is its bitterness, but it becomes more rounded in the mouth. Thereafter, the impression changes, and while it cannot really be described as syrupy, it is more malty against a fruity background. The Bieken is a very calm beer with its own personality, its lacework is only discreet, but it is however active when the bottle is opened (33cl.). For all that, its head is no less dense, on the contrary, its clear honey color is crowned by a full creamy white head. We prefer it when served at a moderate room temperature (12°C/53°F), and primarily as an aperitif.

The Bieken is certainly the most artisanal of the honey beers that we discovered. It has been brewed for three generations by a family of brewers, the Boelen family, who at the same time as running their business in artisanal drinks are involved in a micro-brewery (300 hectoliters per year). Other than this typical honey beer, there is also a triple style beer, the Waas Klok Bier (8.5% vol. alcohol), which is heavily spiced and has a very dense aftertaste.

The BIERE DES OURS

In line with the great end-of-century fashion for producing honeyed beers, this one, the Bière des Ours, comes from the town of Binche with its ancient ramparts. Its category is evident and the label sets the tone, with a (gentle) bear against a background of a nest, on top of the beer's name, accompanied by its honey label.

On first contact, its nose has a very strong aroma, setting the syrupy tone from the outset. On the other hand, its taste is astonishing. To begin with, there is its not inconsiderable bitterness, which is barely cushioned by a suggestion of honey in the aftertaste. Its flavor is however very dense and rich in discoveries. In addition to the honey and the hops in its ingredients, there are certain subtle exotic touches, which according to the brewer are entirely due to the traditional fermentation technique, hops, (pale) malt and

local honey. There is one last surprise to come in the aftertaste, where there is a discreet but nevertheless real impression of Irish Coffee.

The Bière des Ours is fairly strong in its volume of alcohol (8.5%) and its lacework is very active which results in a dense but not too thick head, which is ideal and allows its aroma to express itself fully. Its brewer suggests that it should be served on the cool side (8°C/ 46°F). At a higher temperature it is harder to swallow.

It suits lovers of strong beer, combining a rich bitterness with a powerful effect, which is guaranteed to provide a solid night's sleep. It should be noted that as a digestive it can produce the reverse effect.

The Bière des Ours is truly a sturdy drink, but as yet is an orphan without its own personalized glass, which to be appropriate would be massive.

The BUSH 7% (REPRESENTING TWO HUNDRED AND TWENTY FIVE YEARS OF HISTORY)

The brewery Dubuisson de Pipaix, at Leuze-en-Hainault, celebrated its two hundred and twenty fifth anniversary in 1994. Founded in 1769 by Joseph Leroy, a maternal ancestor of the present Dubuisson family, the business continues to run successfully. Its lead product is the Bush Beer, which is well-known both for its very " British " taste and its distinctive bitterness,

and it is also the strongest beer in Belgium, with a volume of alcohol of 12%, boosted even more during the time it ferments in the bottle. By the hazards of politics (American), it was on the front page of all the Belgian and American newspapers during the investiture of President Bush, who to mark the occasion was presented by the Dubuisson family with a pallet of Bush Beer, of course. The White House spokesman pointed out that " The President had appreciated " [sic]. Bush Beer is the only permanent product of the brewery, which once a year, at Christmas, banks on its Bush Beer.

For the 225th anniversary celebrations, the Dubuisson family, nevertheless wanted to do something special, by introducing a new beer to its guests, the Bush 7%. Initially intended to mark a stage in the brewery's history, this beer stands on its own today as a new product of the brewery at Pipaix.

As its name suggests, it has only 7% in alcohol volume, and is therefore easier to drink than its stablemate with its 12%, thus being the convivial beer that the other bigger Bush could never be.

It is true that this new pale amber-colored brew is intended to be a thirst quencher. It is best served between 5 and 6°C/41-43°F, and possesses a good well-rounded delicate bitterness, with a slightly fruity aroma.

Just like the stronger version, it is top-fermented and filtered. However, lovers of the Bush 12% do not disdain the lower alcohol version, and on the contrary, are its biggest supporters now.

BUSH 12%

It is called " the strongest beer in the country " Indeed, this amber colored brew, which seems peaceful in its glass, as depicted on canvas by Delvaux, is extremely dangerous, for with its 12% volume of alcohol, it is intended for consumers who have been forewarned and have a solid constitution.

Naturally it has a lot of character and can be viewed as a strong English ale, and although there is a bitter caramel aroma in the background, at the finish it is dry. It also leaves a tingling sensation on the tongue as if by way of a warning of its power and the havoc it can create. Very easy to digest and never sickly.

The CAROLUS D'OR (DEDICATED TO CHARLES QUINT)

In Mechelen, the first written document dates from 1369. It represents the accounts that show the contribution paid by the brewer Jean de l'Ancre to the chapter of Saint-Rombaut. Other documents also show the evolution of his brewery. For example, the purchase of new material by his son Mathieu de l'Ancre in 1433.

The Carolus d'Or was created there, and for many generations, with its velvety brownish red color, it has continued to adorn the tables of many taverns in Mechelen. Its label represents the king Charles Quint on his horse. Its taste is not far removed from that of the vineyards, in particular a Burgundy, which is far from due to the whims of chance.

This beer, which is a hundred years old, is not based on any known category of beer. It is a strong beer (7.6% vol. alcohol), in particular through a mellow aroma. Its content is low on hops, and its bitter-sweet taste, which makes it at the same time resemble a traditional Flemish brown ale while retaining its vinous tone, is essentially due to the presence of a caramel malt and coriander.

In general, it is served at a moderate temperature, but it nevertheless loses none of its veracity if it is served a few degrees Celsius cooler. It then becomes positively thirst-quenching, but that is not its essential role, and it would be truly a shame to deprive it of its noble taste.

Its head is not exaggerated, and it is served in a superb regal glass, which has to be treated delicately when being washed. But after all, enjoy its pleasures like a king, as others wait upon you!

The CUVEE DE KONINCK

The traditional De Koninck has to be included amongst the best brews in the whole country, despite its low volume of alcohol of 5%. For dozens of years this beer has flowed generously to the delight of consumers throughout the Belgian metropolis, and has acquired international renown, by word of mouth.

In reality it is a very straightforward beer, and can be classified as an ale. What makes it stand out from English beers in that category, are its slightly peppery, fruity aniseed tangs. Its finish leaves a surprisingly fresh sensation. Its ingredients include amber malts, which are perfectly balanced in the initial approach. It is drunk at a fairly cool temperature (5°C/41°F) and is perfect as a convivial drink, and that is how it became a " must " in Antwerp.

This success led its brewer to ennoble it, with a Cuvée De Koninck that is decidedly much stronger in alcohol content (8%), but has exactly the same ingredients, with however a stronger flavor based on fruit and spices. It also has a hint of exoticism, just enough to serve as a reminder that Antwerp is a truly cosmopolitan city.

And yet, the production of this beer, which was created to coincide with a cultural year (Antwerp '93), was meant in principle to be limited to special occasions and should have been quickly relegated to a corner of the memory. Its destiny, and in particular its quality, decided otherwise, since by popular acclaim it acquired its own status as a new beer.

It was therefore with great pomp that the Vandenbogaert family produced its recipe, this time to be produced on a regular basis and simply renamed the Cuvée de Koninck.

Other than its 75cl. bottle, the brewery also produces a 33cl. version in a highly original form with a double necked bottle, which is very esthetic, which somewhat brings to mind the bottle used to carry urgent messages at sea. Naturally, the De Koninck beer will continue to be available in barrels and 25cl. bottles. Its glass is also new, without being too far removed from its traditional bowl, but with an additional touch of class, which will enable its aroma to be enjoyed even more, despite a rich creamy white head that characterizes it.

The SAISON D'EPEAUTRE

The Saison d'Epeautre is an alliance of circumstances between the spelt, a rustic wheat cereal which is essentially cultivated on the hard ground of the Ardennes, and the fermentation techniques of a white beer.

Spelt contains a natural flavor enhancer, which is in all legality added to the beer that henceforth has that taste. It is also a cereal, which is in great demand amongst the Germans of Fagnes, who use it mainly for baking bread, as well as other bakery products.

In the case of the Saison d'Epeautre, the cereal's flavor is restrained by a discreet bitterness and a slight acidity which results from its top-fermentation. But the spelt reappears in the aftertaste, and leaves a lingering refreshing sensation in the mouth.

It is not filtered, and it is cloudy. There is a slight acidity to the taste, even a slight spiciness on the tongue, but this is very pleasant. It is an authentic beer, which remains faithful to its prime ingredient, which is predominant in the aftertaste.

It is nevertheless, distinctly higher in alcohol content than a traditional white beer (6% vol. alcohol) and extremely refreshing.

That also means that it can be kept for a longer period (at least two years), all the more so since it is not pasteurized.

It is superfluous to point out that it is preferably served cool (5°C/41°F), and is available only in 75cl. bottles, with one or two exceptions where it can be found in barrels.

It also deserves a special mention for its qualities as an aperitif or equally as a digestive. We would imagine that a frugal meal of bread made from spelt accompanied by a soft cheese would serve to highlight even more the qualities of this classic artisanal beer and the know-how of its " mistress-brewer ", since only a woman's hand could bring even more subtlety to a beer which has an optimistic temperament.

NE FLIEREFLUITER (A VERY MISCHIEVOUS BEER)

There are certain beers, which from the first taste, communicate the full meaning of their name. With the Flierefluiter, the brewer intended to stay close to the meaning of a good-for-nothing fun-loving high liver. At least that is the literal translation, as well as the adopted meaning of " flierefluiter ", a name which to begin with has a " sing-song " aspect which, when placed in the mouth of an inhabitant of the Antwerp country from the region of Westerlo, takes on an even more optimistic bearing.

In fact, the " Ne Flierefluiter " is a triple beer in the pure traditional style, pale with an alcohol content that can be described as correct at 7%. Its initial aroma is relatively discreet, on the other hand, the first impression of its taste is truly special. This triple has a marvelous bitterness accompanied by a dry but perfectly balanced flavor. It contains several spices and most likely a rich malt that colors its flavor. It is very lively in its own special glass, small, curved with a long stem. It is full of health and happiness. Its double

165

fermentation means that it can be laid down for relatively long periods, preferably away from direct light.

Its effects are immediate. To begin with, it is excellent from a digestive point of view, and it is ideal as a night cap to ensure a good night's sleep. But be wary, it is faithful to its name, since although its secondary effects may seem to represent a state of well-being, its convivial character, which is decidedly one of its strong points, is not to be neglected. It is rapidly intoxicating, and doubtless loosens many tongues during social gatherings, especially when the tongues are hanging out over a bar.

It can be summed up as an excellent triple, but one that we would recommend drinking with prudence for its innocuous appearance, and preferably at home amongst friends.

A find!

The PANACHE FLORISGAARDEN

Starting with the ingredients for a white beer, it is possible to concoct beers with very diverse tastes. The last of the (great) Ghent breweries is poised to find success with its creation, with its very colorful flowery name. The Florisgaarden, of which the original name comes from Melle a suburb of Ghent renowned for its magnificent flowers (begonias and consorts), has as its base the ingredients of a traditional white beer with a volume of alcohol of 5%.

The Florisgaarden white beer is however different in taste from its fellow white beers, essentially by its very deep bitterness, with an aroma of exotic fragrances. There is a slight suggestion of curaçao and the bitterness of (dried) orange peel. The brewer also confirms the presence of coriander. There are also probably a few spices chosen in good taste which have been added to produce a little extra character. On the other hand, there is no pronounced acidity, which makes it unique as a white beer and particularly refreshing. Its color is very meaningful since it is very clear, almost colorless but slightly cloudy.

That leads us to the fact that the brewery wanted to give priority to the thirst-quenching aspect by completing the range of Florisgaarden beers with three other excellently conceived brews, particularly remarkable for their originality and taste.

First of all, there is the strawberry flavored beer, and this flavor inevitably dominates the beer's tone, commencing with the nose. It does however leave a slight lingering bitterness in the aftertaste, against the reddish backdrop of this beer's color.

Next, the passion-fruit flavored Florisgaarden, which is very well-balanced with once again a bitterness in its aftertaste. Its taste is immediately pleasant, being both refreshing and passionate at the same time. There is also a fairly strong sugary taste, which balances and provides a roundness to its bitterness. Its color reveals its origins as a white beer.

Finally, the one which is particularly seductive, the Florisgaarden Ninkeberry. Created for the export market, it could without any difficulty take its place amongst beers consumed domestically, notably by tickling palates used to the Gueuze. Its ingredients are very exotic, with in particular a mixture of apricots, mangoes as well as a closely kept secret of the brewer. Without too much risk of correction, we detected an astute addition of peppery spices as well as syrupy taste which balances the beer, for there is a slight tingling sensation on the tip of the tongue.

In any event, the last three Florisgaarden beers stand out from the initial white beer, first of all by a very low alcohol content (3%), their exotic and amusing taste, and above all by the pleasure that comes with a new find, which mixes what is useful (very good as a digestive) with what is pleasurable (the exotic aspect).

All the Florisgaarden beers are intended to be served very cool (5°C/41°F) in large flute shaped glasses.

(FOR A WARM WINTER, TRY) THE LIEFMANS GLÜHKRIEK

There is nothing better than a hot drink to combat the harshness of winter. The recipe is not new, but someone had to come up with the idea of adapting the principle to beer.

The idea belongs to the brewery of Liefmans d'Audenhade. The beer in question is the Glühkriek which, as its name suggests, is a Kriek, but top-fermented. Essentially it is based on the house Kriek with several spices added, as well as aniseed and cinnamon. Moreover, drunk cold its taste is not unlike that of the Liefmans Kriekbier. On the other hand, when it is served hot, and to be more precise at 70°C/158°F, its taste is fairly sugary and less acid than expected. It is a well-rounded beer which has much in common with wine, although the brewer is adamant that the spices used are totally different, and that there is no tannin. However, the drink is very pleasant, and is indeed a most effective breath of warm air.

It is served in a simple beer tankard, which it is possible to fill quite easily up to the three-quarters level, for the head lasts only a very short time given the temperature. Its volume of alcohol, at 6.5%, is slightly higher than the traditional Kriek, and is in no way modified by the heat, since at no stage does this reach boiling point, which in any event is not possible. The only drawback when drinking the Glühkriek, is that there is no way of knowing the beer's temperature when it is being heated. A kitchen thermometer is therefore quite a useful accessory for serving and enjoying this beer at its best.

The GAULOISE (IN ITS NATIVE LAND)

The only thing that the Romans never have taught the Belgians was the art of brewing. What is more, they would never have had the idea of calling one of their drinks " gauloise ". Those tribes had caused them far too many problems.

The du Bocq brewery in Purnode: hidden away in the Ardennes forests, this family run business produces three different versions of the Gauloise, the Blonde (7%), the Gauloise Ambrée (6.5%) and finally the Brune (9%), which according to legend was the veritable drink of our ancestors in bygone times.

169

Previously, only the Gauloise Blonde was available, with its rich aroma, which conjures up images of the Ardennes, with a strong, excessively bitter bouquet. The original version of the Blonde has itself been modified and has been made less harsh thanks to a new blend of more delicate hops. The difference is thus more noticeable with its two amber colored fellow beers, which have a distinctly higher hop content and thus a more bitter taste in the mouth, although this quickly disappears in the throat; and finally, the Gauloise Brune, which is the most complex from the point of view of its taste, which produces an intelligent flavor, with its mixture of high quality hops and a roasted malt resulting in a strong, heady taste. Unlike its two stablemates, the Brune is best drunk at room temperature.

It is to be noted that all three have an opulent head, and as if to revive the spirit of our ancestors, the brewer has devised a new glass which is not unlike the traditional mug, but more rounded, which is enough to make those valiant ancestors with their mustaches turn in their graves. If they were to be born again, would they be able to wet their lips?

The GODEFROY
(A TASTE OF HISTORY)

Nestled in the turbulent valley of the Semois, Bouillon attracts tourists who come to visit its majestic, sturdy château, which was formerly the abode of Godefroy, a famous local legend. He was a hero of the first crusade, of which he was one of the leaders, and founded the kingdom of Jerusalem. As a tribute to their hero, in May 1988 the town's inhabitants named a road Jerusalem, being supposedly the road their ancestor had taken almost nine hundred years earlier. In our country, which is so enamored of traditions and carnivals, such an occasion inevitably led to the creation of a beer to mark the occasion. It was quite naturally christened Godefroy. Because the town no longer runs a brewery, this beer is brewed in the north of the country (Moortgat brewery at Beendonk near Antwerp). Just like the per-

son it is intended to commemorate, the beer has a very rugged character.

Its amber color contrasts with the greenery of the rich forests, which are densely populated with fir trees, alongside the Samois. The Godefroy has a strong perfume which is skillfully flavored with hops. Although its taste cannot be described as astringent, it is well-rounded and leaves a lingering bitterness which brings to mind the neighboring Orval. It is a beer that is double fermented, mainly bottle conditioned, which means that it can be kept for at least two years. It is served in a small glass, and that is why pouring this beer requires special dexterity, for very often the chalice will overflow, all the more so since its head is very opulent, and given new life by a generous lacework. It is therefore best to hold the bottle fairly straight, before emptying it all into the glass in one determined movement.

It is not ideal as a night cap, since it is more likely to stimulate your nervous system. On the other hand, as a beer it is primarily intended to be drunk as an aperitif, which is ideal for barbecues in the countryside. Neither are its digestive qualities to be ignored. Generally it is served fairly cool (10 to 12°C/50-53°F),

171

and it is also available, at least in the region, in barrels (30 liters). Its volume of alcohol is not particularly high (5.8% on the label, 5.6% in reality) but it will pay to be wary of its pick-me-up effects since it is capable of transforming many a man into a veritable lion of the Ardennes. It bears the colors of Bouillon, red and black, and its label is both sober and effective. This beer which is named after a legend, and is the pride of its young " brotherhood ", gives the Godefroy a taste that other beers from the Ardennes region do not have...its taste of history.

HOEGAARDEN GRAND CRU

It is sometimes difficult to live in the shadow of a famous name, all the more so when it is the same family. The best proof of this idiom comes from the highly famous Blanche de Hoegaarden. Recognized throughout the world as the best white beer in our country, it hides under its protective wing other secrets, in particular the Grand Cru. As a rising star amongst our national brews, the Grand Cru is not seeking greater recognition in its own right, since it knows how to benefit from the enthusiasm accorded to the famous white beer.

It certainly cannot be blamed, for if the Blanche de Hoegaarden is appreciated when it is drunk as a refreshing beer, the Grand Cru is far too rich to become a beer for every-day consumption. It is also true that its volume of alcohol is already on the high side and consequently it should be drunk in much more moderate quantities.

172

The ingredients used are multiple, and the initial impression left by the Grand Cru is one of exoticism, which for a beer from the Brabant region, it has to be admitted, is fairly strange. In fact, this impression is confirmed by the first taste in the mouth, by retaining it slightly longer than usual and rolling it around the mouth between the palate and the tongue, then by swallowing it in small doses. You will be pleasantly surprised to discover a brew with many different tastes, all of which however belong to the same family. They are all very distinctive. The bitterness which the Grand Cru leaves is that of bitter oranges, or to be more precise that of their dried peel, but modified and improved by the hydration process of a water already brewed using the malt and the special Hoegaarden yeast. During the first fermentation, dried orange peel is added, as well as coriander. It is this subtle combination which makes this beer subtle, diverse, unique and complex all at the same time. To appreciate its aroma at its best, it is preferable to taste the beer at cellar temperature, therefore not too cool. It is doubly fermented, with a second dosage in the bottle, and over the months its taste evolves in a most surprising way, the orange aroma giving way to a more syrupy taste, which after all blends quite logically with its peachy color.

Stupefying for those who discover it, it is very sweet to drink, and its relaxing effects are quickly felt. The Grand Cru is above all a beer to be enjoyed at leisure, and therefore it makes an ideal drink for the evening. It will ensure that you have a good night's sleep, with no nightmares, and will provide you with the necessary vitamins B and C to be fresh and in good form the next morning, on condition of course that you do not drink to excess.

In addition to its very pleasant taste, the Grand Cru has, as an extra, a glass which is a feast for the eyes in its own right, with a cubic joint bearing the badge of the De Kluis de Hoegaarden brewery between the base and the receptacle. When serving, it is recommended to pour the beer into its glass in a single movement, tilting horizontally. You will obtain a 2/3 Grand Cru, that is to say 1/3 head on 2/3 beer. The latter will rapidly reveal its true colors, and you will be able to appreciate all the flavor that the head will have hidden for but a short while. The Hoegaarden Grand Cru is a beer which lives up to expectations, and in its context of a nightcap, will prove itself worthy of its description as a great classic, which is very rare for beers in this category. A beer truly worth discovering.

The GRISETTE

Initially conceived as a household beer, or as it is more commonly known a table beer, the Grisette has come up in the world and has for a long time been appreciated as a beer with its own identity.

Perhaps today it is no longer served primarily as an accompaniment to meals, but its effects are still the same. The Grisette is a summer beer which is served very cool and is ideal as a refresher. Its volume of alcohol is relatively low for a beer of this kind (5.4%), and it can be appreciated as a distinctive craft beer, with a respect for tradition. The fact that it is an every-day drink in the region around the Center (La Louvière) should not make us forget that it is a top-fermented amber beer. One should therefore be wary of its secondary effects.

Its taste is very subtle, and it demonstrates a solid maturity when it is kept in a warm room. Its top fermentation ensures that it has its own personality, and it is pleasantly dosed with hops and is not too bitter, which should appeal to feminine palates. It is filtered after being fermented in casks, and it should be served very cool. Unlike most summer beers, the Grisette does not have a sharp taste. In its aftertaste, one can detect a rich yeast. Given its low alcohol level it is very suitable as an aperitif, but its qualities as a digestive drink should not be neglected, for it should not be forgotten that, in the beginning, its essential role was as an accompaniment to meals.

The Grisette is also an ideal beer to drink with friends and it is merrily drunk in regional cafes.

It is also a symbol of good humor and is often served during traditional festive gatherings in the Center. It is available in 25cl. bottles as well as in 30 liter casks. It keeps for only relatively short periods of time. Its freshness is even more appreciated when it is served as draft beer.

It has a generous thick white head, which serves as an ideal protection against the small flies that appear as invaders during the sticky summer days.

The BINCHOISE (PART OF THE CARNIVAL)

The brewery La Binchoise is situated in the heartland of Belgian national folklore, but it does not claim to be the fruit of the famous carnival. Lying at the foot of the ancient ramparts of the ancient chateau of Queen Mary of Hungary, the old brewing plant has been renovated. It was taken over by a young, ambitious, hardworking couple a few years ago and they are trying to give the splendid town of Binoche a taste of something other than the pastoral Shrove Tuesday festivities. The local brewer has tried to use his imagination to combine not only folklore and culture, but also to integrate the rich historical past of this town in the Hainault, which is also known as the " City of the Ramparts ". As a result we have several exquisite products, including naturally the well-conceived Binchoise which is a worthy daughter of a harmonious but turbulent past.

It has two different appearances for different circumstances, pale (ex-fakir) or brown (Mary of Hungary). Traditionally a " Binchoise " is a pale beer. Its rich, pale yellow color immediately sets the scene. This is a beer of character with lashings of hops with a persistent bitterness. Traditionally brewed and based

175

on an ancestral recipe, it has as its base naturally the essential elements of all beers, malt and hops, but given extra zest by a judicious helping of dried orange peel, which is normal for a carnival town, which gives it this full color, bringing to mind with a touch of imagination the color of the costumes of Gille. The Binchoise undergoes a double top-fermentation and it is bottled with a yeast sediment in a second phase. On top of this, the brewer leaves it to evolve precisely, but slowly, by not filtering it, which does not prevent the beer from remaining very pure. It is advisable to pour it very gently into its brandy shaped glass. Underneath its generous head, the Binchoise has a spicy perfume but which is not discernible in the taste. It is essentially the influence of the different malts that give its taste a certain roundness. Very easy to digest.

The Binchoise is an ideal complement to many dishes, but in particular lighter meals, such as blood sausages for example. Its digestive qualities lie in the active CO_2 to be found in this beer. It is preferably served fairly cool, between 8 and 12°C/46-53°F, and will keep reasonably well for a year. It is available in 33cl. bottles with caps, but beer connoisseurs prefer the 75cl. champagne type bottles which are corked and wired. It should be laid down flat in order for it to reach full maturity in contact with its cork, which will make a very efficient guardian. Nevertheless do not be misled by its relatively low volume of alcohol (at least for a beer of this kind) into drinking too much of this beer, for it works in a roundabout way and is likely to go very quickly to your head. It belongs more in the category of beverages to be enjoyed to the full by the fireside.

A sign of the times, and what could be more normal? The Binchoise has become a symbol of greeting in the city of the Gilles, a town which truly understands the meaning of the word festive, but in its widest sense, warmth and generosity.

176

(LET'S ATTACK) The BARBAR

Officially presented during the 1995 Eurobeer Festival in Strasbourg, the Barbar is representative of a new trend in brewing, not with sugar but with honey. It was well received, and immediately its brewer sought to increase production. Seven countries decided to import it. Amongst them, other than the Bénélux countries, are France, Spain, Portugal, Great Britain and Finland, while three other countries, Sweden, Quebec and Greece also showed a good deal of interest in its future.

Without being really revolutionary, the producers of Barbar honey beer, avoided the trap of taking the easy way out, of making it a beer with lots of sugary flavor.

In reality it is only in its perfume that the honey is discernible, and this is accompanied by an excellent bitterness that is balanced by a very short aftertaste, which all in all is only logical, of a syrupy sweetness which it has to be said is barely perceptible.

It is top-fermented and is brewed in a traditional fashion, except for it being boiled with coal-fired heat, and at the same time includes two types of hops and two types of malt. Its golden yellow honey color is not filtered but appears very clear. The only cloudiness comes from its misty glass tankard. It is to be noted that it is not pasteurized, except for practical reasons when served as a draft beer. It is primarily available in 33cl. bottles. Its head is firm and rich, and makes it even more attractive. The Barbar (vol. alcohol 8%) should be very successful, especially during very hot periods, for it is meant to be served cool, and above all it has the advantage, through its special glass, of remaining cool for a long time. Its qualities as a refresher and as a digestive drink are not to be neglected. It can also be enjoyed as an aperitif.

The BRUNEHAUT (LIBERATED)

In 1944, Rogny, situated on the French border near Tournai, in the province of Hainault, witnessed the arrival of the first American troops who came as liberators.

From that point on, the small companies that existed at that time, could start up their business operations again. Amongst these companies was the Goedembril-Allaert brewery, responsible for a very local beer, the Brunehaut.

The owners from those heroic days have since moved on. The problem is the Brunehaut from Rogny was an integral part of village life and represented an important local tradition. The villagers were then deprived of their beverage. Nothing was as before, and

178

somewhat like the remnants of the Maginot line that runs alongside the border this village shares with France, the faces of the country folk who lived there became surly and seemed to waste away.

Salvation came in 1992, when once again liberators appeared and put a smile back on the faces of the villagers: new brewers were to construct a brand new, ultra modern brewery, and once again brew the famous Brunehaut.

To mark the occasion two new versions were created, a Blonde and an Ambrée, both with 6.5% vol. alcohol. This decision to produce two beers can be explained by two trends, the Blonde (golden) was more aimed at feminine palates, whereas the Ambrée was more intended for masculine consumption. Their tastes are diametrically opposed. The Brunehart blonde (Villages) seems to be a beer that is pleasantly perfumed with a rich aroma of hops, but not quite rounded enough for the masculine palate. It is still a quality beer, for it is perfectly successful as a thirst quencher. The Brunehaut ambrée (Tradition) has a more powerful aroma, and a more distinctive aftertaste, leaving an excellent bitterness as well as a richly complex flavor from its different malts. Both have first rate digestive qualities and can be drunk, according to taste, either cool or at an ambient temperature.

The MONT SAINT-AUBERT

Representing the mountain which overlooks the city of Tournai, this is very much a local beer and is principally consumed in the five taverns within striking distance of the city's five church bells. This beverage succeeds in combining to perfection the tradition of straightforward brewing, from only malt and hops, with real flavors.

Its first impression is a mixture of malt and fruits, while at the same time a bitter tone develops and becomes more pronounced in the mouth. It is however fairly well-rounded, and the bitterness once again reappears strongly, but in the aftertaste this time.

With time it should establish itself as the traditional beer in Tournai, on condition however that it is accepted by a local population which already is spoilt for choice with beers from the Hainault region. It is available in 33cl. bottles and in casks for very special or traditional occasions.

The CARACOLE
(WITH A CHARACTER TO MATCH)

With its somewhat inoffensive label which brings to mind (in image only) a certain sin, the Caracole, brewed by the brewery of the same name, is nevertheless a superb beer with lots of character.

First of all superb, for this beverage, brewed with much passion by two connoisseurs of beer, is remarkable for the richness of its many flavors, which are perceptible immediately with the aroma.

Next, it is a beer of character, because it reveals in a logical manner the depth of its flavors. From the first taste, the palate is invaded by a fairly pronounced bitterness but nevertheless a dry, full tang in the taste gives it more roundness. It is clear that the brewers have used chocolate malt. It can take its place amongst strong Walloon beers reputed for their character, which not so long ago were described as being beers for " real " men.

180

The Caracole exists in two versions. One is a heady amber beer, while the other is a brown beer where the roasting effect is even stronger with a clear taste of licorice in the aftertaste. Both, however, have the same vol. alcohol (7.2%), and are drunk differently depending upon the time of year. They should be savored slowly, accompanied by a soft cheese. To a certain extent they reflect the personality of the citizens of Namur, slow but steady.

They reveal their charms to the full when served at room temperature. In both cases, their appearance betrays a certain cloudiness at the bottom of the glass, as neither is filtered nor pasteurized. The Caracole Ambrée has undoubted digestive qualities, although that is not intended to be its principal function.

The TROUBLETTE

This is a modest, but original, white beer with 5% vol. alcohol. It is a traditional, very soft white beer and is very refreshing, created around small touches of coriander that are barely perceptible. Nevertheless, it does not have enough acidity and character to assert itself as a distinctive beer. It leaves practically no aftertaste. It is light with a neutral taste, but its only real interest is as a thirst quencher. As a mark of respect to its name, it has a cloudy appearance, almost as if out of a sense of decency to hide its lack of character.

The SAXO

Brewed as a tribute to the most famous inhabitant of Dianat, the Saxo (7.2%) is a purebred pale beer, which can be described as very feline.

Its initial taste is very soft, but as if to demonstrate its fidelity to the person and the instrument it is meant to represent, its strength appears in the high notes, with peppery tones that hint at coriander. These elements give more roundness to its bitterness, which blends with its softness. It is only at the close that the bitter taste acquires a drier touch.

The BLANCHE DE DENTERGEMS

As the days grow shorter, the tastes of beer lovers turn to darker, more amber brews, except for white beers, which are in the process of stealing a lead over the traditional Pils. The Dentergems confirms this.

Its roots lie in the " urtyp " of its Flemish ancestors, this being a beverage which was to be found in all the villages in the north of the country. Its recipe was made official in around 1771, and states that white beer should be brewed with barley (50%), wheat (40%) and oats (10%). The hop content is fairly limited, which explains the absence of bitterness, and on the other hand leads to a soft, slightly acid flavor. A touch of mint, but not at all sweet, is barely perceptible. The Dentergems is not as sour as other beers in this category, and has a more pronounced fruity aroma. It is a bottom-fermented beer (just like Pils style beers, by the way) and the result is astonishing. It is slightly cloudy in appearance, because it is not filtered. The fermentation process continues in the bottle and there will be a slight sediment at the bottom of the bottle. It is more often found as a draft beer, when its taste is even less acid, but on the other hand it is easier to drink. Its well balanced blend of cereals, wheat and oats, produces a relaxing beer, with however a slightly tonic effect for those who have a busy schedule. Some people add a slice of lemon, but this is not absolutely necessary.

The BIERE FANTOME

If the forests in the south of our country are more and more haunted by the spirits of those who died during the Battle of the Ardennes, such spirits are not the inspiration behind the creation of the Bière Fantôme which is brewed at Derbuy. In truth, it is not really

182

possible to say precisely where this beer is brewed, since brewing is divided between the Ferme au Chêne at Derbuy and a microbrewery at Erezée. Its brewer is in truth somewhat of a hermit, and only the brewing of his beer seems to fill him with passion.

Everything about this surprising beer is cloaked in secrecy. Its taste is very strong, with a solid bitterness that is, however, eroded by a strong acid undercurrent. Its secrets are hidden behind an amber colored veil, which evokes the fading autumn days. It is, of course, not filtered, and has the same ruggedness as the Ardennes countryside. There is, however, a fruity aroma with also a spiciness not dissimilar to coriander. Its secret formula fuels the imagination of flavors with a generous addition of alcohol (8%).

Its bitterness reappears in the aftertaste. It thus dispels the initial impression, and leaves only a conservative, but darned stubborn, tone.

The GUILLOTINE (FOR EVERYBODY)

To talk of dying for a drink when discussing the Guillotine would be a very tempting and easy play on words. Nevertheless, by giving such a name to this beer, it is not inconceivable that the brewer wanted to make a few hairs stand on end.

Its strength, 9.3% vol. alcohol immediately sets the tone.

Its alcohol content is an important part of its flavor, with a strong bitterness in the background blanketed by a malty aroma.

Its aftertaste fully reflects its character with a lingering bitter-sweet sensation. It was created in 1989 to coincide with the bicentennial celebrations in honor of the French Revolution, and was initially intended for the export market. It was aimed at France of course,

but above all Italy, where it was a tremendous success. However, its tastes and colors convinced many people that it could fill an apparent niche in Belgium, and it has taken its place on the domestic market, which is only fair, for we would have missed out on an accomplished beer that is a success from every point of view.

It is a top-fermented triple beer, and comes beautifully packaged in a 33cl. opaque glass bottle, which is painted to produce a stone-effect. This particularity is not simply a gimmick. Since it was intended for export it needed to be protected against beer's natural enemies, light and heat. Since it is not pasteurized, there was the possibility, during its long journey towards the Italian peninsula for example, that it would undergo an undesirable mutation which would have changed its taste.

The Guillotine can be rightly proud of its digestive qualities.

Its powerful effects mean that the Guillotine is mainly consumed at home, in a calm and relaxing environment.

The GULDEN DRAAK

Beers that come in colored bottles, and effectively hide the contents, are few and far between in Belgium. There is, for example, the Gulden Draak, which surprised us by both the strength and softness of its aroma, but above all by the quality of its entrancing flavor.

By way of a contrast with its white bottle, the Gulden Draak (the golden dragon) is very dark in color, very dense, a reddish amber, and its brewer refers to it as a black beer. Yet we are a long way from an English stout, although its taste has a similar bitterness. It is full-bodied, with a hint of licorice in the aftertaste. Its bitterness helps to retain a good balance in this classic beer, which is powerful and full of character, even initially slightly spicy on the palate. Its bouquet also brings a strong alcoholic flavor, which brings to mind a dark colored Trappist beer. Its vol. alcohol is

shown as 10.5%, but if left to ferment away from the light this can easily be increased by another ½ %.

Ideally it should be drunk at room temperature between 10 and 12°C/50-53°F, and it can be laid down in a cellar and preserved for several years without any problem. It should be poured very delicately into its flared tulip shaped glass, mainly to avoid surprises with the sediment at the bottom of the glass. It is principally a beer to savor and is perfect as an after dinner drink, or to round off an indulgent evening. Neither its relaxing qualities, nor its merits as a digestive drink, are to be ignored.

Certain chefs use the Gulden Draak to prepare sauces for game or red meat dishes.

Compared with other beers of the same style, its quality is above average. It is to be noted that this accomplished beer is a very stable brew and its taste does not evolve during the time it is laid down.

(THE IRRESISTIBLE)
JAN VAN GENT

Jan Van Gent is the name given to the huge seagulls that inhabit the North Sea beaches. As regards the beer of the same name, it is a product of the imagination of the brewers from the Liefmans d'Audenarde brewery in western Flanders.

It was created in 1995, to celebrate the " year of the beer " but uniquely for the inhabitants of the charming capital of the Flemish Ardennes.

185

It is a dark reddish color, as a result of the mix of colored malts and its not being filtered. The basic hops used are English (from Kent), but it is totally unlike the other fruity beers from the Liefmans brewery. Only its well-rounded bitterness could lead to it being classified amongst the soft beers, but make no mistake, it has a tremendous amount of character. For example, its aroma is very distinctive and the aftertaste, which is long-lasting and rich as befits a lively, non-pasteurized beer, is generously endowed with vitamin B and minerals (as a result of the excellent quality of the water in this part of Flanders).

Enormously refreshing and good for the digestion, its vol. alcohol is only 5.5%.

Its very specific diuretic characteristics are also noteworthy, and it is accordingly excellent for the kidneys.

It never goes to your head, and even when consumed generously, let us reassure revelers; it never leaves you with a hangover. The next morning one gets up feeling bright and breezy. But that should not be taken as an invitation to overdo it.

It is to be regretted that at the present time, it is only available in 30 or 50 liter casks. Obviously this is very good for its fermentation, and over the weeks its taste can only get better. It should be a resounding success.

The BIERE DU CHÂTEAU

" A noble beer with the look of an aristocrat " is how the Van Honsenbrouck brewery defines its so-called chateau beer. The brewers from Ingelmunster probably found one of those old beer recipes, which forged the reputation of that part of western Flanders, hidden away in a barn in a chateau-like edifice.

Strictly speaking, the Bière du Château is a very strong beer from every point of view. First of all, its alcohol level (11%) makes it one of the densest beers in Belgium. Its very special licorice taste makes it a very original brew. And of course, just like wine, it is best tasted at room temperature (12 to 15°C/53-59°F).

This last detail is definitely one of the most important aspects, for that is where the beer's subtleties are most perceptible. Some people, on account of its slightly sugary aftertaste, are inclined to compare it with a port. Its bitterness lacks balance, and if it is this taste which is so reminiscent of a Portuguese aperitif which gives the Bière du Château its roundness, this is primarily due to the oxidation process the beer undergoes during fermentation. It is top-fermented, but the process is slow since the yeast is rather unvigorous. It matures in its tank for a dozen or so weeks, and then it will be left for a further 6 to 12 weeks in Ingelmuster's cellars.

It cannot be classified as a digestive beer, nor as an aperitif, although the latter description is not totally inappropriate. We would rather classify it amongst beverages to be savored with great attention, at an appropriate relaxing moment. It is also an excellent table beer, by which we mean it is just as good an accompaniment to a meal based on game or red meat as a vintage red wine. It can be laid down to age in a cellar or another room without any problem, on condition that it is not subject to temperature changes.

As with wines, the label shows the year the beer was brewed, which makes it easier to follow its evolution, should you decide to lay down a reserve of this beer.

Lastly, we must not forget to point out that it is served in one of the most exquisite beer glasses in the world of Belgian brewing...noblesse oblige!

(YOU OLD DEVIL) KASTAAR!

The traditional Gueuze beers are part of the folklore in Brussels, and all foreign tourists visiting the paradise of beer feel duty bound to try them.

And then there are other less well-known beverages, which allude to the " jokes " of the seedy parts of Belgium's capital.

Take a journey through the flat open lands of the Brabant region, and in the northern part you will find a brewery which produces a beer with a very special taste, but very typical in its name, the Kastaar. For those who are not fully familiar with the charms of the local Brussels dilaect, the " kastaar " is not only an awkward mischievous kid, but also a strapping youngster, with a stocky muscular build.

It is a mix of old tradition and a feeling of déjà vu. The Lambic content is perceptible and also a vinous aftertaste. Although its first taste is somewhat weak, it succeeds in creating the impression of a convivial beer, although that is not its initial function. It has only 5% vol. alcohol, which means that it can be consumed in generous quantities. However, after two or three glasses, a change is as good as a rest, for overall it becomes sickly.

When served very cool, it is an original and effective aperitif. It is a top-fermented beer. We would give it three stars when served with a soft cheese, in the style of certain Dutch cheeses. Finally, its digestive qualities should not be overlooked either. Bitterness is

188

certainly not its main characteristic, but it does however leave a long-lasting, sharp aftertaste.

LAMORAL DEGMONT

Despite the industrialisation of brewing, there are
still craft brewers. Lamoral Degmont is a pure product
of one such brewery, being produced by a small fam-
ily-owned brewery in Herzele in eastern Flanders. What
is Lamoral d'Egmont? It is in fact the first name of the
Count of Egmont, Prince of Gavre, a gentleman from
Hainault, born in La Hamaide in 1522, who was beheaded in 1568 in Brussels, together with the Count of

Hornes, following an uprising of the Netherlands against Philippe II. His story inspired, amongst others, Beethoven, who wrote an incidental musical piece under the name of " Egmont ".

In any event, this rich historical past has not stopped the local brewer from producing an impressive beer. First of all, its aroma liberates a powerful, soft, malt perfume, an association of Pils and dry cake. Obviously the bitterness of Lamoral is discernible, without being pre-eminent. It is very pleasant to drink, all the more so for its appearance, which suggests a lively

beer. It is fairly clear with lots of bubbles, as with champagne, and a generous, lively lasting head. The brewery has the advantage of being able to use the spring water from Saint-Leuven, which is not very calcareous, but is very ferruginous, on account of which it is reputed amongst local villagers to have certain medicinal

190

qualities, being in particular good for the kidneys. It should be served at a fairly cool temperature (8°C/46°F). When consumed as an aperitif it is formidable. On the other hand, when considered more as a digestive, it proves itself to be a back-up and most useful. Its taste is very pleasant and well-rounded. Its bitterness is therefore clearly discernible in the flavor but without being overpowering. Its flavor is surprising without being shocking.

Lamoral would be fully entitled to stake its claim to being one of the best triple beers in the country. Its alcohol rate (8%), which is relatively low for this category, is not a distraction in the tasting of this beer. If its qualities as an aperitif and a digestive are obvious, it can also be served as an accompaniment to, not only hot meals, but also cold buffet style meals, particularly those where cooked meats form the basis of the meal. It keeps very well for between one and two years, without any evolution in its taste, which is proof, if it were needed, that from the point of view of fermentation it is fully mature. It is to be found in 33cl. bottles with capsules, and is also available as a draft beer, which for a triple beer has become more and more rare, especially when it undergoes a double fermentation.

Lamoral is a worthy homage to the count after whom it is named, but most fortunately it is unlikely to make you lose your head.

The BIERE SATANIQUE (DEVIL BEERS)

More and more beers allude to the devil. The Satan, which is reddish in color, has a truly strange character. Its sharp vinous taste confirms the presence of Lambic. Its bitterness is discreet but is well-rounded.

It is one of the rare top-fermented beers that is served fairly cool, but this in no way diminishes its strength of character. As a thirst quencher it is

191

marvelous, but on the other hand its alcohol volume, the taste of which is hidden by the sharpness, is sufficiently high to instill a certain wariness as to its secondary effects. It can be kept very easily for several years. Therefore you are recommended to drink it after it has aged for a year in its bottle, in its tall champagne style machiavellian glass (33cl.). It goes very well with all types of cooking, both as an accompaniment, as well as a recipe ingredient. Try a beef carbonade seasoned with pepper and thyme with the Satan and you will be even more bewitched.

LUCIFER (A BEER FROM HELL)

The fact that this beer is called Lucifer should not at all frighten those who wish to discover it. To describe Lucifer as the beer from hell was an irresistible temptation, just like the apple was for Adam and Eve. The only difference, here, is that our beer is a paradise of flavors and artifices, but it is certainly not a forbidden fruit.

We would, however, issue a warning regarding its relative alcoholic strength, which puts it on a level footing with strong pale beers.

The Lucifer is not well known to lovers of pale beers, but behind its attractive appearance it has more than one asset to please lovers of strong beverages, with character and originality in addition.

The Lucifer is a magnificent, very spicy beer, with an admirable aroma that is sharp and dry, which at its height evokes a pungent taste. It is without a doubt a beer that we would describe as hot and having character.

After a sensational initial contact, as an experienced taster, we would describe its aroma as very delicate, full of refinement and subtlety, and indisputably one of the most pleasant. It is healthy and well conceived, with a magnificent bouquet of beguiling mischief. Its pure blonde color has an irresistible charm, which is guaranteed to seduce even the most hesitant. Its taste

is dense and spicy, both initially and in the aftertaste, but Lucifer reveals its secrets progressively during the tasting, to finish on a note of immense satisfaction, with, as a bonus, a polite but spontaneous " reuh ", which is proof if it were needed that one's organism has reacted admirably to this find.

But be warned, the Devil is malicious and can assume the most unexpected forms to hide behind!

The MIROIR (FROM THE BREWER TO THE CONSUMER)

In the suburbs, not far from the main roads that join the inner ring road of Europe's capital, but still sufficiently close to the Basilique de Koekelberg, you will find hidden away one of the most pleasant places in Brussels. Indeed, " Le Mirroir ", which is situated on the Place Reine Astrid in Jette, is certainly the kind of establishment that all Belgians and all tourists should make a point of getting to know.

There are two basic reasons for this. First there is an exceptional beer list, and secondly a beverage which is brewed in this very establishment and is perhaps a classic in its category, but is nevertheless an authentic beer in the pure tradition of such beers.

There are two versions of this beer. Tasting will start with the Miroir (5% vol. alcohol), available in 25cl. or 50cl. sizes. It is a typical white beer, young and very fresh. It has a multitude of qualities, one of which is to prepare your taste buds in readiness for tasting other beers on the list. Next, there is the Miroir Dark (6.5% vol. alcohol) which, as its name indicates, is black. Different roasted malts are used in its preparation, thus explaining its dark appearance, but it also has a very subtle licorice taste. During Christmas time, there is also the Miroir Christmas (8% vol. alcohol).

When all is said and done they are three pleasant beers, not without character, and which are excellent for tasting.

NAPOLEON (THE BEER OF GALLANT MEN)

Without Napoleon, there would never have been Waterloo, and most likely, nor would there have been this beer of gallant men.

Fortunately for beer lovers, history inspired a brewer who named a beer after Napoleon. Yet beer was totally absent during the battle, which took place on June 18, 1815. It was rather the wine that flowed (often the mass wine) to wet the appetite of soldiers of the French Grande Armée for the battle.

This beer is more of a homage to the dead on both sides, for can one speak of a victor?

Its color is that of mourning. It is dark amber with a reddish background, the color of blood, soft in taste and slightly sweet. This initial impression is also increased by a coffee flavor, which is essentially due to its roasted malt. There is a perceptible bitterness, but this is covered by the taste of coffee, and overall it leaves a well-rounded dry aftertaste. It has only a small head and the lacework on the surface of the glass is not particularly active. It is evidently also a top-fermented beer, with an honorable volume of alcohol of 8%.

It is certainly not a beer to be drunk for its digestive qualities, nor for its convivial qualities. The Napoleon is for more intimate occasions when it is almost capable of transposing you to the battlefield and conjuring up the scent of the pipe smoke of the gallant soldiers on the eve of battle. Its glass could be from the same period. This is a discovery waiting to be made!

PAASBIER

Alongside seasonal beers, which are primarily brewed at harvest time, there are also the beers that are brewed periodically for special occasions, such as Christmas beers, or more rarely, Easter beers.

The Paasbier belongs to the latter category.

It is brewed in Ninove, a small town in eastern Flanders, in the area around the Dendre, and provides great joy to those who participate in the traditional carnival, which is always held at Easter time.

It is an excellent bottom-fermented pale beer, very slightly bitter, very clear and straightforward in taste. It is an extremely refreshing drink, and has much in common with a Dortmund style beer, including its glass. Its ingredients include a malt (prisma), a Slav hop (stirie) as well as corn, which is intended to lighten its color. It is to be noted that this is a bottom-fermented beer, and is not pasteurized, since that would probably be considered superfluous, for this beer which disappears very quickly. The whole of the production disappears down the throats of joyous revelers in less than a week.

The PLOQUETTE

The region of Verviers (Liège province) is very prolific in new brewers. Amongst the new discoveries, the Ploquette is one of the most recent creations in the region and is a future great beer in the making. Let us begin with a piece of history, or rather etymology.

During previous centuries, there had been a flourishing wool industry in Verviers. The Ploquette draws its name from the textile industry. Originally the word was used to represent the small pieces of wool that

196

were recovered from around the spikes hooked onto the sheep fur. The men who recovered and transported them were quite simply known as " ploquette " carriers. The word has remained in common usage in the region around Verviers, therefore the brewers decided to give this name to their latest creation which dates from 1992.

Let us turn to the brewers' name. In reality, the brewers responsible for the Ploquette are the Ruwet family, who are particularly well known and enjoy a prestigious reputation in the production of cider. The Ruwet ciders are (and always have been) present on tables throughout the world. Today the family has diversified and now presents a range of products capable of appealing to many different tastes.

The fact is, however, that Joseph Ruwet, the head of the cider dynasty created by the family, was initially trained as a master brewer, which explains his desire to demonstrate his know-how in brewing beer, and what know-how!

The Ploquette (7.5% vol. alcohol) is a very endearing beer, and from the outset its taste has a familiar air. One is immediately aware of an earthy peat odor, and there is a hint of Irish whisky in its aroma.

Its taste is warm and impressive. Its bitterness is afloat in a rich nectar of natural ingredients, where one can detect a hint of caramel, and water, as well as a discreet suggestion of dry sponge biscuits. Its aftertaste leaves an impressive freshness but with no depth to it. It closes gently, but on a major key, like the perfect symphony of a well-balanced and immediately recognizable chef-d'œuvre with a tingling sensation.

It is a vintage beer, which no doubt, over the coming years, will become even better known. It can be laid down in your cellar without any problem, for it is neither pasteurized, nor does it contain any spices. In addition, it is a very efficient digestive drink.

We recommend that you should serve it at a temperature of between 8 and 10°C/46-50°F, with an Ardennes sausage as an accompaniment. I can well believe that the brewer really enjoyed himself in producing this beer. So much the better for us!

197

The STRAFFE HENDRIK

To understand the significance of this beer's name, it has first of all to be understood that in Flemish, the word " straf " means strong, and " Hendrik " is the

equivalent of Henry. You will thus have gathered that " Straffe Hendrik " means " strong Henry ". That obviously implies that the beer in question is a strong beer. In fact, it is not. It is a beer that has a moderate volume of alcohol, barely 5.4% (but 6.5% on the label).

The Straffe Hendrik is brewed by a tiny Brugges based brewery, initially called De Halve Maan, which was established in 1856. It was subsequently renamed Straffe Hendrik and produces only one beer, which has the same name. The brewery is situated in the very heart of Brugges, along the canals, a stone's throw from the famous Beguine convent. Thousands of tourists have not only passed by its walls during boat trips along the canals, but have actually visited the premises. With its first taste, the Straffe Hendrik brings to mind a white beer. But that is only an initial impression, which fades on closer examination. If only from the point of view of its appearance, which is distinctive, and its color, which is a very pure rich yellow, sets it apart from white beers. It has as its base a pale caramel malt with a strong dose of hops, emanating from Czech " Saaz " and the German " Perle Hallertau ". It is full-bodied, but even in its large chalice shaped glass it has little aroma. It is a beer that has to be discovered by the palate and not by its nose. Its bitterness is characterized by its high density in hops, but the aftertaste remains nevertheless mellow and shrewd at the same time. Even in its bottle, the Straffe Hendrik is seductive, with its brilliant blonde color. It should be poured into its glass in one confidently measured movement. Once poured, its rich and creamy head will fluff up like a soft white woolen carpet. Its taste is said to evolve, and this will depend on whether it is served bottled or as draft beer. In the latter case, its bitterness is less distinctive, but on the other hand its dry flavor is more pronounced. The Straffe Hendrik is normally savored at a cool temperature, but it's a relaxing beer. The average beer drinker will probably have never heard of this beer, but it is a classic brew for not only those who live in Brugges, but also for the many tourists who visit the "Venice of the north" every year. Moreover, it is used in several Flemish recipes, in particular mussels and white fish. It really cannot be compared with any other kind of beer, although its initial impression has much to conjure up a wheat-based white beer. However, wheat is not used in the Straffe Hendrik, which throughout the years has had the reputation of being a strong beer, but only in its name and origins. The way its taste evolves is a reminder that it remains an ancestral beer, brewed by traditional methods.

The BIERE DU DIABLE

There are small breweries that, without attracting attention, are very much a part of local life in their region. Then suddenly, at certain special times of the year, they become the focal point of the calendar. That holds true for the small Vanderlinden brewery at Hal (Flemish Brabant).

There are two periods of great activity for the Vanderlinden family, who have taken over this brewery, which was founded in 1895 by the Ghyssels brothers. Paradoxically, it is with its Bière du Diable, that the brewery shows its claws during the traditional pilgrimages to Notre-Dame du Hal, which during the first six-month period of every year unite thousands of pilgrims.

But its glory days come above all during the merrymaking during the Carnival of Hal (the end of February, or the beginning of March). It is the real drink of the princes of the festival and all those involved with it, so much so that as much of the brew is drunk in less than three weeks as is drunk during the entire rest of the year.

Very much in the tradition of old Flemish brown beers, its first taste however is less aggressive. Despite its Lambic base, it is sweet and well-rounded, and very pleasant. That explains how it is drunk readily and without its taste becoming wearisome. It is drunk in great quantities during the carnival festivities, and its volume of alcohol is relatively modest at 5.5%, although, if laid down for six months this figure can rise to nearer 6%. Moreover, unsuspecting beer lovers should be warned that beneath its seemingly inoffensive exterior, its sugary content hidden beneath the beer's brownish color can produce terrible tangs. For wiser heads, its initial approach will reveal a strong fruity aroma. We would recommend it above all as an aperitif, or as a cheerful drink to be consumed in the company of others, in particular amongst card players, who will always find a source of inspiration in it.

PICK-UP WALRAVE (A FRESH PRODUCT)

One of the most famous breweries still existing in Belgium lies hidden in the shadow of the marvelous Château de Larne near Ghent. It is doubly busy, since not only does it brew, but it still has a malt factory and therefore prepares its own malt to use in the recipe to produce its very refreshing Pick-Up.

If the Walrave brewery was founded in 1862 by Auguste Walrave, it has been brewing the Pick-Up " only " since 1947. There are at least thirty or so cafes in the region of Heusden, Laarne, Wetteren, and Zele which permanently stock the small brewery's Pick-Up beer.

It really is an astonishing beer, which I discovered by pure chance during a walking holiday visiting the chateaux in the region around Ghent. It was thirst that led me to discover this Pick-Up. It is a bottom-fermented beer, and it has the special characteristic of being brewed with malts that are produced in-house, with hops from the Asse region (Flemish Brabant), and a healthy yeast.

This beer is brewed by the Walrave family only for local consumption. It is not pasteurized, which means that it must be drunk within a fortnight as freshly as possible.

Its taste has slight traces of bitterness, which is, however, never aggressive, and as a refreshing drink it is perfectly successful whatever the time of the year. It has a traditional 5.4% vol. alcohol. It is extremely tasty and very natural. Its lacework is discreet, which does not prevent the beer from having a generous white head. It will unite all lovers of bottom-fermented beers, primarily through its qualities of ancestral conception.

This beer is a find that must absolutely be consumed locally!

The BIERE DES MOULES

(THE BEER FOR MUSSELS)

Generally, people associate white wine with our traditional national dish of mussels. It cannot be denied that the two marry well together, but the combination is more based on tradition than on logic, which would dictate that our beloved tender shellfish specialty (from Zeeland!) be accompanied by our traditional beverage, namely beer.

The example comes from higher up, at least geographically speaking. In fact it is our northern neighbors, the Dutch, who lead the way. Every year, when to great joy the first mussels appear on the markets, a curious beer appears at the same time, and makes no attempt to hide its purpose. We are talking about the Yersekes Mosselbier, which is listed as a Dutch beer, but is nevertheless brewed on this side of the border.

Its label, which is extremely attractive, confirms that it is a top-fermented beer, with a volume of alcohol which when all is said and done is fairly low, being only 4.5%. Until now the only top-fermented beer with a low degree of alcohol that we have come across is the Courtois (ex-Biertoren brewery) which is no longer produced.

This time we have to reckon with Yersekes Mosselbier, this seasonal beer.

Its name comes from the small Batavian town at the mouth of the river Escaut, on the north coast, and which is the veritable world capital for sea mussels. Around 15th August, more than 100,000 people gather there to taste mussels prepared in every imaginable way, including with the Yersekes Mosselbier, which is not simply intended to be consumed by the thirsty drinkers, but also to give even more taste to the sauces based on green celery.

Its taste is not really distinctive. We would classify it as a beer in the Vieux-Temps or Palm category (amber colored therefore). The Yersekes Mosselbier has a very

202

acceptable bitterness, as well as a lingering, but still bitter, aftertaste, which contrasts with the smoothness of the mussels. Its digestive qualities cannot be denied, and in our view it is far better suited as an accompaniment to mussels than a dry, fruity white wine, which would regrettably be overpowered by a dish which after all is not very delicate. It should be served very cool (5°C/41°F).

The SEZOENS

There was a time when beer was brewed in winter, to quench a summer thirst. Today, beer is also brewed during the hot summer days, not to satisfy the same need, but to remind us of the many different perfumes to be experienced during the balmy summer days.

The province of Limbourg, of all the Belgian provinces, is where the temperature varies the most according to the season.

In the heart of this wonderful part of Belgium, there is a brewery that is known to all the inhabitants of Limbourg province, and that is the Martens brewery in Bocholt.

Its beers are very different in character, ranging from the Pils to a more distinctive beverage, more suited to " tasting " like the Sezoens.

BLONDE

Although it has a relatively soft taste, there is a certain dry acridity, which is a characteristic of inhabitants of Limbourg. Its bitterness is most perceptible in the aftertaste, without however the taste developing in the mouth.

It is the least distinctive of the series (6%).

EUROPE

This beer, which was only recently created (1993), leaves an overall impression of constant bitterness throughout the tasting. No other flavor is discernible during the tasting. The bitterness develops to varying degrees in the mouth, and carries on to the finish. It is a beer with no surprises and without subtlety, but it is dry in character.

QUATRO

This last beer is classified as being one of the brewery's top of the range brews. Its volume of alcohol is 8% and it is a top-fermented beer, which brings to mind the harshness of the climate in Limbourg.

It has lots of body, as do amber beers in general. In addition, however, it has a very pronounced bitterness with a very dense taste, as well as being somewhat heavy, which makes it more of an aperitif. It is served in a glass similar to those used for zabaglione, and this is not simply a question of chance, for it makes an ideal basis for desserts, including zabaglione " à la Soezons Quattro ".

HAPKIN (THE SOOTHING BEER)

This beer was described by its brewer as a " beer that has a soothing effect ". This is somewhat akin to laboring an obvious point, since this applies to most beers based on hops, since the hop plant is soothing above all else.

The Hapkin is produced by a very small brewery in western Flanders, and is situated in Kortemark not far from Dixmude and Roulers. The Hapkin has to be classified as a strong pale beer, with a good dose of bitterness. It is served fairly cool (between 8 and 10°C/46-50°F), in a tall, wide, but delicate glass, not unlike the kerosene lamps our ancestors used (but wider), and asserts its strong personality with its initial aroma. In fact, its aroma will not contradict its delicacy and depth of taste, leaving a very pronounced aftertaste. It is very lively as soon as it is poured, and has a generous head, which is a sign of its good health. Its brewer does not hesitate to describe it as the cham-

pagne of Belgian beers, a more precise label than the initial description. The Hapkin (8.5%) is very easy to digest, and leaves a slight tingling sensation on the tongue. Despite the fact that it is a top-fermented beer, first in casks, then in its bottle, it is perfectly clear, and, well it cannot be denied, is very beneficial to a good night's refreshing sleep, a question of wiping the slate clean and starting from zzzzzzzzzzéro....

LOEBAS (A NOBLE BEER)

Either a beer establishes its pedigree by its strength of character, which will win it acclaim, or else it will be classified as such throughout the long years of its existence.

Neither of these two alternatives applies to the Loebas. In reality, its brewer rediscovered an old recipe in one of those ancient manuscripts that are handed down from generation to generation. As regards the Loebas, its origins go back to the year 1750.

With the first taste, one has the impression of tasting a Gueuze, but rapidly the aftertaste reaffirms this beer's veritable softness and slight bitterness. Its volume of alcohol is slightly above the average (5.8%), and the roasted malt used in its production gives it its amber color. Served cool (6 to 8°C/43-46°F) it is very refreshing but not particularly easy to digest. This beer is to be drunk with restraint since it finishes by becoming sickly.

The Loebas is a " vintage " label designed by the painter Jan Heuninckx, whose work is very much sought after in Flanders. It represents the farm of the ancestors of the brewers who created this beer in the middle of its lands, with in the center of the stage a " loebas ", which in the local dialect means someone who is jovial and a practical joker.

QUINTINE (BEER OF THE HILLS)

Ellezelles and Flobecq, situated at the gateway to the north of the province of Hainault, represent the Belgian equivalent of Normandy, but there is one important difference with that splendid region of France, thanks to a drink which is diametrically opposed to the calvados. It is in this region that the Quintine is brewed. The name finds its origin in the rich folklore of this region with its rolling green hills and their evil spells, Quintine being the name of one of the five broomstick-waving witches of Ellezolles.

The least one can say is that the Quintine has been very well inspired. It is a very accomplished beer. From the first taste, one is aware of its discreet and very strange taste, a mysterious taste in a bouquet full of mischief. Its bitterness is harsh and personalized. It is golden blonde in color, like the ears of corn attached to a witch's broomstick.

It is available in 33cl. bottles with a mechanical cork, and can be taken with you along the paths of the supernatural, but like all unfiltered top-fermented beers it needs to be handled delicately. When seated at the witch's table, it will be served in a tall, tavern style glass.

PAUWEL KWAK (THE BEER WITH A WOODEN STAND)

More commonly called Kwak, this beer which comes from the northern part of Flemish Brabant, on the border of eastern Flanders between Dendre and the river Escaut, simply bears the name of its creator. Mr. Pauwel Kwak was an inn-keeper in 1791. His establishment, or to be more precise his coaching inn, was above all famous for the quality of the beer served there. Travelers, coachmen or the lads responsible for harnessing the horses throughout the years could testify to that, so much so that it still exists today.

Other than its strong alcoholic concentration (8.5%), and its very pronounced bitterness, the Kwak stands out by its very special glass, and in particular its wooden stand, a kind of support to maintain it vertical. It is known as the " coachman's glass ". It has not changed one iota through the centuries. From what was a very practical glass at the time it has now become a collector's item. The Kwak has a fairly bitter taste, which is a testimony to the top-quality hops which are imported from the former Czechoslovakia (Saaz-Zatec), and a malt which corresponds to the beverage and its character. It is a top-fermented beer that undergoes a double fermentation, but is filtered when bottled. From the very first taste, its deep, dry flavor conjures up a feeling of nostalgia with its classic Ambrée taste, which gives a better insight into the reasons why the inn, known as " La Couronne ", was such an irresistible stop-over in the XVIII century for travelers in the region around Termonde.

(FLEMISH BUT) FLANDRIEN

Back in 1877, in the very heart of Flanders, where people lived with the strong winds sweeping in from the north, the calm Louwaege abandoned farming and

devoted himself to brewing beer.He acquired one of the five breweries in Kortemark not far from Dixmude (western Flanders). His first product was the " Louwaege ", which became the veritable star of the 1918 liberation, mainly in this region that had been literally torn to shreds by the confrontations of the " Trenches of Death " alongside the Yser. The Flandrien is a name which is highly symbolic in a region where Flemish extremism tends to put itself on show every year during the pilgrimage to the Yser. It needed courage to give a local agricultural product a francophone name. Its label is also a reference to Placide Louwaege, formerly a farmer. Finally, its glass, a kind of tankard, conjures up an image of a Flemish peasant sitting on a bench, with a pipe in the corner of his mouth.

" The " Flandrien is an unfiltered pale beer, fairly cloudy in appearance. Despite its low volume of alcohol

(5%), it has to be classified with top-fermented beers bottled with a yeast sediment. Its lacework is very lively, and consequently it has a consistent white head. It is difficult to compare its taste with any other beer, and it seems to be unique in its own way, with only a slight bitterness discernible, which improves its flavor even more. " The " Flandrien is a subtle beer that can be enjoyed whatever the season. Besides its delicacy, it is perfect as a digestive, and without being what one could describe as a table beer, it remains very much a beer for social occasions.

THE BREWERIES

BRASSERIE D'ACHOUFFE
Route du Village, 32
6666 ACHOUFFE-WIBRIN
Tél. 061-28 81 47
Fax: 061-28 82 64
· Big Chouffre
· Chouffe
· Cuvé du Tchesté
· Mc Chouffe
· Vieille Salme
· *Bières de Noël:*
· Chouffe-bok 6666
· N'Ice Chouffe

ALKEN-MAES
Waarloosveld, 10
2550 WAARLOOS
Tél. 015- 30 90 11
Fax: 015-31 41 91
· Ciney Blonde
· Ciney Brune
· Ciney spéciale
· Cuvée de l'Ermitage
· Cuvée Christmas
· Cristal
· Eylenbosch gueuze
· Eylenbosch Kriek
· Faro
· Golding Campina
· Grimbergen blonde
· Grimbergen double
· Grimbergen triple
· Grimbergen optimo bruno
· Judas
· Kronenbourg
· Maes Pils
· Mort Subite Gueuze

· Mort Subite Kriek
· Mort Subite Framboise
· Mort Subite Pêche
· Mort Subite Cassis
· Rubens gold
· Rubens rouge
· Spéciale blande
· Tourtel blonde
· Trial
· Watneys
· Zulte

ANDELOT
Doornzelestraat,20
9080 LOCHRISTI
Tél.: 09-356 51 71
Fax: 09-355 31 05
· Reinaert ambrée
· Reinaert triple

HET ANKER
Guido Gezellelaan, 49
2800 MECHELEN
Tél.: 015-20 38 80
Fax: 015-21 21 07
· Carolus d'Or
· Mechelschen Bruynen
Toison d'Or tripleARTISANS
BRASSEURS
Place de la Station 2
5000 NAMUR
Tél.: 081-23 16 94
Fax: 081-22 15 09
· Aldegonde brune
· Aldegonde spéciale
· Marlagne blanche
· Marlagne blonde

ARTOIS
(Groupe Interbrew)
Vaartstraat, 94
3000 LEUVEN
Tél.: 016-24 71 11
Fax: 016-24 74 97
· Brasseur de la Dyle
· Club de Stella Artois
· Dommelsch NA
· Ginder ALe
· Helios
· Hertog Jan Pilsener
· Horse Ale
· Julius
· Jupiler NA
· Krüger Export
· Lamot Pils
· Leffe triple
· Loburg
· Piedboeuf blonde
· Piedboeuf brune
· Safir
· Sernia brune
· Setz braü
· Stella Artois
· Stella Artois dry
· Stella Artois light
· Stella Artois NA
· Supra pils
· Vieux Temps
· Wiel's
Bière de Printemps:
· Mars (bière de)
Bière de Noël:
· Noël (bière de)

BAVIK
Rijksweg, 33
8531 BAVIKHOVE
Tél.: 056-71 90 91
Fax: 056-71 15 12
· Bavik dinner beer blonde
· Bavik dinner beer faro
· Bavik export
· Bavik premium pils
· Bavik triple bock

· Bavik witbier
· Fancy
· Golburg
· Triple Petrus
· Petrus spéciale
· Pony Stout
· Kuurnse Witte
· Witte Ezel

BELLE VUE
(Groupe Interbrew)
Rue Delaunoy, 58-60
1080 MOLENBEEK
Tél.: 02-412 44 11
Fax: 02-410 78 58
Quai du Hainaut, 33
1080 MOLENBEEK
Chaussée de Mons,
1600 LEEUW-ST-PIERRE
· Bécasse framboise lambic
· Bécasse gueuze lambic
· Bécasse kriek
· Belle Vue framboise
· Belle Vue gueuze
· Belle Vue kriek
· Belle Vue kriek LA
· Belle Vue Selection lambic gueuze
· De Koninck gueuze
· De Koninck kriek
· De Neve framboise
· De Neve gueuze filtrée
· De Neve gueuze non filtrée
· Jack-Op
· Mengbier
Bière de Printemps:
Primeur kriekDe BIE
Stoppelweg, 26
8978 WATOU
Tél.: 057-38 86 66
Fax: 057-38 86 66
· Hellekapelle
· Helleketelbier
· Zatte Bie

LA BINCHOISE
Faubourg St-Paul, 38

7130 BINCHE
Tél.: 064-33 61 86
Fax: 064-33 61 86
· Bière des Ours (Médaille d'Or World
Beer Championships 1995)
· Binchoise blonde
· Binchoise brune
· Bruyère brune
· Buxus blonde
· Buxus brune
· Cervoise de l'Ecluse blonde
· Cervoise de l'Ecluse brune
· Cuvée des Tiètes de pipes blonde
· Cuvée des Tiètes de pipes brune
· Fakir
· Iguanodon
· Kelmeser
· Malognarde blonde
· Malognarde brune
· Pir'êye di Licint 6,5%
· Pir'êye di Licint 9%
· Réserve Marie de Hongrie
· St Ferdinand Cuvée fraternelle
· St Quirin blonde
· St Quirin brune
Bière de printemps:
· Bière de Pâques
Bières de Noël:
· La Binchoise spéciale de Noël
(Médaille de Platine World Beer
Championships 1995)
· Réserve de Marie de Hongrie spéciale
Noël

BIOS
Lindenlaan, 25
9940 ERTVELDE
Tél.: 09-344 50 71
Fax: 09-344 54 20
· Augustijn
· Augustijn grand cru
· Bios blonde
· Bios brune
· Bios Vlaamse bourgogne
· Bornem double
· Bornem triple

· Boucanier
· Cuvée de Briqville
· Domein claire
· Domein foncée
· Ever
· Filée
· Groen
· Gulden Draak *184*
· Hoppe ambachtelijke pils
· Keizersberg
· Nounou
· Piraat
· Queue de Charrue blonde
· Rijsel triple ambrée
· Roosenberg
· Sinaaise bok
· Sparta pils
· Steenezel
· Stoeren Bonk blonde
· Stoeren Bonk foncée
· Verrebroekse Flip
· Wilson mild stout
· Yersekes bière des moules *202*
· Zwijntje

BRASSERIE DE BLAUGIES
Rue de la Frontière, 435
7370 BLAUGIES
Tél.: 065-65 03 60
Fax: 065-65 03 60
· Darbyste *142*
· Moneuse
· Saison d'Epeautre
Bière de Noël:
Moneuse Spéciale Noël

DE BLOCK-JOOSTENS
Nieuwbaan, 92
1785 PEIZEGEM-MERCHTEM
Tél.: 052-37 21 59
Fax: 052-37 53 88
· Block export
· Block pils
· Block special
· Kastaar
· Satan Gold

213

· Satan Red
· Timotheus ambrée
· Timotheus blonde
· Timotheus foncée

BOCKOR
Kwabrugstraat, 5
8510 BELLEGEM
Tél.: 056-23 51 71
Fax: 056-22 76 83
· Bockor double blonde
· Bockor export
· Bockor faro
· Bockor ouden tripel
· Bockor pils
· Jacobins framboise lambic
· Jacobins gueuze lambic
· Jacobins kriek lambic
· Kortrijk 800

BRASSERIE DU BOCQ
Rue de la Brasserie, 4
5530 PURNODE
Tél.: 082- 61 07 80
Fax: 082-61 17 80
· Arsoute blonde
· Arsoute brune
· Bergeotte normale
· Bergeotte spéciale
· Blanche de Namur
· Bisounette
· Corsendonk Agnus
· Crupetoise
· Cuvée du P'tit Lu
· Cuvée Li Crochon
· Cuvée St Antoine
· Cuvée St Hadelin blonde
· Cuvée St Hadelin brune
· Deugniet
· Dolmenius
· Gauloise ambrée
· Gauloise blonde
· Gauloise brune
· Gayette
· Geldonia blonde
· Geldonia brune

· Houlette
· Kelottes
· Louvoise
· Rubens rouge
· Saison Régal
· Si Boune blonde
· Si Boune brune
· Ski-rodt biermuseum blonde
· Ski-rodt biermuseum brune
· St Benoît blonde
· St Benoît brune
· St Benoît brune spéciale
· St Benoît triple
· St Feuillien blonde (25 et 75 cl)
· St Feuillien brune (25 et 75 cl)
· St Hubert Cuvée du Bocq
· St Quentin
· Super des Fagnes
· Toine
· Tradition des Moines blonde
· Tradition des Moines brune
· Tricentenaire
· Triple Moine
· Val d'Heure blonde
· Val d'Heure brune
· Val St Lambert
· Vî Keute di Nameur brune
· Vîle Cinse
Bière de printemps:
· Lentebier
Bière de Noël:
· Blanche de Noël
Regal Christmas BOELENS
Kerkstraat, 7
9111 BELSELE
Tél.: 03-772 32 00
Fax: 03-722 09 92
· Bieken
· Waas Klokbier triple
Bières de Noël:
· Belseels kerstbier
· Kerstklok

FRANK BOON
Fonteinstraat, 65
1502 LEMBEEK

Tél.: 02-356 66 44
Fax: 02-356 33 99
· Belgian ale traditional gueuze
· Boon frambozenbier
· Boon gueuze
· Boon gueuze mariage parfait
· Boon lambic
· Lembeek's
· Pertotale faro
· Wentelkriek

BOSTEELS
Kerkstraat, 92
9255 BUGGENHOUT
Tél.: 052-33 22 82
Fax: 052-33 59 56
· Pauwel Kwak
· Prosit pils
· 'T Zelfde

BRABUX
(Groupe Interbrew)
Statiestraat, 31
1861 WOLVERTEM
Tél.: 02 269 12 04
· Bécasse gueuze
· Bécasse gueuze grande réserve
· Bécasse kriek
· Bécasse lambic
· Caves Bruegel gueuze
· Caves Bruegel kriek
· Caves St Pierre framboise
· Caves St Pierre gueuze extra
· Ernest Claes

HET BROUWERSHUIS
Molenstraat, 42
2387 BAARLE HERTOG
Tél.: 014-69 94 03
Fax: 014-69 93 97
· Brave Broeder
· Engeltjes bier
· Lazarus bier
· 992 Milleneir
· Ne Kempenaer

BRASSERIE DE BRUNEHAUT
Rue des Panneries, 17
7623 BRUNEHAUT
Tél.: 069-34 64 11
Fax: 069-34 64 12
· Blanche de Charleroi
· Brunehaut tradition ambrée
· Brunehaut villages blonde
· Ecume des jours 97
· Mont Saint-Aubert

CANTILLON
Rue Gheude, 56
1070 BRUXELLES
Tél.: 02-521 49 28
Fax: 02-520 28 91
· Bruocsella 1990 grand cru
· Cantillon faro
· Cantillon kriek
· Cantillon kriek lambic
· Cantillon lambic
· Cantillon super gueuze
· Rosé de Cambrinus
· St Lamvinus

BRASSERIE CAULIER
Rue de Sondeville, 132
7600 PERUWELZ
Tél.: 069-77 24 71
Fax: 069-77 59 40
Vieille Bon SecoursCARACOLE
Côte Marie-Thérèse, 86
5500 FALMIGNOULE
Tél.: 082-74 40 80
Fax: 082-74 40 80
· Caracole ambrée
· Caracole brune
· Saxo
· Troublette

CHIMAY
Abbaye de Scourmont
Rue de la Trappe, 294
6464 FORGES-LEZ-CHIMAY
Tél.: 060-21 03 11

215

Fax: 060-21 36 96
· Chimay capsule bleue
· Chimay grande réserve
· Chimay première
· Chimay capsule rouge
· Chimay capsule blanche

CLARYSSE
Krekelput, 16-18
9700 OUDENAARDE
Tél.: 055-31 17 21
Fax: 055-31 94 76
· Felix kriekbier
· Felix Oudenaards kriekbier
· Felix Oudenaards oud bruin
· Felix pils
· Felix speciaal Oudenaards
· Oudenaards wit trawebier
· St Hermes abdijbier

CNUDDE
Fabriekstraat, 8
9700 EINE
Tél.: 055-31 18 33
· Cnudde kriek
· Cnudde Oudenaards bruin
· Lowie V

CONTRERAS
Molenstraat, 115
9890 GAVERE
Tél.: 09-384 27 06
· Contra-pils
· Rafexport
· Tonneke
Bière de printemps:
· Contreras martzen bier

BRASSERIE CORSENDONK
Steenweg op Mol, 118
2360 OUD-TURNHOUT
Tél.: 014-45 33 11
Fax: 014-45 33 38
· Corsendonk Agnus
· Corsendonk Pater

CROMBE G
Hospitaalstraat, 10
9620 ZOTTEGEM
Tél.: 09-360 02 40
· Artisan Reuzebier
· Cezarken
· Egmont Zottegemse tripel
· Manneken Pis
· Oud Kriekenbier
· Oud Zottegems bier
· Oud Zottegems bier hergist
· Pee Klak grand cru
· Pee Klak special
· Zottesgemse grand cru
Bière de Noël:
· Christmas-Beer

DECA SERVICES
Elverdingestraat, 4
8640 WOESTEN-VLETEREN
Tél.: 057-42 20 75
Fax: 057-42 36 86
· Een Molleke
· Harings Orgelbier
· St Amandus blonde
· Kortenbergs abdijbier
· St Amandus Kortenbergs abdijbier
· Vlet alt
· Vleteren super 8
· Hooibier

DE KEERSMAEKER
Lierput, 1
1730 KOBBEGEM
Tél.: 02-452 47 47
Fax: 02-452 43 10
(voir Alken-Maes)

DE KONINCK
Mechelsesteenweg, 291
2018 ANTWERPEN
Tél.: 03-218 40 48
Fax: 03-230 85 19
· Cuvée De Koninck
· De Koninck

DE KROON
Beekstraat, 20
3040 NEERIJSE
Tél.: 016-47 71 04
· De Kroon dubbel wit
· Leuvens witbier

DE SCHUUR
Gobbelsrode, 75
3220 KORTRIJK-DUTSEL
Tél.: 016-62 19 60
· Meneer

DE SMEDT
Ringlaan, 18
1745 OPWIJK
Tél.: 052-35 99 11
Fax: 052-35 83 57
· Abbaye d'Aulne 6 sur lie
· Abbaye d'Aulne 8 sélection
· Abbaye d'Aulne 10 superbe
· Abbaye d'Aulne blonde Pères
· Abbaye d'Aulne triple
· Abbaye de Brogne foncée
· Abbaye de Brogne triple
· Abbaye de Florival blonde
· Abbaye de Florival brune
· Affligem blonde
· Affligem double
· Affligem triple
· Blanche du Delhaize
· Celis pale bock
· Celis white
· Dikkenek
· Napoléon
· Ne Flierefluiter
· Op-ale
· Postel double
· Postel triple
· *Bières de Noël:*
· Abbaye d'Aulne super Noël
· Boxer Christmas beer
· Delhaize Christmas
· Postel kerstbier
· Affligem Christmas ale
· Affligem patervat

DEVAUX
Rue de l'Eglise St Philippe, 1
5600 PHILIPPEVILLE
Tél.: 071-66 63 47
· Schwendi

DE TROCH
Langestraat, 20
1741 TERNAT-WAMBEEK
Tél.: 02-582 10 27
Fax: 02-582 72 41
· Chapeau exotic
· Chapeau faro
· Chapeau fraise lambic
· Chapeau framboise
· Chapeau gueuze
· Chapeau kriek
· Chapeau mirabelle
· Chapeau pêche
· Chapeau tropical
· De Troch gueuze non filtrée

DOLLE BROUWERS
Roeselarestraat, 12B
8600 ESEN-DIKSMUIDE
Tél.: 051-50 27 81
Fax: 051-510337
· Arabier
· Dulle Teve
· Lichtervelds blonde (uniquement
tous les deux ans)
· Oeral
· Oerbier
· Snoek
· *Bière de printemps:*
· Boskeun
· *Bière de Noël;*
· Stille Nacht

DOMUS
Tiensestraat, 8
3000 LEUVEN
Tél.: 016-29 18 68
Fax: 016-20 64 36
· Bugel

· Domus
· Fonske
· Leuvense witte
· *Bières de printemps:*
· Domus double honingbier
· Domus meibok
· Domus paaskriek

DE DOOL
Eikendreef, 21
3530 HELCHTEREN
Tél.: 011-52 29 99
Fax: 011-52 13 18
· Ter Dolen
Bière de Noël:
· Ter Dolen kerstbier

DRIE FONTEINEN
H. Teirlinckplein, 3
1650 BEERSEL
Tél.: 02-331 06 52
Fax: 02-331 07 03
· Drie Fonteinen gueuze
· Drie Fonteinen kriek
· Drie Fonteinen kriek au tonneau

DUBUISSON
Chaussée de Mons, 28
7904 PIPAIX
Tél.: 069-66 20 85
Fax: 069-66 17 27
· Bush beer
· Bush 7
Bière de Noël:
· Bush de Noël

DUPONT
Rue Basse, 5
7904 TOURPES-LEUZE
Tél.: 069-67 10 66
Fax: 069-67 10 45
· Abbaye de St-Ghislain
· Anvinoise
· Belgo
· Broqueroise de l'Abbaye de St-Denis
· Bière de Beloeil· Cervesia

· Cervoise de Leptines
· Cervoise de St Gery
· Cervoise des Francs-Gaulois
· Dupont biologique
· Dupont Vieille provision
· Gaillarde de la Posterie
· Gougnies
· Joyeuse blonde
· Joyeuse brune
· Laplaignoise
· Les Feuilles Mortes
· Moinette biolégère
· Moinette blonde
· Moinette brune
· Moinette des Iguanodons de Bernissart
· Moinette des Sorcières de Warquignies
· Oelegems Titsenbier
· Vieille des Estinnes
· Vieillotte du Hurlevent
Bière de Noël:
Avec les bons voeux de la Brasserie

ELLEZELLOISE
Guinaumont, 75
7890 ELLEZELLES
Tél.: 068-54 31 60
Fax: 068-54 37 16
· Hercule
· Quintine
Bière de Noël:
· Quintine de Noël

EUPENER BIIERBRAUEREI
Paveestrasse, 12-14
4700 EUPEN
Tél.: 087-55 47 31
· Caramel bière de table
· Eupener caramel
· Eupener export
· Eupener extra light
· Eupener klosterbier special bock
· Eupener pils

EYLENBOSCH
(Groupe Alken-Maes)
Ninoofsesteenweg, 778
1703 SCHEPDAAL
Tél.: 02-569 14 76
(voir Alken-Maes)

FACON
Kwabrugstraat, 27
8510 BELLEGEM
Tél.: 056-22 07 69
Fax: 056-25 93 47
· Bellegems witbier
· Bière du Château de Ramegnies-Chin
· Facon export
· Facon extra stout
· Facon oud bruin
· Facon pils
· Facon bière de table blonde
· Facon bière de table brune
· King's pils
· La Mouscronnoise
· La Scaldienne
· La Spéciale de Calonne blonde
· La Spéciale de Calonne brune
· L'Obligeoise
· Punch blonde
· Punch foncée
· Satcheu
· *Bière de Noël:*
· Facon scotch Christmas

FANTÔME
Rue Preal, 8
6997 SOY
Tél.: 086-47 70 44
Fax: 086-47 70 44
· Bière des jumeaux ambrée
· Bière des jumeaux blonde
· Black Gosh
· Campagnarde blonde
· Campagnarde brune
· Cuvée de la Gate
· Cuvée de 'l Sin Djosef
· Fantôme

· Fantômette
· Green's beer
· La bière des Abeilles
· La Canebière
· La Queue de Chat
· La St Gabriel
· L'Européenne
· L'Héliante
· Pissenlit
· Saison d'Erezée Automne
· Saison d'Erezée Eté
· Saison d'Erezée Hiver
· Saison d'Erezée Printemps
Bière de Noël:
· Le Fantôme de Noël

LE FERME DU CHÊNE
Rue du Comte d'Ursel, 36
6940 DURBUY
Tél.: 086-21 10 67
Fax: 086-21 10 67
· Marckloff

FRIART
Rue d'Houdeng, 20
7070 LE ROEULX
Tél.: 064-66 21 51
· Fax : 064-67 67 30
· St Feuillien blonde
· St Feuillien brune
· *Bière de Noël:*
· St Feuillien cuvée de Noël

'T GAVERHOPKE
Steenbrugstraat, 187
8530 HARELBEKE-STASEGEM
Tél.: 056-25 86 70
Fax: 056-25 86 70
· 't Gaverhopke blonde
· 't Gaverhopke brune
· 't Gaverhopke 8%

BRASSERIE DU GEER
Rue d'Elmette, 39
4300 OLEYE-WAREMME
Tél.: 019-33 04 35

219

· La Hesbaye ambrée
· La Hesbaye blonde
· La Hesbaye brune

GIGI
Grand-Rue, 96
6769 GEROUVILLE
Tél.: 063-57 75 15
Fax: 063-57 75 15
· Gaumaise blonde
· Gaumaise brune
· Gigi double blonde
· Gigi Spéciale
· Super brune
· Unic

GIRARDIN
Lindenberg, 10
1700 ST-ULRIKS-KAPELLE
Tél.: 02-453 94 19
· Girardin framboise
· Girardin gueuze 1882
· Girardin kriek 1882
· Girardin kriekenlambic
· Girardin lambic
· Ulricher lager

DE GOUDEN BOOM
Langestraat, 45
8000 BRUGGE
Tél.: 050-33 06 99
Fax: 050-33 46 44
· Blanche de Bruges
· Brugse tripel
· Daiselnaere
· Steenbrugge dobbel
· Steenbrugge tripel

GOUDEN CAROLUS
Guido Gezellelaan, 49
2800 MECHELEN
Tél.: 015-20 38 80
· Carolus d'Or
· Mechelsen bruynen
· Triple Toison d'Or

HAACHT
Provinciesteenweg, 28
3190 BOORTMEERTBEEK
Tél.: 016-60 15 01
Fax: 016-60 83 84
· Abbaye de Malonne brune
· Adler
· Aro pils
· Bavaro
· Bockhauser pils
· Charles Quint
· Coq Hardi blonde
· Coq Hardi bock
· Coq Hardi pils
· Coq Hardi spéciale
· Derby pils
· GB bière de table
· Gildenbier
· Haacht blonde
· Haacht export
· Haacht pils
· Haacht blanche
· Maltosa
· Munck pils
· Pater brune
· Primus
· Prisma pils
· Samwell pils
· Star blonde
· Star brune
· Tongerlo blonde
· Tongerlo double
· Tongerlo triple
· Very Diest
Bière de Noël:
· Tongerlo Christmas

BRASSERIE ARTISANALE
DU HAMEAU
Rue d'Erbaut, 10
7870 LENS
Tél.: 065-22 52 92
· Bière des Trinitaires
· Dorée de l'Hamio
Bière de Noël:
· Cuvée de Noël

HANSSENS
Vroenenbosstraat, 15
1653 DWORP
Tél.: 02-380 31 33
· Hanssens gueuze
· Hanssens kriek

HOPDUVEL
Coupure links, 625
9000 GENT
Tél.: 09-225 20 68
Fax: 09-224 14 06
· Blondine
· Brunette
· Cuvée Château des Flandres
· Gentse tripel
· Stropken

HUYGHE
Brusselsesteenweg, 282
9090 MELLE
Tél.: 09-252 15 01
Fax: 09-252 29 31
· Aardbeien witbier
· Aarschotse bruine
· Abbaye des Dunes blonde
· Alfa
· Artevelde
· Artevelde grand cru
· Astor
· Blanche des Neiges
· Bière des Nonettes
· Biertoren bruno
· Biertoren special
· Bobeline
· Campus
· Campus gold
· Carioca
· Charlemagne
· Corsaire bière rouge
· Corsaire cuvée spéciale
· Cuvée de Namur blonde
· Cuvée de Namur brune
· Cuvée des Flandres triple
· Delirium Tremens

· Drossaard
· El Coco
· Fire Fox
· Florisgaardren blanche
· Florisgaarden fraise
· Florisgaarden fruit de la passion
· Florisgaarden Ninkeberry
· Golden Kenia
· Guillotine
· Huyghe blonde
· Huyghe brune
· Huyghe export
· Huyghe faro
· Karibik pils
· Lotus
· Marquise
· Match blonde
· Match brune
· Match triple
· Mateen Belgian ale triple
· N'Balens Kruierke
· Mc Gregor
· Minty
· O'Connell's Dublin ale
· Poiluchette blanche de Thy
· Poiluchette blonde
· Poiluchette brune
· Rétro ancienne méthode
· Rubbel sexy lager
· San Michael triple
· St Gregory
· St Idesbald blonde
· St Idesbald brune
· St Idesbald triple
· Trap 40 grand cru
· Verlinden special blond

JAWADDE
Karel Van Den Doorenstraat, 18
9600 RONSE
Tél.: 055-20 77 77
Fax: 055-20 83 30
· Jawadde gemberbier
· Jawadde kriek
· Jawadde triple
Bière de Noël:
· Jawadde sleedoorn kerstbier

JUPILER
(Groupe Interbrew)
Rue de Visé; 243
4020 JUPILLE-SUR-MEUSE
Tél.: 041-62 78 00
· Ale Braü
· Derby blonde
· Derby brune
· Gambrinus bock
· Gambrinus pils
· Jupiler
· Kurstenbraü
· Platzen pils
· Vega pils

KERKOM
Naamsesteenweg, 469
3800 KERKOM-ST-TRUIDEN
Tél.: 011-68 20 87
· Bink

KLUIS
(Groupe Interbrew)
Stoopkensstraat, 46
3320 HOEGAARDEN
Tél.: 016-76 76 76
Fax: 016-76 76 91
· Hoegaarden blanche
· Hoegaarden grand cru
· Hoegaarden spéciale
· Fruit Défendu
· Julius

LEFEBVRE
Rue de Croly, 54
1430 QUENAST
Tél.: 067-67 07 66
Fax: 067-75 02 38
· Abbaye de Bonne Espérance
· Abbaye de Dieleghem ambrée
· Abbaye de Dieleghem blonde
· Abbaye de Dieleghem foncée
· Auveloise
· Barbar
· Bière de l'abbaye de Gembloux

· Blanche de Bruxelles
· Blanche de Floreffe
· Blanche de Francorchamps
· Blanche du Zafke
· Blonde du Menhir
· Bousval blonde spéciale
· Bousval brune spéciale
· Cuvée de Francorchamps
· Cuvée de l'Ascension blonde
· Cuvée de la Pucelette
· Cuvée du Spartacus blonde
· Cuvée du Spartacus brune
· Cuvée Melletoise
· Cuvée Saint Roch
· Cuvée St Berthuin
· Durboyse ambrée
· Durboyse foncée
· Durboyse blonde
· Floreffe blonde
· Floreffe double
· Floreffe la meilleure
· Floreffe triple
· Foudroyante de Bruxelles
· Four Chapitre
· Freutche
· Lefèbvre blonde
· Lefèbvre brune
· Lefèbvre triple blonde
· Malmedy blonde
· Malmedy brune
· Manon des Sources
· Moeder Overste
· Perle d'Hastière
· Quenast
· Raisinoise
· Saison 1900
· Seigneurie
· Soleilmont double
· Spéciale des Géants
· St Berthuin brune
· St Léger
· Student
· Super Houblo
· Vî Keute di Nameur blonde

LEROY
Diksmuideseweg, 406
8904 BOEZINGE
Tél.: 057-42 20 05
Fax: 057-42 39 70
· Crack pils
· Katje special
· Kerelsbier donker
· Kerelsbier licht
· Leroy blonde
· Leroy brune
· Leroy stout
· Old Musketerr
· Paulus
· Peter Benoit
· Pompeschitter
· Prima
· Ridder
· Sas export
· Sas pils
· Sasbraü
· Suma pils
· West pils
· Yperman
Bière de Noël:
· Leroy Christmas

LIEFMANS
(Groupe Riva)
Aalstraat, 200
9700 OUDENAARDE
Tél.: 055-31 13 92
Fax: 055-31 94 86
· Jan van Gent
· Liefmans frambozenbier
· Liefmans goudenband
· Liefmans kriek
· Liefmans odnar
· Liefmans oud bruin
· Liefmans glühkriek (bière chaude!)

LINDEMANS
Lenniksebaan, 1479
1602 VLEZENBEEK
Tél.: 02-569 03 90

Fax: 02-569 05 10
· Foudroyante framboise
· Foudroyante gueuze
· Foudroyante kriek
· Foudroyante myrtille
· Foudroyante pêche
· Lindemans cassis
· Lindemans faro lambic
· Lindemans framboise
· Lindemans kriek
· Lindemans kriek lambic
· Lindemans lambic
· Pécheresse
· Tea Beer

LOUWAEGE
Markt, 14
8610 KORTEMARK
Tél.: 051-56 60 67
Fax: 051-57 05 95
· Akila pilsener
· Flandrien
· Hapkin
· Louwaege double blonde
· Louwaege export
· Louwaege faro
· Louwaege stout
· Louwaege's pils
· Thouroutenaere

BRASSERIE DU MARAIS
Rue de Ligny, 9
7530 GAURAIN-RAMECROIX
Tél.: 069-22 69 45
Fax: 069-22 69 45
· Cuvée du Marais blonde brut
· Cuvée du Marais brune brut
· Cuvée du Marais spéciale brut

MARTENS
Reppelerweg, 1
3950 BOCHOLT
Tél.: 089-47 29 80
Fax: 089-47 27 00
· Karlsquell pils
· Martens pils

· Martens tafelstout
· Sezoens quattro
· Sezoens blond
· Sezoens Europe

MEESTERS
Hoogstraat, 50
1570 GALMAARDEN
Tél.: 054-58 84 80
· Meesters bier
· Gamlaardsen tripel

MIROIR SPECULUM s.a.
Place Reine Asrid 24-26
1090 JETTE
Tél.: 02-424 04 78
Fax: 02-424 22 01
· Miroir spéciale
· Miroir spéciale dark
Bière de Noël:
· Miroir Christmas
Bière de Pâques:
· Miroir bière de Pâques

MOORTGAT
Breendonkdorp, 58
2870 BREENDONK-PUURS
Tél.: 03-860 94 00
Fax: 03-886 46 22
· Bel pils
· Duvel verte
· Duvel
· Godefroy
· Godefroy premium pils
· Maredsous 10
· Maredsous 6 blonde
· Maredsous 6 foncée
· Maredsous 8
· Maredsous 9
· Sanctus
· Vedett
· Wonder premium light beer

NINO BACELLE
Brugstraat, 43
8560 WEVELGEM
Tél.: 056-41 82 41
· Guldenberg

BRASSERIE DU GEER asbl
Rue d'Elmette, 39
4300 WAREMME
Tél.: 019-33 04 35
· L'Amélie
· Bière des Moines de Pousset
· La Charlemagne
· La Hesbaye ambrée
· La Hesbaye blonde
· La Hesbaye brune
· L'Ourteye bière à l'Ortie
· La Plope ambrée
· La Plope blonde
· La Plope brune

ORVAL
Brasserie d'Orval
Orval, 2
6823 VILLERS-DEVANT-ORVAL
Tél.: 061-31 12 61
Fax: 061-31 29 27
· Orval

PALM
Steenhuffeldorp, 3
1840 STEENHUFFEL
Tél.: 052-30 94 81
Fax: 052-30 41 67
· Aerts 1900
· Bock premium pils
· Palm green
· Special Palm
· Steendonk
Bière de Noël
· Dobbel Palm

PATER VAN DAMME
Jacob Van Maerlanstraat, 2
8340 DAMME
Tél.: 050-35 71 92
· Pater Van Damme

PIESSENS
Oostberg, 52
9140 TEMSE

Tél.: 03-771 03 53
Fax: 03-771 03 53
· De Wandeling
· Kaailoper
· Nieemerke
· Promesse
· Sublim
· Sublim kriek
· Sublim light
· Witbier van Temse

PIRON
Rue Battice, 93
4880 AUBEL
Tél.: 087-68 70 29
Fax: 087-68 79 78
· Légende d'Aubel
· Val-Dieu blonde
· Val-Dieu brune

BRASSERIE DE LA PRAILE
Rue de la Praile, 3
7120 PEISSANT
Tél.: 064-77 16 43
· Blonde de la Praile
· Brune de la Praile
· Campagnarde brune
· Cuvée d'Aristée au miel
· Saison de la Praile
Bière de Noël:
· Cuvée d'Aristée spéciale de Noël

RIVA
Wontergemstraat, 42
8720 DENTERGEM
Tél.: 051-63 36 81
Fax: 051-63 62 08
· Baptiste
· Billekarreke
· Dentergems
· Lucifer
· Riva Bavière
· Riva brune spéciale
· Riva pils
· Riva triple abdij
· Royal pils

· St Arnoldus triple
voir Br Caulier
· Vondel
· Wittekop

ROBERG
Rodebergstraat, 46/53
8954 WESTOUTER
Tél.: 057-44 44 55
Fax: 057-44 71 27
· Roberg classic
· Roberg dark
· Roberg junior

ROCHEFORT
Abbaye Notre-Dame-de-
St-Rémy
Rue de l'Abbaye, 8
5580 ROCHEFORT
Tél.: 084-22 01 40
· Rochefort 6
· Rochefort 8
· Rochefort 10

BRASSERIE DE L'ABBAYE
DES ROCS
Chaussée de Brunehaut, 37
7387 MONTIGNIES-SUR-ROC
Tél.: 065-75 99 76
Fax: 065-75 99 76
· Abbaye des Rocs
· Autreppe
· Bière du Jumelage
· Blanche des Honnelles
· Cuvée cent ans Domaine du Bois
· d'Anchin
· Cuvée Jean d'Avesnes ambrée
· Cuvée Jean d'Avesnes blanche
· Domaine du Bois d'Anchin
· Essen Bakkersmolen Wildert
blonde
· Essen Bakkersmolen brune
· Matagnarde
· Montagnarde
· Regain
· Schaerbeekoise

225

· St Hubert
· St Lenderik
Bière de Noël:
· Abbaye des Rocs spéciale Noël

RODENBACH
Spanjestraat, 133
8800 ROESELARE
Tél.: 051-22 34 00
Fax: 051-22 92 48
· Alexander Rodenbach
· Rodenbach
· Rodenbach grand cru

ROMAN
Hauweret, 61
9700 OUDENAARDE-MATER
Tél.: 055-45 54 01
Fax: 055-45 56 00
· Abbaye d'Ename double
· Abbaye d'Ename triple
· Alfri
· Hotteuse
· Hotteuse grand cru
· Mater blanche
· Prik pils
· Roman spéical
· Roman blonde
· Roman brune
· Roman Dobbelen bruinen
· Roman export
· Roman Oudenaards
· Romy luxe
· Romy pils
· Sloeber
· Triplor

BRASSERIE RUWET
Rue Victor Besme, 27
4800 VERVIERS
Tél.: 087-30 04 36
Fax: 087-44 61 54
· La Clermontoise
· Papy Jo

· La Ploquette

(DE) RYCK
Kerkstraat, 28
9550 HERZELE
Tél.: 053-62 23 02
Fax: 053-63 15 41
· De Ryck special
· De Ryck kriek
· Molenbier
· Rochus
Bière de Noël:
· De Ryck Christmas pale ale

SILENRIEUX
Rue Noupré, 1
5630 SILENRIEUX
Tél.: 071-63 32 01
Fax: 071-66 82 04
· Joseph, bière à l'Epeautre
· Sara, bière au Sarrasin
· Pavé de l'Ours
· Foire verte de l'Eau d'Heure cuvée
spéciale
Bière de Noël;
· Supernoël

BRASSERIE DE SILLY
Ville Basse, A 141
7830 SILLY
Tél.: 068-55 13 51
Fax: 068-56 84 36
· Brave Broeder
· Brug ale belge
· Cervoise de l'Avouerie
d'Anthisnes
· Double d'Enghien blonde
· Double d'Enghien ambrée
· Grisette bière du cayoteu
· Gueule Noire
· La Divine
· Royale blonde
· Saison de Silly
· Scotch Silly
· Silbraü dort urtyp
· Silly bock

· Silly pils
· Silly triple bock
· St Christophe blonde
· St Christophe brune
· Super
· Titje
· Villers-St-Ghislain
· Villers-St-Ghislain brune
· Vitus spezialbier

SLAGHMUYLDER
Denderhoutembaan, 2
9400 NINOVE
Tél.: 054-33 18 31
Fax: 054-33 84 45
· Ambiorix Dubbel
· Drongens plesierke
· Helles export
· Slag lager pils
· Slaghmuylder's oud bier
· Slaghmuylder's tafel hell
· Witkap pater dubbele
· Witkap pater stimulo
· Witkap pater tripel
Bière de Noël:
· Slaghmuylder's kerstbier
Bière de Pâques:
· Paasbier

ST BERNARDUS
Trappistenweg, 23
8978 WATOU
Tél.: 057 38 80 21
Fax: 057-38 80 71
· St Bernardus abt 12
· St Bernardus blonde
· St Bernardus pater G
· St Bernardus prior
· St Bernardus triple

ST GUIBERT
(Groupe Interbrew)
Rue de Riquau, 1
1435 MONT-ST-GUIBERT
Tél.: 010-65 57 71
· Leffe blonde

· Leffe brune
· Leffe radieuse
· Leffe triple
· Leffe vieille cuvée

ST JOZEF
Itterplein, 19
3960 OPITTER
Tél.: 089-86 47 11
Fax: 089-86 74 19
· Bokkereyer
· Bosbier
· Brussels gold
· Keyser
· Limburgse witte
· Molenbier
· Ops-ale
· Pax pils
· Ras super pils
· St Jozef kriekenbier

STEEDJE
Schoolstraat, 45B
8460 ETTELGEM
Tél.: 059-26 50 30
· Grande bière de Blondine
· Hoge Bier
· Oogst blond
· Oogst bruin
· Oudenburgs abdijbier
· Oudenbrugs bruin
· Polderbier bitter
Snellegemsen
· Steedje special
· Steedje tripel
Bière de Noël:
· Steedje kerstbier
Bière de Pâques:
· Paasche

STERKENS
Merdorp, 20
2321 MEER
Tél.: 03-315 71 45
Fax: 03-315 94 20
· Aarschots kruikenbier

227

· Boals kruikenbier triple
· Bokrijk hoevelbier 6
· Bokrijk hoevelbier 8
· Bokrijks kruikenbier
· Carnav-ale
· Cervoise des Ancêtres grand cru
· Kapel van Schoor
· Keerse tripel
· Klooster Zusters Annonciaden
· Kluyserbier
· Molenbier van Tesenderlo
· Oelegems kruikenbier
· Oregon rodeo beer
· Pastorijpoort Balen/Olmen
· Poorter
· Smokkelaar
· St Adriaan kruikenbier dark
· St Adriaan kruikenbier grand cru
· St Denise dark
· St Denise grand cru
· St Laurent double
· St Laurent triple
· St Paul double
· St Paul triple
· St Sebastiaan dark
· St Sebastiaan grand cru
· Stadhuis Lommel
· Ser Ale
· Taverne 'Berghuis - Muizen
· Taverne Old Time -Veltem
· Topmolen - Balen
· Tremeloos Damiaanbier
· 'T Veltems kruikje grand cru
· Watermolen
· Zaal Kapelhof

STRAFFE HENDRIK
(Groupe Riva)
Walplein, 26
8000 BRUGGE
Tél.: 050-33 26 97
Fax: 050-34 59 35
· Straffe Hendrik

STRUBBE
Markt, 1

8480 ICHTEGEM
Tél.: 051-58 81 16
Fax: 051-58 24 46
· Couckelaerschen Doedel
· Dikke Mathilde
· Dobbelken
· Edel-Braü
· Ensor
· Hoeve bier
· Ichtegem's oud bruin
· Pee klak Moorsels bier
· Strubbe export
· Strubbe faro
· Strubbe oud bier
· Strubbe pilsen
· Strubbe stout
· Super pils
· Teugelbier
· Trammelantbier
· Wastobbeke
· Yves pils
· Zedelgemse Martelaar

TEUT
Stationstraat, 97
3910 NEERPELT
Tél.: 011-80 17 31
· Breda's Begijntje dubbel
· Breda's Begijntje tripel
· Breda's Begijntje witbier
· Donkere Dikke
· Witte Dikke
· Eersels Menneke
· Rembrandt's bier
· Teutenbier
· Teutenbock
· 'T Paterken
· Witte van de Teut

TIMMERMANS
(Groupe John Martins)
Kerkstraat, 11
1701 ITTERBEEK
Tél.: 02-569 03 58
Fax: 02-569 01 98
· Bourgogne des Flandres

· Timmermans blanche lambic
· Timmermans cassis lambic
· Timmermans faro lambic
· Timmermans framboise lambic
· Timmermans gueuze caveau
· Timmermans gueuze lambic
· Timmermans kriek lambic
· Timmermans lambic
· Timmermans pêche lambic

BRASSERIE DE LA TOUR
Rue Chera, 9
4180 COMBLAIN-LA-TOUR
Tél.: 04-369 38 87
· Magonette

BRASSERIE DE L'UNION
(Groupe Alken-Maes)
Rue Derbèque, 7
6040 JUMET
Tél.: 071-35 01 33
Fax: 071-34 02 22
Voir Alken Maes

VAN DEN BOSSCHE
Sint-Lievensplein, 16
9550 SINT-LIEVENS-ESSE
Tél.: 054-50 04 11
Fax: 054-50 04 06
· Amuzantje
· Arjaun
· Buffalo
· Hoofse Gaffel
· Kamilleken
· Lamoral Degmont
· Lamoral tripel
· Pater Lieven
· S-pils
· Zwarte Flesch
Bière de Noël:
· Van Den Bossche kerstbier
Bière de Pâques:
· Deins paasbier

VAN EECKE
Douwieweg, 2

8978 WATOU
Tél.: 057-42 20 05
Fax: 057-42 39 70
· Bakelandt
· Beselaars Heksenbier
· Bière de la Bonde
· Bleeken Moriaen
· Bruynen Moriaen
· Coy'Heimsen
· Fiertelbier
· Harelbekenaar van de abdijhoeve pater
· Harelbekenaar van de abdijhoeve wit
· Het Kapittel abt
· Het Kapittel dubbel
· Het Kapittel pater
· Het Kapittel prior
· Livinus blonde
· Livinus brune
· Ne Kempenaer
· N'Aalbeeksen St Corneluisbier
· N'Slijpke
· Poperings hommelbier
· Watou's wit bier

VAN HONSEBROUCK
Oostrozebekestraat, 43
8770 INGELMUNSTER
Tél.: 051-33 51 60
Fax: 051-31 38 39
· Bacchus
· Brigand
· Kasteelbier triple d'or
· La Bière du Château de Ingelmunster
· La Bière du Château de Ooidonk
· St Louis cassis kir royal
· St Louis framboisé
· St Louis gueuze fond tradition lambic
· St Louis gueuze lambic
· St Louis kriek lambic
· St Louis pêche lambic
· Triple de Val-Dieu
· Vieux Bruges blanche

229

· Vieux Bruges framboise
· Vieux Bruges gueuze lambic
· Vieux Bruges kriek lambic
· Vieux Bruxelles gueuze lambic
· Vlaamsch wit
Bière de Noël:
· Brigand Christmas

VANDER LINDEN
Brouwerijstraat, 2
1500 HALLE
Tél.: 02-356 50 59
Fax: 02-360 01 17
· Duivels bier
· Vander Linden faro
· Vander Linden frambozenbier
· Vander Linden lambic
· Vieux Foudre faro
· Vieux Foudre gueuze
· Vieux Foudre Kriek

VANDERVELDEN HENRI
Laarheidestraat, 230
1650 BEERSEL
Tél.: 02-380 33 96
· Oud Beersel gueuze
· Oud Beersel lambic
· Sherry Poësy old Beersel

BRASSERIE A VAPEUR
Rue de Maréchal, 1
7904 PIPAIX-LEUZE
Tél.: 069 66 20 47
· Anpavi
· Ballotil
· Bière de la Taupe
· Bière Vache
· Caza cuvée spéicale
· Cuvée de Winamplanche
· Cuvée des Moissons blonde
· Cuvée du Tronquoy
· Cuvée spéciale du 80e
· Cuvée spéciale Patro Salette
· El Vert Doudou
· Frenette
· Jobarde

· Kirally
· La Drontalière
· La Folie
· La spéciale Etoile
· La Vezonnoise
· La Vive Vie
· La Woise
· La Cochonnette
· L'Hercule à Vapeur
· L'Incartade
· La Jamelovienne
· La Nationale
· La Pétouille
· O Mac Kot -Bière de Blaton
· Saison de Pipaix
· Vapeur Cochonne
· Vapeur en Folie
· Vapeur Légère
· Vapeur Rousse
· Verne en Folie
· Verne Rousse
· Viking

VERHAEGHE
Beukenhofstraat, 96
8570 VICHTE
Tél.: 056 77 70 32
Fax: 056-77 70 32
· Cambrinus
· Caves
· Duchesse de Bourgogne
· Ezel
· Gapers bier
· Pandoer
· Queue de Charrue
· Vera Dubbel blond
· Vera export
· Vera ouden bruinen
· Vera pils
· Vera special
· Verabraü urtyp
· Verhaeghe echte kriek
· Verhaeghe triple blonde
· Vichtenaar
· Zandberg braü
· Zerewever

Bières de Noël:
· Ninoviet
· Noël-Christmas-Weihnacht

BRASSERIE VERVIFONTAINE
Vervifontaine, 100
4845 JALHAY
Tél.: 087-64 83 03
Fax: 087-34 01 11
· La Bière du Lion
· La Rousse des Fagnes

VILLERS
Liezeledorp, 37
2870 LIEZELE-PUURS
Tél.: 03-889 88 00
Fax: 03-889 99 30
· Fumée d'Anvers
· Loteling blond
· Loteling bruin
· Mercator
· Paranoia groen
· Paranoia roze
· Villers double ambrée
· Villers triple

WALRAVE
Lepelstraat, 36
9270 LAARNE
Tél.: 09-369 01 34
· Pick-up pils
· Walrave export
· Walrave extra tafelbier

WELDEBROEC
Mechelsesteenweg, 53
2830 WILLEBROEK
Tél.: 03-886 12 44
Fax: 03-886 12 44
· Vaartlander

WESTMALLE
Abbaye des Trappistes
de Westmalle
Antwerpsesteenweg, 496
2390 MALLE

Tél.: 03-312 92 22
Fax: 03-312 92 27
· Westmalle double
· Westmalle extra
· Westmalle triple

WESTVLETEREN
Abbaye de St Sixtus
Donkerstraat, 12
8640 WESTVLETEREN
Tél.: 057-40 03 76
· Westvleteren 4
· Westvleteren 6
· Westvleteren 8
· Westvleteren 12

WIEZE
Nieuwstraat, 1
9280 WIEZE
Tél.: 053-21 52 01
Fax: 053-77 58 40
· Hei-Kneuter
· Royal type ale
· Upper
· Wieze kriek lambic
· Wieze pils
Bière de Noël:
· Wieze Christmas

GLOSSARY

ABBEY BEERS

(*see Trappist and Abbey Beers*)

ABBEY BEERS

The abbeys at Leffe, Grimbergen, Floreffe, Postel are the names of Premonstratensian abbeys, which were founded respectively at the beginning of the XIII century, before being destroyed by and subsequent to the French Revolution. As with the Trappist abbeys, some of them were reconstructed and presently live as best they can thanks to different activities, using the revenues obtained from the use of their name under license to ensure the prosperity of their community or others situated in regions where there is hardship. This is the case of the communities at Grimbergen and Tongerlo, to cite two well-known examples. In other cases, all that remains of the abbey is the site. The Premonstratensian communities have their origins in the Order of Regular Canons founded in 1120 by the future Saint Norbert. After a somewhat hectic youth, Norbert was converted and became a Benedictine monk. After unsuccessful attempts to reform the Xanten chapter (near Cologne), he left the community and became an itinerant preacher. As a radical preacher he rid himself of all his belongings. In 1118 he met Hugues who was eventually to become his successor. During his pilgrimages, Norbert traveled through Picardy and intended to settle in Prémontré. Because of the need to recruit companions, he took to the road again in 1119 and with fourteen companions, he founded in 1120 the Abbaye de Prémontré.

In 1121, this community adopted the rules of Saint Augustine. They were cannons who, while looking after the spiritual needs of local inhabitants, lived as monks in a community, not within an abbey, but in the outside world, by training the clergy of a church where they celebrated the divine office as a collegiate. Just like Benedictine monks, certain families of canons, known as " regular canons " took vows of poverty, chastity and humility. These are not to be confused with " secular canons " who had the right to have belongings, and generally lived alone as parish priests or within educational institutions. They were in a separate category to the clergy who had parish responsibilities, generally a cathedral or a collegiate church. The Premonstratensian families involved in brewing are those that had formed or form a monastic community of " regular canons ". It is worth noting at this point the importance of the Abbaye de Floreffe, which was founded in 1121 by Norbert himself at the request of the Counts of Namur, and the prosperity in the XII and XIII centuries is mentioned in several reference books. At Floreffe, as with all three other more rustic settlements, the calling of the Premonstratensians was to reform the parish clergy by themselves supplying priests. It was the period when the Templars invented the notion of " monk-soldier " that the Premonstratensians, under the leadership of Fhugues de Fosse, mobilized their efforts to become " monks-priests ". The names of these abbeys are used by lay brewers to market a certain kind of beer in agreement with, and sometimes even at the specific request of, monastic communities.

ACID

(See taste)

ACID BEER

This applies to spontaneous-fermentation beers (*see Gueuze*), or on a top-fermentation basis, but in the latter case the acidification is more often than not the result of long aging in oak tuns (for example the acid beers of Roeselaere of which the most famous is no doubt the Rodenbach). The two most important acids present are lactic acid (from 2 to 7 g/l) and acetic acid (from 0.5 to 2 g/l), the first producing above all a smooth tone, whereas the other can produce a frankly vinegary aspect if there is too much of it. (*see Spontaneous Fermentation*).

ACRID, ACRIDITY

The acridity is the sensation in the mouth felt when consuming fruits covered with a thin layer, rich in tannins, for example nuts, chestnuts. This sensation is typical of certain aged beers and is due to the presence of an important quantity of oxidized polyphenols, natural compounds which emanate from the hops and the barley. (*see Taste*).

ALE

The term is English in origin and indicates the type of fermentation used to produce the beer. In contrast to bottom-fermented beers known as " Lager ", beers categorized as " Ale " are top-fermented. Depending upon their respective colors, there are Pale Ales, or slightly amber colored beers which are very popular in certain regions in this country (Vieux Temps, Palm, or more typically British such as Bass and Whitbread) as well as the Dark Ales, amongst which Guinness is certainly the most famous. (*see Fermentation*).

AROMA

The aroma is the olfactory sensation emanating from drinks or food perceived through the back of the nose (by the canal that links the mouth to the nose). It is therefore a matter of solid or liquid bolus present in the mouth and which release molecules that by their presence stimulate the olfactory cilia, these signals being decoded as odors by the olfactory bulb located in the brain. While the range of tastes has a relatively simplistic structure, the complexity of odors must be underlined. It is of the utmost importance to emphasize that the notion of sensation introduces the notion of perception and that the human body is not equally sensitive to all odors; that is why a perception threshold has been established for each compound and why this differs according to the type of molecule. The scented compounds found in beer are of the following types: acids, alcohol, aldehydes, ketones, sulfur compounds, esters, lactones and phenols. A beer's aroma is quantified by its aromatic strength expressed in " flavor units ". The intention is to classify each compound according to its real importance in terms of odor, that is to say to divide its concentration by its perception threshold and to add up the number of the flavor units found. A beer is considered to be aromatic when its concentration in molecules with a pleasant odor is greater than 4 flavor units.

BARLEY

Barley, with corn, is the easiest cereal to cultivate in our country. For the brewer, it has several technological advantages, which have led to it being the ideal raw material for producing beer. There are two types of barley; winter barley and summer barley. Beers produced from the latter are reputed to be more subtle, probably because this barley proportionally has fewer straws. However, the barley grains cannot be used in their existing form in the production process, for the extractable matters it contains have a structure which makes it completely impossible for them to be assimilated by the yeast.

That is why the barley grains must be germinated and dried beforehand, that is to say malted. The malting process includes successively the phase whereby the grains are left to soak in water, then germinated, and finally they must be dried, which is completed with a blast of heat of around 80°C/176°F. The last operation is called the kilning. The malt thus obtained is used to produce " Pils " style beer. It is moreover possible to produce a darker colored malt by drying it at a higher temperature, either by caramelizing it in a roaster where it is dried, which produces a caramel malt, or by simply roasting the malt, which will have been dried beforehand, which produces a roasted malt. The malting stage is indispensable to obtain the best possible results during the brewing and facilitate the transformation of approximately 80% of the extract into fermentable sugars. That is why the production of beer by traditional methods always requires the utilization of at least 50% of malted barley of the " Pils " type. The rest of the ingredients that are added in the brewhouse consist of malt or other non-germinated grains called dry grains and are made up of unsorted rice, corn meal, wheat, untreated barley, or even other sources of starch.

BEER GLASSES

Given the notion of brand image that has developed in Belgium in the beer sector, each brewery tends to promote the association between a beer and its individual glass. Hence, it has become imperative for breweries to choose a glass which is specific to the brewery and this has become even more important, given the pressure from the important distribution networks to standardize all containers (bottles and racks). At the present time, three criteria are applied in selecting a glass: the esthetic aspect of the glass and whether it suits the product's image, the practical aspect from the point of view of its utilization (weight and cleaning) and finally the economics (cost price). Beer glasses come in a multitude of forms ranging from the classic straight glass to the most complicated forms such as spin-offs from " tulip " glasses, even " flared tulip " glasses. All the glasses have typical parameters: the diameter of the glass where it comes into contact with the mouth, the widest diameter of the glass, the height of the glass, the total volume, the nominal volume and finally the relative volume (Total volume/nominal volume x 100). The glasses vary in shape from the tall, thin glass (ratio surface of the glass/volume of beer: maximum) to spherical (ratio surface of the glass/ volume of beer: minimum). Before selecting the ideal glass, each brewer carries out tests in these different types of drinking vessels.

BITTER ORANGE (CURACAO)

Bitter oranges are the fruit from the orange tree *Citrus aurantium* L. whereas the typical sweet orange is the fruit of the *Citrus sinensis Osbeck.* They are cultivated in particular in Sicily, Spain, India and Russia.

In brewing, bitter orange peels are a frequently used ingredient and they are very indentifiable by their aroma. The latter comes from essential oils lodged in innumerable small oval sacs that are scattered at different depths over the cuticle of the fruit.

The quantities used depend on the type of beer to be produced and the quality of the peels; one value capable of being used as a basis for testing being from 5gr/hl to 20gr/hl.

BITTERNESS

The bitterness of a beer reflects the degree of intensity of a specific taste, which is felt on the back of the tongue. The bitterness can have different origins: the most common source in beer is the hops, more precisely the alpha acids which are present in the lupulin grains, that is to say the yellow powder which is to be found in the malt cones. In beer, the bitterness emanates from the hop compounds (alpha acids) which undergo a slight transformation (isometrization) when the wort boils; in special darker beers it can also have its origins in the utilization of roasted malts. In other drinks, the bitterness can come from other natural substances, for example quinine. (*see Hops*).

BOTTOM FERMENTING YEAST

· it is never utilized at temperatures above 10°C/50°F and generally ferments at around 8°C/46°F;
· it is slightly smaller and a little less spherical than top yeast;
· the budding is markedly less branchy than in the case of top yeast;
· it does not rise to the surface, whatever the temperature at which it is treated;
· the beer thus produced is completely different from that obtained with top yeast.

The predetermined production of top-fermented beers with a pure culture is not particularly ancient, but the imagination which Belgian brewers have shown proof of in their efforts to produce original and authentic beers deserves applause. This irrefutable fact deserved to attract the attention of science. It was thus becoming indispensable to record in book form the basic know-how and its organoleptic characteristics that are an integral part of Belgium's national brewing heritage, of which it is rightly proud. (*see also Fermentation*).

BOTTOM-FERMENTATION

Bottom-fermentation is thus called because it occurs at a low temperature, that is to say at a cellar temperature, or to be more precise between 6°C/43°F and 14°C/57°F. What is specific to this process is that at the end of fermentation, the yeast remains at the bottom of the vat. The most famous beers produced in this way are the Pils style beers, which originated in the town of Pilsen, in the former Czechoslovakia. Given the temperatures that this technique requires, it was impossible to produce these beers in our country without the availability of " special industrial cooling facilities ". That is why, until the end of the XIX century, bottom-fermented beers were either imported or sold more expensively than ordinary beers, which in general were top-fermented. It goes without saying that the two events which had the greatest impact on the closing of many breweries at the start of the 1920s were on the one hand the First World War and the requisitioning of all copper equipment (for example brewing rooms), as well as the fact that the brews produced did not correspond to the demands of consumers, who displayed a growing preference for bottom-fermented beers. From an aromatic point of view, the characteristics of these beers are often based on the basic ingredients, namely malt and hops, as well as certain sulfurous notes which evoke the odors and aromas of certain green vegetables (onions, celery, cabbage). Sometimes, in beers that have not been allowed to mature sufficiently, there is a trace of butter, in truth margarine. On the other hand, in beers that have been left to age, it is above all a taste of papier-mâché which is the most prominent. All of these aromas are inherent in the ingredients and the yeast function. The scientific name of the micro-organism at the heart of the bottom-fermentation process is *Saccharomyces cerevisiae var. carlsbergensis;* depending on the conditions of the medium and the environment, it is capable of developing and fermenting between 4°C/39°F and 35°C/95°F. These micro-organisms are added to the wort, once it has been cooled after boiling.

BREWING (THE MASH TUB)

Brewing is the phase in the production of beer that consists of producing the wort, that is to say the sweet liquid which, once it has been boiled, will be cooled and fermented by the yeast. It is acknowledged that this operation includes the milling of the grain, its soaking in the brewing water, the heating of this mixture at varying standard temperatures (45°C/113°F, 62°C/143°F and 72°C/161°F) to degrade the nitrogenous material, the sugar, as well as the other compounds vital to the fermentation of the wort by the yeast. There are three types of brewing: by infusion, which consists of heating the contents of the mash tun to different temperatures; by decoction, which consists of heating the mash tun while removing part of its contents, in boiling it in another vat and in re-heating the contents of the first while pumping in again the boiling wort; finally, mixed methods, which combine the two processes. Subsequently, the wort is filtered into a filtering tank or a filter press and collected in the boiler. It is at this stage that the hops are added. The brewing process, including the boiling, generally lasts between 6 and 10 hours.

CENTRIFUGAL FORCE

The process used to separate a solid compound from a liquid solution or two liquid compounds of different specific weights by accentuating the difference of the specific weights by using the force that results from rotating the mixture at a high speed.

CORIANDER

Coriander is the fruit of an umbelliferous plant, *Coriandrum sativum* L. which originated in Mediterranean countries but is now found in regions with temperate climates. The dry fruit is very pleasant and is even used to flavor sweet aperitifs to which it gives an aroma of muscat. It has been described as having a warm, sweet and fruity odor, as well as a very distinctive spicy aroma, which is slightly fruity and endowed with a flowery tone in the background. The indicative values concerning its utilization vary between 1.5gr/hl and 4gr/hl;coriander should be used fresh and finely ground. It should be added five minutes before the end of the boiling phase.

Other spices that were formerly used in brewing are the grains of paradise and camomile leaves. And let us not forget licorice, which is still used in dark beers, in the " Scotch " style.

DEGREES BALLING & DEGREES PLATO

Degrees Balling and Degrees Plato, which are synonymous for most people who are not brewers, are named after their creators. They express, in grams of sucrose/100 grams of wort, the quantity of compounds present in a solution; generally they are used to quantify the extract content. In the brewing room, they quantify the soluble substances extracted from the raw materials and dissolved in the wort during the brewing; after boiling and cooling, they are used to determine beer's basic extract content; this value multiplied by 0.45 is an effective way in most cases of establishing the final alcoholic strength of the beer in percentage vol. (that is to say alcohol/beer). Utilized in fermentation, they are a way of quantifying the yeast activity; finally, in regards to the finished beer product, they indicate the quantity of matter that the yeast in the wort will not ferment. The essential difference between the two degrees lies in the accuracy of their definition. Balling invented the concept which aims to establish the correlation between the wort's specific weight, a value which is difficult to utilize on a practical basis, and a sucrose solution with the same specific weight but which has a much more practical utilization (for example: the density of a wort is 1.04646, which corresponds to 12.0 Plato or the equivalent of a solution containing 12 grams of sucrose per liter). This inventor of genius forgot however to subtract the weight of the air contained in the standardized volume used to determine the specific weight of the solutions; this error, although not unduly important, is not however completely negligible; it was corrected by Plato who thus published his own tables.

DOUBLE

The terms " Double " and " Triple " are generally used to describe beers of which the basic extract content (and consequently the alcoholic strength) is superior to the average in that category. In this way, there are " Doubles " and " Triples " in table beers (alcohol content: from 2.5 to 3.0 percent alcohol in volume) just as with stronger beers like the " Spéciale ". The production process of a " Double " or a " Triple " is simple: either the quantity of raw materials utilized is higher, or the quantity of water utilized to extract the raw materials and to wash the spent grain when it is filtered from the mash tun is lower. In most cases, it concerns brown beers produced from a base of amber, even caramel malts, and decidedly dark and thus more often than not produced using sugars or coloring syrups. The basic difference between the " Double " and the " Triple " is twofold: color and alcoholic strength. The " Double " being almost always darker but less strong than the " Triple ".

DRY GRAINS

(*see Malt*)

FARO

(*see Gueuze*)

FERMENTATION

Fermentation is the metabolic mechanism by which the yeast transforms the fermentable sugars (glucose, sucrose, fructose, maltose, maltotriose) into ethanol and carbon dioxide. Fermentation enables the yeast to form the necessary energy to survive and multiply. There are different types of fermentation: bottom-fermentation, top-fermentation and spontaneous fermentation. The fact that fermentation is assured by a living micro-organism which is the result of exterior contamination was first described by Pasteur around 1860. That assertion, although correct and proven, was vehemently contested by the German scientist von Liebig, which resulted in scientists from that period witnessing an acrimonious debate between these two famous research scientists.

FLOWERY

The flowery odors and aromas of beers are linked to roses and their perfume. They may be either of the type " Fresh Roses " or " Mature Roses ". The compounds responsible for these odors are formed by the yeast during the beer's fermentation and are respectively phenylethanol and phenylethanol acetate.

FRUITY

The fruity aroma found in most beers relies on subtle variations based on the following fruit: pears, bananas, apricots, peaches, and tropical fruit such as mangos or pineapples. Sometimes the fruity sensation can be more pungent and bring to mind a solvent. The compounds responsible for these aromatic subtleties are primarily compounds of the ester kind, formed from an interaction of a radical " alcohol " and a radical " acid ". In most cases, the quantity of ester present is proportional to the concentration of its two basic radicals. Given that in beer the alcohol most present is ethanol and that the predominant radical acid is acetate, the prevalent ester will be acetaldehyde (typical odor of a solvent). But, except in certain acidic beers, this aroma is very rarely perceptible since its perception threshold by a human being is relatively high (from 30 to 50 mg/l). On the other hand, certain esters, such as the acetate d'isoamyle (aroma of pears and bananas) that is present in beer, but in much smaller concentrations, and which has a much lower perception threshold (1.6 mg/l), are distinctly perceptible. In this connection, the most typical beers are the Trappist beers, such as Westmalle Triple, Chimay Bleue, the Duval and Bush special beers, as well as Abbey beers such as Leffe Blonde, Affligem and to a lesser extent Grimbergen. It has to be pointed out that the presence of these compounds is a result of the yeast function (metabolism) during fermentation and that, consequently, the concentration of these compounds in the beer also depends on the mash tub and the characteristics of the yeast.Certain acidic beers also have a very specific fruity aroma: cherry, raspberries, blackcurrants, etc. If the first two still result, in certain cases, from the addition of fresh fruit in barrels of acid beers (50 kg/250 l for the cherries and approximately 150 kg/250 l as regards the raspberries), it cannot be denied that most are the result of the addition of extracts or natural aromas, which is a far easier technique, but definitely does not produce the same subtleties.

GUEUZE, LAMBIC, FARO, KRIEK

Gueuze, Lambic, Faro, Kriek [adapted from: Dc CLERCK, J., *Cours de Brasserie,* Ed. Chaire de Clerck, Leuven-la-Neuve, 1984, page 885].

The Lambic is a beer that originated in the province of Brabant, in particular in Brussels and Pajotteland (south west of Brussels). It is produced with 60 per cent malt and 40 per cent raw wheat. The different brewing methods are more or less complicated. For the hopping process, a generous dose (approximately 600g/hl) of aged hops is used (2 or 3 years old). It is left to cook for a long time (from 4 to 6 hours). Its essential characteristic is the spontaneous fermentation it undergoes. The wort is pumped into tuns without bacteria being added. There it is fermented by natural yeast elements, lactic bacteria and bacteria in the ambient air, *Brettanomyces* (that is to say different from the types of yeast commonly used in brewing). The fermentation process develops during the first few weeks but it cannot be too lively otherwise there is a danger that it will produce ill-balanced and over acidic beers: that is why brewing takes place only during the cold seasons. Fermentation lasts several months and when it is finished, the casks are sealed and preserved for 1, 2 or 3 years. However, the microbial process continues actively in the cask. Then tuns of Lambic of different ages are blended to obtain a representative flavor, which is vinous but always acidic, and then it is bottled. It is from this time on that the product is called " Gueuze ". As with champagne, in the case of traditional Gueuzes which are not filtered, the beer is refermented in its bottle and consequently the carbonation continues. In time, all the sugars may be fermented, so much so that the aged Gueuzes can be drunk by diabetics.

Certain typical beers are known as " blended beers ". In the case of beers produced by spontaneous fermentation, some beers to which Lambic has been added have too hard a taste to be sold as such, so by means of dilution, the sharp taste is lessened and the beers acquire the Lambic aroma. An important category of beers produced in this way is the Faro, which is a light beer, blended with sugar and residual Lambic. The Kriek comes from the addition of Morello cherries to the young Lambic produced the same year. (*see Fruity and Spontaneous fermentation*).

HOPS

The hop is a climbing plant, in which there are both male and female plants, which are distinct. Brewers use the flowers from the female plant. Its flowers, or cones, consist of petals, and at the base of each petal there is a yellow powder, known as lupulin. This powder has two aspects which are of particular interest to brewers: the bitter acids that provide beer with its bitterness, and oils which give certain beers their characteristic hop aroma. The bitter acids are non-volatile compounds which become even more bitter during the boil (through their structure being modified: isomerization) and which in the finished product are concentrated in the head; it is moreover significant that a beer's head is far more bitter than the beer which it covers. The essential oils that contain the hop's typical aroma are volatile compounds which escape during the boil if the hops are added too soon. That is why, in the case of beers with a distinctive hop aroma, brewers add part of the hops to the boil at the last minute, or add dry hops at the end of fermentation. This is a typical practice for certain beers, like the Trappist Orval beer or the Sezoens Mertens, which is brewed in the province of Limburg. There are different types of hops and, depending upon their characteristics, they are classified as either bitter or aromatic hops. The best known zones where hops are cultivated are Bohemia (in the Czech Republic), in Styrie in Austria, in the Duchy of Bade north of Lake Constance in Germany (Tettnang variety), in the region of Lublin (Poland), in the regions around Spalt and Hallertau (Germany) and in England with the Kent hops, which are characterized by the cheesy aroma which they give to certain Pale Ales (for example Bass, Martin's). The Alsace region in France also produces hops, but as far as Belgium is concerned, it has to be admitted that this is very small scale, probably because of the low percentage of land given over to their cultivation and the difficulty in mechanizing their cultivation. Nevertheless, the region of Poperinghe (western Flanders) deserves mention in this connection. There are other countries that produce hops including the United States and Australia, as well as China, which by the quality of its produce is starting to attract the interest of brewers.

LACEWORK

Lacework is a term used to describe the way in which carbon dioxide that is present in beer is released. In this connection, a distinction has to be drawn between the bubbles which are formed along the sides of the glass, and which are noteworthy by their large numbers and by their quality (rough or delicate), and the lacework that characterizes the delicate release of carbon dioxide from the bottom of the glass and which is sometimes highlighted by brewers who mark the bottom of the glass with a tracer. Ideally the lacework is light and delicate.

MALT

(*see Barley*)

PASTEURIZATION AND STERILIZATION

Sterilization is a principle of microbiological stabilization of a substance or a body by thermal means. For liquids, it is recognized that the application of a temperature of 121°C during approximately 20 minutes in surroundings saturated with steam helps to achieve a sterile environment. If the environment is a gas like air, it needs a higher temperature. Sterilization is therefore an absolute law.

On the other hand, pasteurization is not an absolute law. It is a law of logarithmic destruction, which can be defined as being the proportion of micro-organisms destroyed at predetermined temperatures and in the physico-chemical conditions applying to an ambient medium. Pasteurization is far less destructive of the typical aroma of beers than an intense thermal treatment. It is generally recognized that in order to stabilize a beer from a microbiological point of view, it requires between 15 and 25 Pasteurization Units or PU (1 PU corresponds to the destructive effect by thermal treatment of micro-organisms produced when the liquid is left during 1 minute at 60°C/140°F). There are two types of pasteurization; flash-pasteurization and tunnel-pasteurization. Tunnel-pasteurization consists of heating the beer which has already been filled in bottles or cans that are placed on a conveyor belt which circulates through a tunnel where they are sprayed with hot water in order to heat the contents to the requisite temperature for a predetermined time in order to satisfy pasteurization standards. In breweries, pasteurization is generally carried out at around 62°C/143°F and lasts approximately 10 minutes. The bottles or cans are subsequently cooled by jets of cold water. Flash-pasteurization consists of heating the beer before it

244

has been bottled by using a heat exchanger. This is done at temperatures approaching 72°C/161°F and the treatment lasts approximately 30 seconds.

PILS STYLE BEER

Since the beginning of the century, Pils style beers have undoubtedly become the preeminent beer style in the eyes of consumers. Whereas back in 1880, such beers were essentially imported from Nordic countries (Prussia and Denmark), Belgian brewers began to produce their own, especially after the First World War. Unfortunately, many brewers have fallen victims to this change in tastes, either because the necessary capital expenditure was too great, or simply because their breweries had been razed by the Prussian army during the First World War. This beer is obtained by fermenting the wort using bottom-fermentation techniques. It accounts for almost 70% of the volume of beer consumed annually in Belgium; world-wide, this figure exceeds 95%. (*see also : Fermentation, bottom-fermentation*).

REFERMENTED BEER

In beers, the carbonation, or CO^2 content (carbon dioxide), is obtained through fermentation, kept pressurized and finally the concentration is adjusted by injecting gas. In refermented beers, the carbonation is obtained using the same techniques applied in the production of champagne. At the time of decanting, sugar and yeast are added to the beer in the requisite quantities, generally around 10 grams of glucose sugar per liter and 1 million cells of yeast per milliliter of beer. As with champagne, there is a phase where the beer is refermented in the bottle (where it acquires its head), a phase where it is left to mature and finally a phase where it is left to age. Contrary to the champagne production process, the yeast is not eliminated from the bottle before it is offered for sale. Depending on their type, beers can be kept for periods of up to 24 months after the decanting; beyond that, their flavor becomes " oxidized " or downright acrid.

SEASONING

(see *Spices*)

SPICES AND HERBS

The expressions " herbs " and " spices " are often used as synonyms; there is however a shade of meaning which separates them. In fact, the Robert dictionary gives the following definitions; we note that the term " herb " covers a far vaster concept than " spice ", the latter being above all used to refer to vegetables or parts of vegetables used in food.

Herb: Fragrant vegetable substance; ancient. Perfume (incense, myrrh), medicine; mod. Spice, condiment: artemisia, basil, cinnamon, caraway, cumin, tarragon, fennel, juniper, ginger, cloves, hyssop, bay leaves, marjoram, oregano, chillies, pepper, horseradish, rosemary, saffron, thyme.

Spice: Substance of vegetable origin, aromatic or pungent, used to season food. Principal spices: aniseed, betel, cinnamon, curry, cubeb, cumin, ginger, cloves, mustard, nutmeg, paprika, chillies, pepper, saffron, sage, vanilla.

The herbs most commonly used in the drinks industry are the natural herbs. They are characterized by the part of the plant or fruit utilized. We shall make particular mention of bitter orange (curaçao) and coriander.

SPONTANEOUS FERMENTATION

Spontaneous fermentation is referred to in this way for, contrary to standard brewing practices, neither wheat, nor consequently yeast, are added to the wort after boiling. The wort is left to cool in shallow, wide vessels, and when the desired temperature has been reached, it is transferred to casks where it is left to ferment. Thus, the fermentation is the consequence of the contamination of the wort by the micro-organisms in the environment: in the air and the walls of the wooden casks. Traditional brewing yeast is used, but there is also a complex mixture, including certain types of yeast that are capable of using sugars that commonly used types of yeast are not capable of fermenting. That is why, when they are produced in the traditional way, they can, after three years of aging in a cellar, be drunk in moderation, but with no danger for diabetics. These beers are also characterized by an acid taste which originates from the presence of lactic, acetic bacteria which, by their activity, bring about the presence of perceptible quantities of lactic acid (flavor of soured milk) and acetic acid (vinegar flavor). The beers most commonly associated with this type of production are those in the Gueuze, Lambic style, as well as those containing fruit, such as the Kriek. (*see Gueuze and Fruity*).

STARCH

Starch is the method used by plants to store sugar and therefore energy. It is in fact a complex molecule that is present in the form of multiple globules in barley grains. One of its properties is that it swells (starches) under the joint effect of heat and humidity to the point of bursting if there is sufficient humidity, or becoming stiff in the opposite case. In grain, the starch is stored in reserve cells; these cells are destroyed during the malting (germination of the grain); as regards the starch structures which are also released, during the brewing these are 80% transformed into fermentable sugars (glucose, sucrose, fructose, maltose, maltotriose).

SUGAR

The term " sugar " is an generic expression which applies to a multitude of molecules. It is often used as a synonym for carbohydrates. As regards beer, the most important sugar is glucose and its polymers, of which the most complex is the starch, a form of storage by the barley. For the brewer, there is a crucial difference between sugars which are fermentable and those which are not, and he must also distinguish between those which influence the physico-chemical properties of the wort and the beer, such as their viscosity. All these parameters depend upon the variety of malted barley and dry grains used as well as the brewing technique applied. (*see Starch, Brewing, Fermentation, Barley*).

TASTE

Taste is the oral sensory perception at the level of the tongue. There are four typical sensations felt in very specific parts of the tongue; sweetness on the tip of the tongue, salty elements on the sides at the front of the tongue, acidity at the level of the lateral median surface and finally bitterness at the back of the tongue. The center of the tongue is thus a zone that is insensitive to the different tastes. Finally, certain authors refer to a fifth taste, known as " umami ", and which characterizes certain oriental dishes cooked with soy sauce. It must however be said that this taste is not really part of our western culture and is not at all present in beer. A distinction has to be made between the notion of taste and certain sensations of texture, such as well-rounded or smooth, which are typical of certain top-fermented beers (for example Palm) or the acidity found in certain very old beers which seem to " stick to the palate or in the throat ".

TOP FERMENTING YEAST

In any comparison of top yeast with other alcoholic yeasts, the following characteristics are apparent in this category:
· the cells are slightly bigger in diameter;
· they are generally more globular in form;
· they exhibit a very branchy method of budding.furthermore, he noted that:
· for an identical quantity of sweetened wort, the weight of top yeast is considerably greater than for other yeasts;
· top yeast is more plastic;
· top yeast produces a special beer with its own distinctive taste;
· it rises to the surface during fermentation and forms a thick layer which is called a cap;
· it ferments at around 20°C/68°F.

TOP-FERMENTATION

Top-fermentation is thus called because it takes place at an ambient temperature (between 18°C/64°F and 32°C/89°F), depending on the properties of the yeast and because, at the end of the fermentation, the yeast rises to the surface of the vat. In Belgium, until the end of the XIX century, most of the beers available for every-day consumption were produced by this method. Today, one can state without fear of contradiction that the vast majority of special and regional Belgian beers are fermented using this technique. The odors and aromas of top-fermented beers are rich and generally flowery, even fruity. The different subtleties that one perceives are of the following type: rose water, pear, banana. They are produced naturally by the yeast function. The scientific name given to the micro-organism on which top-fermentation is based is *Saccharomyces cerevisiae var.cerevisiae.* Depending on the condition of the medium and the environment, it can develop and ferment at between 14°C/57°F and 35°C/95°F. It is therefore not possible to produce bottom-fermented beers with this kind of micro-organism. As with top-fermented beers, these micro-organisms are added to the wort, once it has cooled after boiling.

TRAPPIST

To appreciate fully the phenomenon of Trappist beers, it is indispensable to look at the historical background and the structure of the monastic world and its religious context. Religious congregations living in monasteries can be divided according to their main occupations, into " contemplative orders " and " spiritual orders ", with both devoted to carrying out the divine will, on the one hand by physical effort and prayer, on the other hand by mental effort above all. Consequently, while one group was to be found settled in the countryside, in poor agricultural regions or buried in quiet forests where they devoted themselves to helping the poor or pilgrims, the others were situated in or near large towns, close to the universities where their expertise was placed at the service of science. As regards the " Trappist " monks in particular, it is worthwhile referring to the genesis of the order [according to Le BAIL, A. and BOCK, C., *Abbaye Notre-Dame de Scourmont de l'Ordre de Cîteaux à Forges-Lez-Chimay,* Ed; the Abbaye Notre-Dame de Scourmont, Forges, 1950, page 131]. In the VI century AD, Saint Benedict of Nursie traveled throughout Europe and created an austere monastic movement: the Benedictine movement. In around the year 500 he founded the abbey of Subiaco (Italy) and around the year 530, the abbey of Mont-Cassin (Italy). He died around the year 547. The rules of Benedict of Nursie were codified in a seventy five chapter capitular by Saint Benedict of Aniane (750-821). The latter was most successful in recruiting for the order and the rules also met with great success. Finally, in 817, the monastic synod of Aix-la-Chapelle proclaimed that the Benedictine rules, which were largely inspired by the rules drawn up by Saint Benedict of Nursie during his life, would be followed everywhere. From a political point of view, the movement was unique in that its Abbot was initially designated by his predecessor, then elected amongst his peers. Although from a hierarchical point of view he was supervised by the local bishop, he nevertheless enjoyed great freedom vis-à-vis the Church's traditional structure. This privilege was granted for the first time in 815 by Louis le Pieux to the Benedictine community of the Abbaye de Saint-Gall in Switzerland, which was founded in 747 on the site of a hermitage created around the year 610. The Abbot of a Benedictine abbey still in fact wears the ring. Following what can best be described as human failings, an initial reform, which was intended to centralize and increase control to provide greater discipline in their activities, was implemented at the start of the X century by the Abbaye de Cluny, which was the largest Benedictine abbey (at its summit, in the XII century, the community had almost 3,000 members). However, very rapidly, this reform soon proved to be insufficient, and under the leadership of Robert de Molesmes, certain Benedictine monks conceived the foundation of the Abbaye de Cîteaux, which was realized the 21st March 1098. This represented a revival of the rule of Saint Benedict in its purest form. The new Order no longer took the name of its founder, Saint Benedict having been elevated to the rank of Father of the Order, but was instead known as the Cistercian Order (derived from the Latin *cisterciunum:* of Cîteaux). However, the young abbey had great difficulty in prospering and therefore it was with great relief in 1112 that it welcomed the support of the person who was to become Saint

Bernard, and thirty or so of his supporters and friends. This person was particularly dynamic and he gave the abbey a new lease on life and, amongst other achievements, he founded the famous Abbaye de Clairvaux (France). On the death of Saint Bernard, the Order had more than 340 abbeys in France and neighboring areas. That was its golden age and represented a period of unimaginable prosperity, which finally went into decline in the XIV and XV centuries. There were subsequent attempts at reform, to revive the initial fervor. In the XVII century a commendable movement took the name of " Strict Observance ", but in this case also, a mixture of controversy and the revolutionary fervor which prevailed in France detracted from the movement's aims. It was left to another reform to perpetuate the spirit of the movement. This heavy responsibility fell to a Norman abbey, called the Trappe de Soligny (Orne), an ancient abbey which had no more than a dozen monks, when in 1664, the abbot of Rancé endeavored to implement the " Strict Observance " reform there. Weary of the internal quarrels, he drew up special rules, the " the Rules of La Trappe " well-known for their austerity and which drew their inspiration from the Fathers of the Desert.

The abbot of Rancé wanted to revive the Cistercian movement as it was in bygone times and to revert to the practices which were common in the days of Saint Bernard. In other words, he wanted to apply the " Rules of Saint Benedict " to the letter. For the uninitiated, the Trappe movement may seem to be a renewal with the Cistercian traditions. And completely unexpectedly, this initiative was successful, and on the abbot of Rancé's death, the Trappe movement had grown to 300 members. What is remarkable, is the movement's timelessness. Its stamp of austerity, together with a profound piety represented, as it were, the backbone of the movement and prevented it from wavering from its ideal. It survived the revolutionary turbulence of the XVIII century, not without courage, it may be added. Indeed, in 1790, the Revolutionary Council decided to enact a law to suppress all monasteries, first in France, then progressively in all the occupied territories (for example in Belgium: the Benedictine monasteries of Orval, Rochefort, Villiers-la-Ville). As a consequence of this revolutionary fervor, the community's members were dispersed, but twenty two monks settled in Switzerland in a former Carthusian monastery, the Val-Sainte, only to be expelled from there by the revolutionary armies and to be forced to wander throughout Europe. It was from there, however, that the Order built a new structure and resettled in 1815. The old ruins left by the Revolution and destroyed by the governing body of the Napoleonic Empire, had seen the abbeys being used as virtual quarries for building work carried out in the surrounding areas. Others however took the road northwards and found refuge at Westmalle in Belgium. It is therefore these monks, known as " Trappistes " and who were Benedictine-Cistercian monks belonging to the Strict Observance of the rules of Saint Benedict, who at the end of the XIX century and the XX century, were responsible for the renovation of abandoned sites or the foundation of new communities. That is also how the Abbaye Notre-Dame de Scourmont was founded in 1850, near the town of Chimay, by monks who originally came from the Cistercian-Trappist Abbaye de Westvlteren. In this economically backward region and given the infertile land, the monks decided to construct a brewery in 1861 to promote the activity and develop social cohesion in the region. It was they who used the expression " Trappist Beer " for the first time, and this name was subsequently adopted by the five other such abbeys. Since 1962 the name has been recognized legally as a registered trade-mark. With the help of lay workers, it is there that they produce the different Chimay Trappist beers. On the other hand, the Abbaye Notre-Dame d'Orval had already been founded in 1132 by Cistercian monks, but like the majority, it had been destroyed in the wake of the French Revolution. In 1926, it rose from the ashes and, in 1931, the monks decided to construct a brewery to help finance the cost of building the new monastery and to help towards the cost of maintaining it. The particular beer that is produced there is the Orval Trappist Beer.

As regards the Abbaye Saint-Remy in Rochefort, this was founded in 1230 and was initially occupied by cloistered nuns; then from 1464 to 1794 by monks. It was once again taken over by Benedictine monks in 1887. They decided to set up a brewery in 1899 and it is there that the Rochefort Trappist Beers are produced. The Abbaye de Westmalle is a typical case for, as already explained, its creation in 1794 was a direct consequence of the French Revolution. It was for reasons similar to those already mentioned that the monks decided to open a brewery there in 1836, but it was only from 1872 that the Trappist Beers from Westmalle began to enjoy success in the outside world. The Abbaye de Westvlteren was founded in 1831 and in 1838 the monks had the possibility of acquiring a second-hand brewery, but this activity never developed to the same extent as in other Trappist abbeys. This can be explained by their deliberate decision to limit sales of their beer exclusively to those who actually visit the brewery. Its financial resources being derived from allowing the abbey's name to be used by a local lay brewery, which has since become the Saint-Bernard brewery in Watou.

A close examination of the rule of Saint Benedict helps to understand clearly the basic aim of the Trappist communities and their approach to brewing activities. In effect, the Cistercian concept is based on a highly structured way of life. This included time (prayer, work, sleep), space (every space had a precise function) and the community (abbot, prior, the person responsible for food and drink or bursar, the master of the novices, priests-monks, monks, novices, lay brothers).

The rules adopted by monks are fundamentally based on three vows: stability, obedience and conversion to a specific way of life. Stability signifies that the monk is committed for life to his abbey and can only leave for good if he is dispensed from his undertaking by the Holy See. By his vow of obedience, the individual sacrifices himself to the overall good and accepts the hierarchy. Finally, the third vow is destined to lead the monk closer to God by respecting poverty, chastity, as well as the monastic observances which emphasize prayer, charity and manual work. It is herein that the Trappist monks found the justification for their brewing activities.

TRAPPIST AND ABBEY BEERS

TRIPLE

(*see Double*)

VOLUME OF ALCOHOL

The volume of alcohol or percentage alcohol in volume or °GL (Gay-Lussac) represents the quantity of ethyl alcohol (ethanol) in milliliters contained in 100 milliliters of liquid. Given that the specific weight of ethanol (0.79 kg/l at 4°C/39°F) is lower than that of water (1kg/l at 4°C/39°F), the percentage of alcohol in volume in beer will always be higher than if it were to be expressed in percent weight, that is to say in grams of ethanol per 100 grams of solution. In the scientific world, as well as in industry, it has been decided to favor the utilization of the degree Gay-Lussac, that is to say the expression of the ethanol content of drinks in percent volume.

WHEAT

Wheat, which is the cereal used as the basis for baking bread, is one of the typical raw materials used in producing white beers and Brussels acid beers in the Lambic style and its offshoots such as the Gueuze and the Kriek. Unlike barley, where the dried germs (called malt) are used, in our country dried corn kernels are used which makes the beer well-rounded and smooth.

WHITE BEER

Cloudy beers have a long tradition in certain regions and their production is very typical. Although in the past, most beers must have had an obvious tendency to opalescence, white beer was the result of a typical technological application. Lacambre points out that in 1850, the most famous white beers were those of Leuven, the wheat beers of Hoegaarden were only known locally; it is a very pleasant white beer in summer. The ingredient mix practiced was 5 or 6 parts of malted barley, 2 parts wheat, and 1 to 1.5 parts of oats. The wort was placed in casks without any addition of yeast and the beer was consumed while it was still in the middle of the fermentation process in the tank in such a way as to produce a better froth in the tank, unless it " turned ", which could be detected by its acidity after 8 to 15 days. When they were fresh, the Hoegaarden beers, like most of the Leuven beers, were very blue in color, due to the starch, but this disappeared in time (probably on account of a microbiological fauna capable of utilizing the starch as a source of carbohydrates). Lacambre, who viewed this way of brewing and fermentation as being unsound, adds that from an organoleptic point of view, the Hoegaarden beer is not as smooth as that of Leuven, which he attributes to the fact that it contains more oats, less wheat and the fact that the boiling of the soft beer does not last as long as that of the same name which is used to prepare the Leuven white beers. Otherwise it is lighter in color but equally cloudy and with a similar bouquet. Today, it is undeniable that the most famous white beer in Belgium is the Blanche de Hoegaarden. The brewing history of this village, which is situated on the linguistic border between Tirlemont (Tienen) and Jodoigne and which is now part of Flemish Brabant, not very far from the province of Liège, is worth a little of our attention. Through the centuries, Hoegaarden was a domain in the principality of Liège in the Duchy of Brabant, which gave rise to a multitude of tax advantages for the town and facilitated the implantation and development of a thriving brewing industry. The zenith of this success was reached when the town had thirty or so breweries for just over a thousand inhabitants. From that point in time, as always, the glory days gradually disappeared, and in 1958 an all time low was reached when the town's last brewery in operation, Tomsin, decided to close down. It was in 1964 that a dairyman, who had already shown his ability to break new ground by promoting and producing a particularly hygienic milk (AA milk), decided to produce white beer anew in the town. Pierre Célis began by applying the principles he had learned at Tomsin, when as a youngster, he helped out there in his spare time. He rapidly realized that the " traditional " production techniques were no longer compatible with his intention to distribute a consistently high-quality product. He enlisted the help of Marcel Thomas, who had graduated in 1932 from the Ecole de Brasserie at the

Catholic University of Leuven, as his technical advisor, and restarted production of the " white " beer with a new amended method. The present-day version of Hoegaarden's white beer is different from that of olden days in that it keeps better, has a richer aroma and is exported throughout the world but, just as in the past, it is still drunk cloudy and its carbonation (saturation in CO_2) is obtained through further fermentation in the bottle.

YEAST

The different types of yeast used in brewing are complex single cell micro-organisms, which are original in their organization. While they are programmed to reproduce sexually, the yeasts used by brewers have lost this faculty and multiply only by reproducing a quasi mirror image, which is reproduction by budding. Furthermore, whereas in the presence of oxygen and fermentable sugar, they should be able to use the sugar by breathing it, brewers have selected yeasts which have the distinctive feature of not being able to utilize sugars by breathing when air is present. They can only do so by fermentation, which obliges them to produce ethanol and carbon dioxide even when oxygen is present. The first person to appreciate that yeast is a living micro-organism was Pasteur. He asserted that yeast was a micro-organism that lived in the air, whereas von Liebig maintained that it was the fruit of a spontaneous generation due to the " life forces present in the environment ". In a nutshell, there are two main types of yeast: top yeasts and bottom yeasts.

It is only since Pasteur that we are able to isolate and distinguish top yeasts from bottom yeasts, and we shall use his words to describe them. To begin with, that is to say before 1870, brewers who very often were traditionalists unwittingly used mixed fermentation methods, whether using top or bottom fermentation, and the observations of several scientists of that period are particularly enlightening in this connection. First, let us quote Payen, a member of the French Health Regulatory Body, who in 1870 evoked " the disastrous effect of heat on the preservation of beer ". In April 1871, Pasteur visited the Kuhn brewery at Chamalières (France) in order to broaden his knowledge on the art of producing beer. The information he gleaned, whether from the owner or the workers, was confined to the following three elements:

· everything is carried out in accordance with a secular tradition;
· when there is a production problem, we change the leaven which we obtain from a fellow brewer;
· in most cases, brewers are only aware of problems in the quality of their production when a customer complains.

At that stage Pasteur decided to devote his research to obtaining a pure yeast and to trying to explain the reasons behind the modifications which occurred from time to time. It has to be borne in mind that the scientist had already carried out research into the problems connected with the production of vinegar and wine.

He very quickly ascertained that there were two types of beer, top and bottom beers. He noted that all the English beers were top-fermented (pale ale, stout, bitter beer, porter, ale) whereas the bottom-fermented beers which had originated in Bavaria were also to be found in Austria, Prussia, Bohemia and France, the transition from top-fermentation to bottom-fermentation having taken place only from 1860 onwards.

As regards top-fermented beers, he noticed that they were produced at 20°C/68°F, and that while they were easier to produce than bottom-fermented beers, they were above all more liable to alteration; in addition, they did not travel well. On the other hand, bottom-fermented beers which were manufactured at 5°C/41°F and had to be preserved at that temperature, did not need to be consumed immediately; that is why they were called long-life beers. Such beers could therefore be produced at any time of the year, and he added that in addition to keeping them in cold cellars, they also had to be kept in barrels, preferably not too large, because they had to be emptied quickly to avoid harming the beer. Finally, Pasteur's observations regarding the distinction between top and bottom yeasts are worth noting.

Professor Guy DERDELINCKX,
Doctor of science.
Lecturer at the Catholic University of Leuven,
joint holder with Professor DELVAUX,
Doctor of science, of the chair of brewing-malting.

BIBLIOGRAPHY

BERGER, Christian et DUBOË-LAURENCE, Philippe, *L'Amateur de Bière*, Editions Robert Laffont, 1985.

BEYSEN, Edward, *Bier op tafel*, Uitgeverij Helios nv., 1981

BUREN, Raymond, *Trappistes et bières d'Abbayes*, Glénat Benelux, 1990

BUREN, Raymond, *Gueuze, Faro et Kriek*, Glénat Benelux, 1992.

BOLOGNE, Jean-Claude, *Histoire des Cafés et des Cafetiers*, Editions Larousse, 1993.

CELS, JOS, *Les Brasseurs du Hainaut*, Vif Editions, 1994.

CELS, JOS, *Het Brouwersgeslacht Maes 1880- 1990*, Uitgeverij De Vlijt, 1990.

CELS, JOS, *Het Mysterie van De Gueuze*, Roularta Books, 1992.

CROMBECQ, Peter, *Bier Jaarboek 1995 - 1996*, Uitgeverij Kosmos Z & K, 1995

DARCHAMBEAU, Nicole, *La Bière ça se mange!*, Editions Les Capucines, 1994

DARCHAMBEAU, Nicole, *La Bière c'est la santé*, RTL Editions, 1986.

DARCHAMBEAU, Nicole, *Flavours from Orval*, Editions les Capucines, 1995.

DARCHAMBEAU, Nicole, *Het Genot van Orval*, Editions Les Capucines, 1995.

DARCHAMBEAU, Nicole, *La Gueuze Gourmande,* Editions les Capucines, 1995.

DARCHAMBEAU, Nicole, *Saveurs d'Orval,* Editions les Capucines, 1994.

DELOS, Gilbert, *Les Bières du Monde,* Editions Hatier.

ELEGEER, Jill, *Antwerps Caféboek,* Copyright Niveau Management.

GOCAR, Marcel, *Cette Bonne Vieille Bière,* Editions Marcel Gocar, 1969.

GOCAR, Marcel, *Histoire vraie et comique de la Bière,* Glénat Benelux, 1987.

GOEDBIER, *Arnoldus, Bierverleden te Brugge,* 't Hamerken, 1994.

HELL, Bertrand, *L'homme et la Bière,* EC Editions, 1982.

HENDRICKX, Bob, *143 Originele Cafés in Vlaanderen,* Uitgeverij Van Hemeldonck, 1995.

HERMAN, Paul, *Bistrots Bruxellois,* Glénat Benelux, 1986.

HERMAN, Paul, *Bistrots Bruxellois, 2e tournée,* Glénat Benelux, 1988.

HERMAN, Paul et RODRIGUEZ, Jean, *Cuisine facile à la bière,* Glénat Benelux, 1989.

JACKSON, Michael, *La Bière,* Glénat Benelux, 1990.

JACKSON, Michael, *Les Bières,* Guide Mondial, 2e édition, Editions Vander, 1985.

JACKSON, Michael, *Les Grandes Bières de Belgique,* Editions M.M.C. CODA, 1992.

LATOUR, Achille, *Les Brasseurs et la Bière,* Editions Créer, 1989.

LEMAIRE, Anne-Marie, DITS Jean-Louis et BOSSEAUX, Hervé, *La Brasserie à Vapeur,* Edition J.-L. Dits, 1990.

PATROONS, Wilfried, *La Route Belge de la Bière,* Copyright nv Scriptoria Antwerpen, 1984.

PERRIER-ROBERT, Annie et MBAYE, Aline, *La Bière*, Editions Larousse, 1988.

SCHAIK VAN GRASDORFF, Gilles, *Il était une fois les Brasseurs*, RTL Editions, 1986.

SIMARD, Jean-François, *Comment faire de la bonne Bière chez soi*, Editions du Trécarré, 1992.

DETHEE, Simon, *Brasseries '94*, Polaroïd.

SPARMONT, Jean-Louis, *Les Routes de la Bière*, Editions Labor, 1995.

VAN LIERDE, Geert, *Bier in België*, Uitgeverij Lannoo, 1992.

VAN LIERDE, Geert, DE MOOR, Piet, GROSEMANS André et RENSON, Serge, *In het Spoor van de Trappisten*, Roularta Books, Infotex en VAR, 1993.

VAN REMOORTERE, Julien, *Belgisch Bier*, Uitgeverij de Keyser, 1985.

VAN SCHAIK, Jan, *Bier dat moet je proeven!*, Uitgeverij J.v.

VERDONCK, Guy, *Verdwenen Brouwerijen in en rond Antwerpen*, Edition Verdonck, 1994.

VLAM, Dave, *Benelux Bier Gids*, Uitgeverij Elmar nv, Rijswijk, 1989.

WEBB, Tim, *Good Beer Guide to Belgium and Holland*, Alma Books Ltd., 1992.

COMIC STRIPS

Since 1986, Louis-Michael Carpentier, cartoonist at the Editions Dupuis, together with Raoul Cauvin, the matchless scriptwriter, also at the Editions Dupuis, have combined their talents to produce a series of comic strips devoted to beer. The first was published in 1986 to coincide with the world beer year. Subsequently, it was through the character of Poje, and the sparkling text, that these comic strips really caught on with the public at large.

It is to be noted that these comic strips have been adapted into different languages and dialects: Flemish (not Dutch!), the local dialects of Brussels (by Paul VAN KEUKEN), Liège, Alsace, " cht'i ", Tournai, Antwerp,

259

Luxembourg, Picardy, and in the not too distant future Quebec and its dialect will be honored.

L'Année de la Bière, Editions Les Archers, 1986.
La Tournée des Grands Ducs, Editions Les Archers, 1987.
Crédit est mort, Editions Dupuis, 1990.
La Tournée du Patron, Editions Dupuis, 1991.
Le Lendemain de la veille, Editions Dupuis, 1992.
On Ferme!, Editions Dupuis, 1993.
Patron sous pression, Editions Dupuis, 1994.
Un monde flou, flou, flou, Editions Dupuis, 1994.
Bière précieuse, Editions Dupuis, 1996.

GAME

" My Round ": the most refreshing game you have ever tasted!
Tournée Générale, Deshker Productions, Rue de Perck, 72, B-1630 Linkebeek.
Tel - fax: 02-358 39 56

SENSORY EVALUATION AND TASTING BEER

Tasting was for a long time considered to be a relatively abstract exercise given the complexity of the sensory mechanisms involved and the multitude of aromatic compounds which are present in beer. Thanks, however, to the analytical means and methods available today, its has become a science in its own right and has to be treated as such.

DEFINITION OF TASTING

Tasting is the sensory evaluation and description of solid or liquid food which the taster sees, and from which he extracts the volatile components through his nose and the back of his nose, the non-volatile components being more discernible on the tongue, or in the mouth. Given the precision of the vocabulary that is used in this matter where shades of meaning are primordial, we shall begin by defining the four essential concepts, which are appearance, odor, aroma and taste.

DEFINITION AND PROPERTIES OF THE NOTIONS OF APPEARANCE, AROMA , TASTE AND ODOR

Appearance: Visual sensation perceived by the retina in the eye.
Odor: Olfactory sensation perceived by the olfactory bulb through the nose.
Aroma: Olfactory sensation perceived by the olfactory bulb through the back of the nose. A food's aroma is almost always richer than its odor; for someone tasting non-sparkling drinks (wines, juices) this stems from the fact that the wine trapped in the oral cavity gets warmer which, thanks to mastication, facilitates the release of volatile compounds in the gaseous part of the mouth and the back of the nose. For someone tasting saturated drinks (beers, lemonades, sparkling wines) it is the mouth temperature and the tongue's surface, which is very uneven, that together leads to the release of the CO_2 and consequently emanation of volatile compounds.

It is to be emphasized that the perception of aromas is more often than not accompanied by a gustatory sensation on the tongue, which cannot be taken into consideration when defining the aroma. It is often very difficult for an inexperienced taster to consider them independently. *Taste:* Oral sensation perceived on the tongue. There are also related tastes that result from specific sensations on the palate.

The sensory evaluation of beer is the conscious reaction of an individual (the taster) vis-à-vis a product (beer). The difficulty most often lies in describing and quantifying this reaction. In fact, quite frequently, the taster allows himself to be influenced, even dominated, by the beer he is supposed to evaluate, whereas normally he should be in control and question his senses (eyesight, touch, sense of smell, taste) in order to describe the beer objectively. The following explanations are intended to underline the theoretical elements and scientific basis underlying the sensory evaluation of beer.

THE STIMULUS

All individuals, whenever they come into contact with an object, experience a series of signals which are given out by the body in question and are likely to arouse his senses; these signals, which are known as stimuli, provoke different sensations.

STEVENS' equation is used to connect the logarithms of the intensity of the stimulus (1n I) and the sensation perceived (1nS) and is expressed by:

$S = kIn$

where

S	=	the intensity of the sensation;
k	=	typical constant of the saturation threshold;
I	=	the intensity of the stimulus (defined on a scale varying between 0 and 1);
n =		the coefficient expressing the way in which the sensation varies when the stimulus is varied.

This law enables different sensory thresholds to be defined in respect of individual tasters. Three zones can be distinguished:

- if n > 1: the relation obeys an exponential law: an increase in the stimulus leads to a proportionally greater increase in the sensation (S) (zone 1 of the curve);
- if n = 1: the relation is linear, which signifies that an increase in the stimulus (I) leads to a proportional increase in the sensation (S) (zone 2 of the curve);
- if n < 1: the relation obeys an exponential law where an increase in the stimulus (I) leads to a proportionally smaller increase in the

sensation (S) (zone 3 of the curve).This curve enables different sensory thresholds to be defined in respect of individual tasters.

THE DIFFERENT THRESHOLDS

The tasting of a liquid (beer, wine, juice or others) can be carried out through the different sensory receptors, which function through the eyes, nose and mouth. Perception results from the response of these nervous receptors to a given stimulus.

For the sensory receptors to register such stimuli, the latter must reach a minimum quantitative value known as *the perception threshold.*

The second phase in the tasting consists of identifying the stimulus; the minimal quantitative value necessary to identify the stimulus is called the *identification threshold.*

A complementary notion is the description of the intensity of the stimulus; the smallest quantitative value from which a variation in intensity of a stimulus can be detected is known as the *nuance detection threshold.*

Finally, the last threshold to examine is the *saturation threshold;* this is defined as being the smallest quantitative value beyond which no increase in intensity is felt.

Perception threshold.

The perception threshold is a characteristic of compounds. It is determined as being the concentration above which 50% of tasters perceive a change in the odor or taste of the test vis-à-vis a witness who acts as a reference. The perception threshold varies a great deal according to the compounds (from a few ng (nanograms) to several g per liter). It can also vary considerably from one individual to another. Certain individuals are insensitive to certain stimuli (case of anosmia). It follows, therefore, that it requires a group of people (a tasting jury) who correspond to certain criteria, in order to reach an objective definition of a perception threshold. In particular, these people must be clearly interested in the sensory evaluation of the product, be in good health and must not have any manifest anomalies from a sensory point of view. Furthermore, during evaluation tests carried out on solutions, they must demonstrate an acceptable level of sensitivity with regard to a series of basic stimuli. The group must therefore be in a position to supply a series of evaluations and opinions that tally in order to be able to establish an average and analyze the deviations. The results obtained have to be analyzed using statistical methodology in order to establish any significant deviations in relation to a predetermined probability. These principles can be used to determine the perception thresholds of a whole series of beer constituents.

Identification threshold

Whereas the perception threshold is above all a property of the compound, the same is not true in respect of the identification threshold, which is more a qualitative characteristic of the individual taster. In reality, identification corresponds to the establishment of an analogy between the sensation perceived and a recognizable sensation which has been committed to memory at an earlier stage. It is therefore possible to train tasters in such a way that they can develop a sufficient organoleptic basis to enable them to be able to identify permanently the stimuli perceived. Indeed, special tasting kits that provide a variety of specimen odors are available and provide a basis on which to educate one's senses to identify the stimuli. It requires practice to improve one's tasting skills and the aim should be to bring the perception and identification thresholds as close as possible together. Ideally, these two thresholds should become one and the same. The level of a taster's identification thresholds reflect his " expertise ", and the disparity will be wider in the case of someone who is off form or is unaware of the techniques.

Nuance detection threshold

In practice, the nuance detection threshold is very important for it represents the essential starting point in any complete sensory evaluation of a product, that is to say the identification and quantification of the stimuli. The very definition of the perception, identification and nuance detection thresholds implies the existence of a quantitative relationship between the value of the stimuli (concentration of the substance acting on the senses) and the intensity of the sensory perception, which also involves a degree of appreciation of the product.

Saturation threshold

This threshold depends on both the compound and the taster. It is characterized by the fact that an increase in the stimulus no longer leads to an increase in the sensation. From a theoretical point of view, this corresponds to fixing $n = 0$ in STEVENS' formula. In practical terms, this means that the sensory receptors are saturated. In certain cases, this effect has been observed to produce reactions such as a feeling of sickness or rejection linked to phenomena of irritation, or even allergies.

OBJECTIVE CHARACTERISTICS OF TASTING

Beer, which for our purposes, is the object which gives out the stimuli, possesses its own inherent physico-chemical characteristics. These characteristics depend not only upon the ingredients used, but also upon the technology applied. Each beer, whether it be a special or Pils style beer, and whether it be served in bottles, small bottles, cans or as draft beer, has its own specific characteristics. During a tasting, many different stimuli are perceptible, ranging from purely visual stimuli, to those associated with different flavors or tactile in nature. The principal visual characteristics are the head, the color, the brilliance, the effervescence and the lacework. In the case of special beers, consumers will sometimes judge the form of the bottle as well as its label or the shape of the glass. As regards the aroma and taste, these are evaluated in terms of units of flavor (concentration in relation to the perception threshold). It must not be forgotten that most stimuli that are present depend upon outside factors such as the temperature, the light, or the shape of the glass.

BEER'S VISUAL CHARACTERISTICS

When we are served a glass of beer, we study it and our initial opinion is based on four essential visual elements: its head, its color, its brilliance and the saturation, which influences its effervescence and the level of gas.

Head

The head of a beer is a complex network composed essentially of carbohydrates and protein in which there is also a concentration of isahumulones (bitter compounds emanating from the hops). That is why the head always has a more pronounced bitter taste than the beer that it covers. The head is generally white in color, but it can sometimes be brownish, as in the case of certain Scotch type beers and other very dark British beers. In such cases this color comes from the special malts used (caramel malts and/or roasted malts). It must be emphasized that thick heads such as those that we see on white beers, and other special beers which are bottle conditioned, are the result of the quality of the manufacturing process (scrupulous attention paid to filtering the wort, sufficient boiling, the right treatment of the cooked wort, sufficient cooling) and/or the utilization of dried cereals (wheat, rye, unmalted barley) in the production of these beers.

Any appreciation of the head therefore consists of evaluating the following:
-        the color;

265

- the stability and firmness;
- its structure and the size of the bubbles;
- whether it sticks to the surface of the glass;
- how it covers the beer while it remains in the glass.

Color

Beer's basic color comes from the malt. Normally it is a cross between a pale yellow and a golden yellow color formed by a slight caramelization of the sugars during the mashing which is increased as the wort is boiled. Darker colors can also be obtained by using malt and roasted caramels that also develop an odor, an aroma and a specific taste, or by adding coloring syrups, some of which are neutral from the olfactory point of view and as regards taste.

A beer's color is a fundamental characteristic of its category and it is therefore imperative to describe it correctly.

To be precise, the color of a special beer must be assessed on the basis of:
- its basic color (yellow, red-brown, black);
- shades of this color (gold, ochre, orange, amber);
- the intensity of this color (pale, neutral, dark).

Brilliance

In principle, beer is brilliant. Its brightness results from a perfect filtration of the untreated beer at a low temperature (< 2°C/35°F). This filtration is intended to remove the yeasts but also the colloidal cloudiness, which is due to a formation of low energy bonds (hydrogen bridges) primarily between proteins and polyphenols. It is these bonds that are responsible for the appearance of the reversible cloudiness, that is to say the cloudiness which appears at low temperatures (less than 6°C/43°F) but which disappears at an ambient temperature. These bonds are in part responsible for the cloudiness of traditional white beers and other special beers the temperature of which, prior to bottling, never dropped below 14°C/57°F.

As regards clear beers, the yeasts are eliminated by filtration on a bed of diatoms (kieselguhr) and the colloidal stabilization (elimination of protein and sensitive polyphenol compounds) can be carried out by using, prior to filtration, technological additives without organoleptic effects, such as silica gels, tannins and nylon by-products. In certain refermented beers, the yeast can also be responsible for the appearance of a cloudiness when they are poured from the bottle; from a sensory point of view, it is however preferable to taste these beers without the yeast which was used for refermentation purposes, and after all that is the practice with the most famous refermented drink: champagne!

Often consumers base their appraisal of a drink, whether it be water, wine or beer, exclusively on its brilliance. That is why professional tasters are supposed to examine a product's brilliance with the utmost attention and to describe with precision the nature of any cloudiness that is discernible.

The terms which are normally utilized to characterize a beer's brilliance are clear or brilliant, while the different shades of meaning in this connection are expressed by such terms as veiled, opalescent, or cloudy. It is equally important to describe the kind of impurity and indicate whether it can be described as flecks, particles which perform like acrobats or even an homogeneous kind of impurity which forms no sediment; it is also interesting to note how it reacts at different temperatures.

In this connection, it has to be borne in mind that the opalescence, even a cloudy appearance, is not considered a defect in all types of beer, for white beers, for example, whether from Bavaria, Berlin, Leuven, Hoegaarden or other regions, this characteristic is an integral part of the beer's reputation. On the contrary, these beers are considered as not being up to standard if they are limpid or insufficiently cloudy. The texture (composition) of the cloudiness depends upon the technology utilized and can equally be starchy in nature, or other carbohydrates (for example gum arabic), even polyphenols. Accordingly, the following elements have to be taken into account when evaluating a special beer's brilliance:

-     its limpidity;
-     the temperature at which it is tasted;
-     the appearance and characteristics of any discernible cloudiness.

Saturation and effervescence

The bubbles that are discernible in a beer when it is served cool come from the release of a gas (CO_2) from a liquid (beer) where it is in a state of super-saturation. In beer the CO_2 content varies from 4.5 g/l to 5.0 g/l for casks and from 5.0 g/l to 9.5 g/l for bottles, while the concentration of balance in the water at atmospheric pressure corresponds to approximately 1.5 g/l. This gas results from the fermentation (that is to say from the transformation of sugar into ethanol and CO_2 for example by the yeast) and an adjustment through the addition before decanting in the case of filtered beers. It can also be due to the beer being conditioned in casks or bottles in the case of certain special beers. Finally, the sparkling aspect also depends upon the surface of the glass, which according to whether or not it is smooth leads to an infiltration, which is more or less intense, and hence CO_2 is released, which is not long-lasting but is more intense. A beer's effervescence is characterized by the release of CO_2 that is discernible in the glass.

Ideally, there should be a trickle of bubbles rising from the bottom of the glass as well as a little " lacework " as the gas sticks to the surface of the glass. These two elements influence consumers enormously in their appreciation of a beer. It goes without saying that these two criteria concern the beer's saturation which should be neither too low nor too high, because the latter would undoubtedly make the beer heavy and difficult to digest on account of the degassing which takes place in the stomach. It is preferable to reach values varying between 5.0 g/L and 7.5 g/L although certain brewers do not hesitate in the case of special beers to go as high as 9.5 g/L. It is to be noted that as a general rule stronger beers require a greater saturation, and they release their CO_2 much more slowly. Nor is it to be forgotten that the best results are incontestably obtained by bottle conditioning. This phenomenon is just as clearly discernible when one compares the carbon dioxide released from a champagne compared with a sparkling wine which has been artificially saturated.

Accordingly, from a tasting point of view, a beer's saturation has to be examined with regard to:
- its sparkle;
- its lacework;
- its digestibility, (which is evaluated during the gustatory test).

TACTILE CHARACTERISTICS

Although they are often neglected, these characteristics however are essential as regards the primary organoleptic evaluation of the product. In fact, after eyesight, it is the sense of touch which plays the most important role in the sensory evaluation of beer. In this connection, the two most important parameters are the temperature and the effervescence, which depends upon the level of saturation. Although brewers can easily control the latter, the same does not hold true in respect of the temperature which overall depends upon the skills, the technical means and " good will " of the licensed dealer or the bar owner.

The thermic sensation is mainly felt in the hands that hold the glass and provides the consumer with an idea of whether or not the product conforms to his expectations. The first point to be made in this connection is that drinking habits vary according to the type of beer, and consumers like " Pils " style beers to be served very cool, that is to say between 3°C and 5°C/37-41°F, other beers they prefer to drink at cellar temperature (10°C to 12°C/50-54°F), while special beers are served very much at room temperature (18°C to 20°C/64-68°F). It has to be said however that some beer lovers prefer to drink their fermented beers, even dense beers, straight out of the refrigerator. The thermic sensation, whether felt through the hands, or in the mouth, has a very important influence on the beer's thirst quenching qualities as well as the sensation of roundness, as the case may be.Without fear of contradiction, we can affirm that it is recognized that a beer with relatively few aromatic characteristics, that is to say the total of the FU relative to the compounds resulting from the fermentation is less than 2, is generally better drunk at a low temperature (FU: Flavor Unit; the quantity of FU represented by a compound in a solution corresponds to its concentration in that solution divided by its perception threshold). On the other hand, those where the total of FUs relative to the compounds resulting from the fermentation is higher than 4, that is to say generally top-fermented beers, are characterized by a much wider range of drinking temperatures which, according to the requirements of an objective sensory evaluation, or quite simply depending upon an individual consumer's preference, can vary between 5°C and 20°C/ 41-68°F. On this point, it all depends upon priorities, the refreshing thirst quenching aspect at low temperatures, the smooth, mellow character of the beer and its rich bouquet at a higher temperature, as with wines tasted at room temperature. A final point that we would make is that tasting a drink at an ambient temperature does highlight its defects, whereas cold temperatures do tend to cover up such defects.

The sensation involving the beer's effervescence is linked to its saturation and to the intensity of the bond between the liquid and the gas. The fact that the sensation disappears on the tongue is due to its rough surface and the temperature in the mouth. This phenomenon gives rise to a tingling sensation due to the bursting of the bubbles on contact with the surface of the tongue, but above all the palate, and an acid sensation due to the presence of CO^2. From an organoleptic point of view, this produces a refreshing effect which leaves a favorable impression. It should also be noted that if the beer is lacking in effervescence, this is considered a defect and leads to beer being downgraded, and being described by tasters as " flat ". But nor should the effervescent aspect be too prevalent, since in such cases beers tend to become difficult to digest, and this is felt in a malaise akin to a heavy weight in the stomach. In conclusion, we would point out that the sensation perceived depends upon the type of beer tasted, dense beers tending to have a better CO^2 bond than light beers, the sensation perceived could therefore be identical even though the CO^2 content is different.

OLFACTORY CHARACTERISTICS

Olfactory perception in human beings

Human beings have a sense of smell that is particularly sensitive to certain compounds and relatively insensitive to others. In addition, sense of taste is more acute in some tasters than in others and depends upon the environment. That is why it is normally recommended to draw the tasting jury from a wide range and to classify tasters according to their sensitivity to different principal compounds and accordingly their respective qualities; it is to be noted that despite a possible divergence with the accurate response, certain tasters can be particularly sensitive to different molecules.

The olfactory characteristics which are specific to beer are set out in the tasting CHART. For this to be used in a satisfactory manner tasters must have been trained to distinguish between notions of odor and aroma and to describe correctly the olfactory sensations perceived.

Any olfactory appreciation of a beer is the synthesis of the sensations perceived by the sense of smell, which plays a twofold role during a beer tasting. First of all, it is stimulated by fragrant molecules that are perceptible in the gaseous phase when the gases are released from the beer; they reach the olfactory mucous membrane through the nose and the sensation perceived by this channel is called the ODOR.

Then, during consumption and while it remains in the mouth, beer will gradually release the CO_2 it contains, with the latter accompanied by volatile compounds. This phenomenon is aided by the tongue's rough surface and the oral cavity's high temperature (close to 37°C/99°F). The fact that the beer's saturation is partially lost in the mouth also explains why its tasting does not require the same vigorous mouth movements as a wine. The gaseous phase, which is released at that time and which comes into contact with the olfactory bulb via the throat and the channel at the back of the nose, produces the sensation which is called AROMA.

Odor and aroma are perceived by the same receptor but are the consequence of sensations perceived from gases that arrive in different ways.

The origin of beer's olfactory flavors

Beer's olfactory flavors are many and complex. The different compounds responsible for the odor or the aroma are generally sub-divided into 8 groups or categories based on their origin or their olfactory characteristics. The sub-division in general use is attributed to MEILGAARD (a Danish author working in the United States) and is the following:

270

1st Category

0110; 0111; 0112: alcoholic (ethanol produced during fermentation; perceived from 14 g/l), spicy (vanilla, cloves, sage... resulting from spices being added or the use of aromatic hops), vinous.

0120; 0121; 0122; 0123: solvent (resulting from the fermentation).

0130; 0131; 0132; 0133: esterified.

0140; 0141; 0142; 0143; 0144; 0145; 0146; 0147; 0148: fruity
As regards the last two categories, the olfactory notes result above all from the esters produced during the fermentation of the wort by the yeast. Their concentration depends not only upon the type of yeast but also on the fermentation method which influences the growth in the yeast, such as the temperature, the primary density, the carbon dioxide pressure, the oxygen content, the content in lipids or the degree of movement. By way of example, a wort which has been only slightly aerated at the start of fermentation, or a low acid content, can encourage their presence. High CO^2 content (pressurized fermentation) will restrict acetate type esters (ethyl acetate: odor of solvent and isoamyl acetate: aroma of bananas) but will sometimes encourage the production of fatty acid esters (caproat or ethyl caprylate: aroma of apples). Fusel (superior alcohol) produced during fermentation, such as isoamylic alcohol (aroma of bananas) as well as many oxygenated terpenes can equally produce fruity notes.

0150; acetaldehyde (aroma of green apples; produced during fermentation) is a normal by-product of fermentation but is also to be found in aged beers, the acetaldehyde being a product of the oxidation of the ethanol.

0160; 0161; 0162; 0163: flowery. This aroma, which in general is not particularly popular in beers, is the 2-phenyl-ethanol, which is characterized by an intense rose flavored odor. It appears during fermentation, in particular when the yeast develops to an important degree (high temperature, a lot of movement, low pressure...), leading to the utilization of third family aminoacids, such as phenylalanine.

0170; 0171; 0172; 0173: hop odors. These are obtained by adding aromatic hops (Saaz type) at the end of the cooking of the wort or while it is left to mature in the cellar. The chemical compounds, which are responsible for this fruit are often present in only small quantities. Mainly they are terpens (myrcens: odor of bays; a-humulene; b-carophyllene: odor of turpentine, oxygen by-products...) and possibly sulfuric compounds which have an unpleasant odor.

2nd Category

0210; 0211: resin odors. This olfactory note can derive from different terpens (a- and b-pinenes...) or phenols (eugenol...).

0220; 0221; 0222; 0223; 0224: an aroma of nuts. The pyrazines produced during the mashing can, amongst others, be the cause of this flavor. The benzaldehyde can produce an almond aroma.

0230; 0231; 0232: an aroma of greenery. Most of the aromas in this category are produced by the linear aldehydes arising from the oxidation of the lipids (nonadienal...). Moreover, certain pyrazines produced by the Maillard reactions also give off an aroma of this type.

3rd Category

0310; 0311; 0312; 0313; 0320; 0330: cereal odors. These are more intense when a slightly mashed malt is used. These aromas are more prevalent when the brewing is based on 100% malt (with no utilization of dry grains) and when winter barley is used. The Stecker aldehydes (isobutanal, 2- and 3-methylbutanal) are mainly responsible for this olfactory note.

4th Category

0410: caramel odor. This is obtained by using special malts such as caramel malts, which are rich in isomaltol and furanone, during brewing.
Note: the presence of a caramel aroma in a " Pils " style beer can be the sign that the beer has been over-pasteurized, or an indication that it is starting to age.

0420: odor of burning. This is a consequence of using special malts such as roasted malts during the brewing, or the heating of the boiling tank by a naked flame.
Note: the presence of this aroma of roasting in certain German special beers is obtained by introducing a superheated heat-resistant stone into the boiling wort.

5th Category

0501; 0502; 0503; 0504; 0505: phenolic odors. These can result from the utilization of a percentage of malts from which the peat has been removed (obtained by distilling the peat under the malt during the mashing) as raw materials during the brewing process.
Note: a phenolic or medicinal odor in beers can result from the beer accidentally coming into contact with disinfectants containing chlorine, which can react with the polyphenols to produce chlorophenols.

6th Category

0611; 0612; 0613; 0614: fatty acid aromas. These come from the metabolism of the yeast.

0620; 0630;0640: stale odor. The yeast metabolism of the amino-acids, and in particular the leucine and the isoleucine, can lead to the production of diketones such as diacetyl which give off an unpleasant, rancid odor. This will be produced in important quantities if the wort is rich in first family amino-acids or poor in second category amino-acids. Normally, this flavor will be eliminated during the storage of the beer (transformation into organoleptically inactive acetoin). However, it can persist if it is not left for a sufficient period of time in the cellars to mature before decanting. It is to be noted that this compound can also arise from a bacterial contamination of the beer (for example by Pediococcus cervesiae or Pediococcus damnosus), the metabolism of these micro-organisms being characterized by the production of diacetyl.

7th Category

0710: odor of sulfur. The sulfurous anhydride results from the metabolism of the amino-acids treated with sulfur during the fermentation, or the presence of KMS (*potassium metabisulfite*) previously added after fermentation to restrict the aging.

0720; 0721; 0722; 0723; 0726; 0727: mercaptan odors. These are also produced during the yeast metabolism of the amino-acids. Logically, they are eliminated during storage, but can appear in beers that were bottled too young. Notes: **0724.** The taste of light which is found in beers exposed to the light (mainly in green bottles) results from a degradation of the bitter substances in the hops. **0725;** An odor of autolysis can occur when the beer has been preserved for too long a period on an aged yeast and autolyzed at a high temperature (above 17°C/63°F), during fermentation and/or storage.

0730; 0731; 0732; 0733; 0734; 0735; 0736: aroma of boiled vegetables. The dimethylsulfide can persist in abnormally high quantities in malts that have been insufficiently mashed. Certain special malts, rich in dimethylsulfoxides, can also, through reduction, lead to a greater volume of dimethylsulfide during fermentation. The fact that the wort is insufficiently boiled (the evaporation rate per hour less than 5%) is a third possible cause for an over-persistent odor of cooked cabbage/onions.

0740: odor of yeast. This can arise if it is left to ferment for too long a period and/or if it is kept on fresh yeast at a high temperature (>17°C/63°F).

8th category

0800; 0810; 0820; 0830: odors of cat's urine, paper, leather or mold. In particular, the " taste of paper " appearing during the aging of the beer is likely to be the result of the production of trans-2-nonenal (odor and aroma of papier-mâché), a compound from the oxidization (degradation) of the lipids.

GUSTATORY CHARACTERISTICS

Gustatory perception in human beings

Our body is capable of detecting 5 basic flavors, which are perceived in specific parts of the tongue and in the mouth; acid, sweet, savory, bitter and umami. As regards beer, we shall assess the first four and what are known as secondary tastes. The latter are usually specific oral sensations: *acridity*, that is to say, a bitterness perceived on the palate and not on the tongue; *Astringency,* that is to say, a sensation that leaves a dry aggressive sensation on the teeth, and finally the *post-bitterness* which indicates the length of time that the bitter taste is perceived to persist on the tongue.

Any gustatory analysis inevitably focuses on the mouth since that is where the different gustatory receptors are to be found.

As a general rule the four primary tastes that are perceptible are the following:

- **Savory** taste
This is perceived on the sides of the front of the tongue and on the palate; the compounds which act as stimulants are primarily the cations K, Na and Li.
- **Acid** taste
This is perceived on the sides of the back of the tongue and the palate; most Brönstedt acids are stimulants.
- **Soft** taste
There are two particularly sensitive zones, depending on the nature of the compound at the origin of the sensation:
the **soft taste** which derives from sugars and certain amino-acids (for example the L-Alanine) is perceived on the tip of the tongue;
the **sickly sweet taste** which derives from certain phenolic compounds (for example dihydro-chalcone) is perceived at the back of the tongue.

- **Bitter** taste
There are also two particularly sensitive zones as regards this taste, depending on the nature of the compound at the origin of the sensation:
the **bitter taste** which derives from phenolic compounds, isohumulones and certain salts (for example $MgSO4$) is perceived on the back of the tongue; the **bitter taste** which results from certain amino-acids (for example L-Tryptophane) is perceived on the front of the tongue and on the palate.

Secondary tastes
There are certain oral sensations which strictly speaking are not gustatory; for example astringency, the sensation of smoothness, the thirst quenching sensation, etc. These characteristics essentially come from the polyphenolic compounds, dextrins and certain polypeptide compounds. They are felt on the palate and at the back of the mouth and are part of the overall oral sensation experienced during the tasting.

Origin of the beer's gustatory flavors

Acid flavor
In bottom-fermented beers, this taste primarily comes from the cells of the yeast and/or the utilization of an important proportion of dry grains (source of sweetness other than malted barley). In special beers, such as " white " beers and certain English beers, the acidity comes from the lactic acid resulting from a contamination of the beer by bacteria of the Lactobacillius sp. Type. In beers such as " lambic " and " gueuze ", as well as the acid beers of Roulers, acetic acid (vinegar) is also present due to contamination by Acetobacter sp. and Acetomonas sp.
Note: While the presence of these micro-organisms is deliberate in the above-mentioned special beers, they are prohibited in most breweries where acidification corresponds to a modification in the taste and indicates a lack of cleanliness. It is to be noted that they can also be found in the pipes of barrels of beers served on tap in bars and can lead to a beer being downgraded. That is why breweries attach particular importance to the installations in hotels, cafes and restaurants where draft beer is served.

Sweet (soft) flavor
This taste comes from the sugars present in the beer and results from the brewing method. If it is a question of sugars which can be fermented by the yeast (glucose, fructose, maltose, maltotriose), these come from elements added after the fermentation-storage and prior to pasteurization in order to

275

soften the beer (for example beers which are too acid); if it is a question of non-fermentable sugars, these occur as a result of a brewing method which strongly reduces the saccharification stage (activity of the b-amylase at 63°C/ 145°F). The chloride content can also provoke a sensation of softness when combined with sodium (approx. 200 mg/l).

Savory taste

This taste principally comes from the beer's concentration of NaCl (it is perceived if the content is higher than 500 mg/l). Beer's salt composition essentially comes from the water used in the brewing process, the malt contributes mainly potassium and phosphates; in fact, from a mineral point of view, beer contains essentially phosphates. It also contains trace elements (for example Zinc, Copper, Aluminum and Iron).

Bitter taste

The intensity of the bitterness comes from the quality of the hops used and the pH at the time of boiling, a higher pH leading to a more arresting, but less subtle, bitterness. The quality of the bitterness also depends upon the quality of the hops utilized (the most refined come from the former Czecho-slovakia, Poland, Austria and Germany, and are the Saaz, Tettnang, Styrie, and Hallertau types).

Secondary tastes

Above all, they come from the sensations felt in the oral cavity. The tannic taste, which is relatively thirst quenching, comes from non-oxidized polyphenols. On the other hand, if they are oxidized, they are astringent, even acid. The " smoothness " comes from the proteins, the dextrins and certain amino-acids (for example glutamic acid).

Professor Guy DERDELINCKX

<table>
<tr><td colspan="2" rowspan="3">Keys</td></tr>
</table>

Date :	**Keys** 1 = Absent 2 = Only slightly perceptible 3 = Average intensity	4 = Significant/ Influential presence 5 = Dominant characteristic

SENSORY EVALUATION CARRIED OUT BY:

Odor and aroma	1	2	3	4	5
of the malt					
pils					
caramel					
roasted					
of the hops					
fresh hops					
aged hops					
cheesey hops					
...					
of flowers					
rose					
of fruit					
pears					
bananas					
pineapples					
apples (green - ripe)					
peaches					
apricots					
...					
of spices					
coriander					
orange					
licorice					
...					
of solvent					
varnish/acetone					
...					
of vegetables					
onions/celery					
of sulfur					
matches (SO2)					
special comments					
Fresh yeast					
Old yeast (autolysed)					
Butter-margarine					
Rancid-yogurt					
Metallic					
Rubber					
Disinfectant					

Taste	1	2	3	4	5
of the malt					
bitter					
soft					
sweet					
savory					
acid					
refreshing					
smooth					
...					
...					

Special comments	1	2	3	4	5
taste of the yeast					
medicinal					
post-bitterness					
acrid					
licorice					
metalic					
papier-mâché					
oxidized					
smoke-phenolic					
...					
...					

Appereance

Color		Straw colored	Golden yellow	Ochre
		Amber	Brown	Dark
Head	Color	White	Brownish	
	Structure	Creamy	Compact	Labile
	Adherence to the glass	Solid	Average	Labile
CO2	Saturation	Abundant	Average	Weak
	Lacework	Abundant	Average	Weak
	Size of bubbles	Abundant	Average	Weak

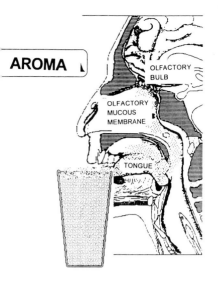

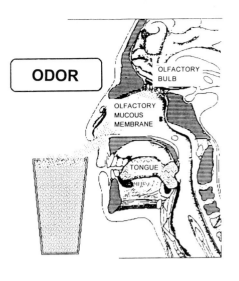

Schematic guide to the sensitive zones/receptors as well as a few notions of aroma and odor.

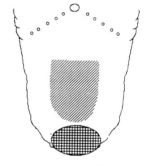

Zone which is particularly sensitive to SWEET SICKLY tastes

Zone which is insensitive to SWEET SICKLY tastes

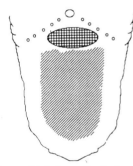

Zone which is particularly sensitive to BITTER tastes

Zone which is insensitive to BITTER tastes

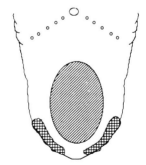

Zone which is particularly sensitive to SAVORY tastes

Zone which is insensitive to SAVORY tastes

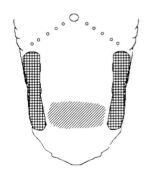

Zone which is particularly sensitive to ACID tastes

Zone which is insensitive to ACID tastes

Printed by :

Gutenberg Editions

Rue Marconi 173 - 177
1190 Brussels Belgium
☎ + 32.2.343.89.89